# TRANSICIONES

# TRANSICIONES

*Pathways of Latinas and Latinos Writing in High School and College*

**TODD RUECKER**

UTAH STATE UNIVERSITY PRESS
*Logan*

© 2015 by the University Press of Colorado

Published by Utah State University Press
An imprint of University Press of Colorado
5589 Arapahoe Avenue, Suite 206C
Boulder, Colorado 80303

All rights reserved

 The University Press of Colorado is a proud member of
The Association of American University Presses.

The University Press of Colorado is a cooperative publishing enterprise supported, in part, by Adams State University, Colorado State University, Fort Lewis College, Metropolitan State University of Denver, Regis University, University of Colorado, University of Northern Colorado, Utah State University, and Western State Colorado University.

ISBN: 978-0-87421-975-3 (paperback)
ISBN: 978-0-87421-976-0 (ebook)

Library of Congress Cataloging-in-Publication Data

Ruecker, Todd Christopher.
  Transiciones : Pathways of Latinas and Latinos writing in high school and college / Todd Ruecker.
      pages cm
  Includes bibliographical references and index.
  ISBN 978-0-87421-975-3 (pbk.) — ISBN 978-0-87421-976-0 (ebook)
  1. English language—Rhetoric—Study and teaching. 2. English language—Study and teaching (Higher)—Spanish speakers. 3. English language—Study and teaching (Secondary)—Spanish speakers. 4. Language arts—Remedial teaching. 5. Hispanic Americans—Education (Higher) 6. Hispanic Americans—Education (Secondary) 7. First-generation college students—United States. I. Title.
  PE1405.U6R76 2015
  808'.042071—dc23
                              2014007955

Cover photographs (clockwise from top left): photo by author, © Alan49/Shutterstock, © arek_malang/Shutterstock, photograph by author, © Andresr/Shutterstock.

# CONTENTS

*Acknowledgments   vii*

1   Introduction   1
2   College Decisions and Institutional Disparities   24
3   Struggling Transitions   44
4   Difficult but Successful Transitions   65
5   Smooth Transitions   99
6   An Unpredictable Transition   128
7   Contextualizing Transitions to College   141
8   The Role of Composition Researchers, Teachers, and Administrators   154

*Epilogue and Final Thoughts   174*
*Appendix A: Student Surveys and Interview Protocols   184*
*Appendix B: Teacher and Administrator Interview Protocols   193*
*References   199*
*About the Author   211*
*Index   213*

# ACKNOWLEDGMENTS

First, I would like to thank all the students who participated at some point in this project. Without their willingness to share their lives with me and take the time to meet and answer innumerable questions, this project would not have happened. As revealed within this book, their stories are diverse, but they all have unique talents and I am confident that all have bright futures ahead of them.

In addition to the participants, the other foundation for this project has been my mentor, Kate Mangelsdorf. An excellent mentor, she has built my confidence as she guided me through a number of successful projects. Along the way, many others provided feedback on various iterations of this manuscript: Linda Adler-Kassner, Beth Brunk-Chavez, Brooke Cholka, Yasko Kanno, Christina Ortmeier-Hooper, John Scenters-Zapico, Alfredo Urzua, and two anonymous reviewers. I also value the editorial guidance provided by Michael Spooner at USUP throughout this process along with his unflagging support of my proposed book project and my ability to undertake it.

A number of others, including the principal of the high school where I did my research, the senior English teacher I collaborated with, and the other people I interviewed with or worked with throughout the duration of this project, also deserve credit. I also thank my previous institution's Graduate School for providing multiple research grants to support the transcription work associated with the project.

I would like to thank my family, especially my parents who provided many opportunities and supported me in multiple ways throughout my life. Finally, I would like to thank my partner Brooke who has been with me throughout this process, and who was patient and supportive as I spent endless hours in front of the computer transcribing interviews, analyzing data, writing, and revising.

# TRANSICIONES

# 1
# INTRODUCTION

> *"I don't know who you blame. I don't know if you blame the school. I don't know if you blame the system. I don't know if you blame the teacher . . . it doesn't seem to me that students are coming out with the ability to communicate at all sometimes, you know, either spoken or written."*
> —A first-year composition instructor on
> why students were not coming to college prepared

In El Paso, Texas, the largest port of entry from Mexico into the United States, transition is a way of life. Every day, people line up on the arched bridges spanning the Rio Grande, coming by car, bike, or on foot to the United States to shop, study, or work. Looking across the border from the University where part of this study took place, one sees hillsides of dilapidated houses, many home to workers at *maquilidoras*—factories run by US corporations in Mexico to take advantage of lower production costs. At the time of this study, drug violence rates in Mexico had skyrocketed, with Ciudad Juárez, just across the border from El Paso, having the highest murder rate in the world. Conversely, El Paso consistently has one of the lowest crime rates among large cities in the United States (KVIA 2013). Crossing the bridge into downtown El Paso, one enters some of the poorest neighborhoods in the United States, where 62 percent of residents live below the poverty line and almost 80 percent lack a high school diploma (Ramirez 2011). Moving away from here, one passes through middle class neighborhoods before coming across communities with large manicured lawns and swimming pools, both luxuries in the desert. In transitioning from the city center to suburbs, one passes from neighborhoods where people only know Spanish to ones where many only know English. On the University campus, hearing conversations in both languages, including the variety of Spanglish spoken in El Paso, is the norm.

The uniqueness of El Paso's setting as the largest port of entry to the United States initially drew me to the region. Soon after arriving, I came across applied linguist Linda Harklau's (2000) "From the Good Kids to the Worst," which focused on an important academic transition: high school to college. As the title implies, the multilingual students in her study grappled with very different identities moving through the two environments, labeled as excellent students by high school teachers but considered slackers in college. A search for work like Harklau's (2000) closer to rhetoric and composition turned up little. Villanueva's (1993) classic autobiographical narrative *Bootstraps,* gave us some insight into a Latino transitioning through various levels of the US educational system. Beyond that, most studies on transition have focused on writing transfer from first-year composition (FYC) to other university classes or beyond (e.g., Beaufort 2007; Frazier 2010; Leki 2007; Wardle 2007; 2009).

Instructors I talked with over the course of this study made comments like the one quoted in the epigraph above: we know there is a problem but who or what is to blame? I have often witnessed colleagues lamenting the writing abilities of their first-year students along the lines of those seen above. Recent articles in the flagship composition journal have called for our field to pay more attention to what happens before college (Addison and McGee 2010; Williams 2010). There have been similar calls in the flagship journal for second language writing (Harklau 2011). For many college writing instructors, what happens outside FYC classrooms is often a mystery. I rarely studied adolescent writers in my doctoral seminars yet taught students matriculating from the same educational system with varying writing abilities, English proficiencies, and many with seemingly little understanding of the basic conventions of academic writing. Students entered my class struggling to participate in discussions and engage in more complex writing tasks like rhetorical analyses. Their grades suffered or, even worse, they disappeared from class. Maybe they returned to another FYC class next semester. Maybe they delayed it until they were ready to graduate. Maybe they never returned to college.

With limited research guiding these initial phases and limited personal knowledge of what actually goes on in high schools, much less high schools in the borderlands of a state long known for a history of high stakes assessment in K–12 schools, I sought a way to begin exploring this topic. I drafted research questions oriented to exploring the challenges and successes students faced in making transitions as writers from high school to college. As I reflected on the study design, I realized that research on transitions between educational institutions were rare for a few reasons: after working closely with a participant for a semester or more, they may decide not to go to college or go to college out of town. Moreover, high schools are foreign environments to most university researchers outside of education departments. In such spaces, it takes time to build trusting relationships where one is given access to observe classes or is able to form connections with adolescent students.

With these challenges in mind, especially the last one, I started slowly. The school site came fairly naturally as I wanted something unique to the border region. Samson High School (SHS),[1] the focal school in this study is located close to the border, which means some students would cross every day to attend school in the United States, this complex transition a part of their daily life. I initially became involved through a program called Gear Up, which placed volunteers in school to support teachers as they worked to prepare students for college. After a semester working with lower-level ESL classes, I began working with the senior English teacher, Mr. Robertson, because of a desire to find students interested in attending college. By regularly attending classes a couple days a week, my face became familiar to students and teachers. Thanks to informal interactions and observations that took place over the course of this first year, I was able to develop more focused research questions:

- How are the writing demands different at the high school, community college, and university levels and what contributes to these differences?
- What curricular and extracurricular challenges do Latina/o linguistic minority (LM) students face in making the transition between high school and college writing?[2]
- What resources do students draw on to support their college transitions?

Too often ignorance of student experiences in varied contexts leads to an endless cycle of assigning blame without sufficient knowledge, as evident from the teacher quoted at the beginning of this chapter. High school teachers blame students' home lives. FYC instructors blame high school teachers. University faculty blame two-year colleges. College professors in other disciplines blame FYC. This book helps break down these barriers by detailing curricular and extracurricular successes and challenges that seven Mexican/Mexican American students faced as they transitioned from high school to a local community college or university. The stories shared within reveal the complexities shared by some of the teachers above: the impact of social polices like No Child Left Behind (NCLB) on writing instruction, divides between the type of writing expected at different institutions, and home lives where students care for dependents, work full time, and speak a different language than is expected of them at school. In sharing these stories, I explore what writing teachers across institutions can do to support the success of increasingly diverse students, especially Latina/o LM students.

Given the integral role that writing plays in college and the almost universal requirement that students will have a writing class in their critical first year of college, it is essential that composition researchers and teachers gain a fuller understanding of the role we play in supporting and hindering students' transitions to college. This study is an attempt to build this understanding. It explores the disconnect between students' writing experiences in high school, community college, and the university while recognizing that our role in the lives of students making this transition may be smaller than we would like to think.

## INCREASING LATINA/O STUDENT POPULATIONS

In the past, composition teachers and scholars have held a "myth of linguistic homogeneity" and have largely ignored the diversity present in their classroom, at worst pushing an "English only" agenda that can serve to marginalize students (Canagarajah 2006; Horner, NeCamp, and Donahue 2011; Horner and Trimbur 2002; Matsuda 2006; Schroeder 2011). As Schroeder (2011, 201) noted, adherence to a standard English ideology throughout educational institutions as well as organizations like NCTE have framed "ethnolinguistic differences as educational obstacles to overcome rather than intellectual resources to exploit." It is time for composition researchers to pay attention to the dramatic demographic shifts taking place in the United States and transform the ways we teach writing.

Mexican American immigrants or children of immigrants, like the students profiled in this study, are contributing to a demographic shift in the United States largely precipitated by the growth in the Latina/o population. From 2000 to 2010, the Latina/o population in the United States increased from 35.3 to 50.5 million, accounting for 56 percent of the nation's population growth in this decade (Passel, Cohn, and Hugo Lopez 2011). While most Latinas/os still live in Arizona, California, Colorado, Florida, Illinois, New Mexico, New Jersey, New York, and Texas, their numbers are dramatically increasing in states where they have not traditionally been a significant part of the population, such as South Carolina with a 148 percent increase and Alabama with a 145 percent increase over the past decade, meaning that composition researchers and teachers at all institutions need to attend to supporting the success of diverse student populations. Accounting for over 65 percent of Latinas/os as of 2009, Mexicans and Mexican Americans (the focus of this study) play a huge role in this growth story (Passel, Cohn, and Hugo Lopez 2011).

As their population has increased, Latinas/os have become an increasing presence in the school system, comprising 23.3 percent of K–12 students as of 2010, up from 16.7 percent in 2000 (Fry and Lopez 2012). In Texas, the state in which my study was conducted, Latinas/os comprised 50.3 percent of the students in the K–12 system in 2010, accounting for over 90 percent of the enrollment growth in Texas schools over the decade (TEA 2011a). Latina/o enrollment at the college level has similarly surged, from 10 percent of total college enrollment in 2000 to 15 percent in 2010 (Fry 2011; Llagas and Snyder 2003). Although Latinas/os are entering the education system and graduating from college in greater numbers (Fry and Lopez 2012), there is a continued problem of retention and Latinas/os are still the "least educated major racial or ethnic group in terms of completion of a bachelor's degree" (Fry 2011).[3]

A commonly referenced Lumina Foundation (2007) statistic notes that for every one hundred Latina/o elementary school students, fifty-two graduate from high school, twenty go to a community college, eleven go to a four-year institution, ten graduate from college, four of them earn a graduate degree, and one earns a doctorate. Unfortunately, Latina/o and other LM students often lack the resources to succeed. They often attend segregated, underfunded, and underperforming schools, are denied access to advanced coursework, have parents who do not possess the language skills and knowledge to help them with homework or navigate unfamiliar educational systems, and are viewed through a lens that sees their multilingualism as a deficit (Callahan and Shifrer 2012; Enright and Gilliland 2011; Harklau 2011; Llagas and Snyder 2003; Mosqueda 2012; Nuñez and Sparks 2012; Suárez-Orozco and Suárez-Orozco 2001; Suárez-Orozco, Suárez-Orozco and Todorova 2008; Villanueva 1993; Wolfe 1999). As a result, many students, despite coming from families with high aspirations for their education, never make it to college. Of those who do, many never graduate.

## STUDENT ENGAGEMENT AND THE FIRST-YEAR EXPERIENCE

The first year of college is generally regarded as the most critical point of determining a student's likelihood to graduate from college, with the 2001 first-year retention rate at 73.9 percent at four-year institutions and only 54.1 percent at two-year colleges (Ishler and Upcraft 2005, 29). For instance, of the seven students in the study presented in this book, three dropped out and restarted classes their first year, with a few of these transferring to private technical colleges looking for a quicker path to completion. Looking further out, the commonly cited four-year graduation rate is a goal consistently achieved by a minority of students nationwide (Chronicle of Higher Education 2013).

The last few decades have brought more first-year initiatives, more scholarship, and more collaborations between college departments to promote first-year success and student retention (Evenbeck, Smith, and Ward 2010; Upcraft, Gardner, and Barefoot 2005). However, while writing teachers have engaged in some of the best practices validated by this research, composition studies has been largely absent from these discussions. A notable exception has been relatively recent work by scholars in basic writing focused on examining the positive impacts of basic writing programs on student retention (Baker and Jolly 1999; Glau 2007; McCurrie 2009; Peele 2010; Webb-Sunderhaus 2010). This research has largely arisen out of the need to defend programs increasingly at risk in an era of shrinking funding for higher education, a challenge that all those involved in postsecondary education will face moving forward.

Tinto (1975; 1988; 1993; 1997) was one of the earliest researchers focusing on students' first-year experience and causes behind student dropout. In 1975, he proposed a dropout theory based on Durkheim's model of suicide, in which he divided the college into two components, the academic and the social: "This theoretical model of dropout . . . argues that the process of dropout from college can be viewed as a longitudinal process of interactions between the individual and the academic and social systems of the college during which a person's experiences in those systems . . . continually modify his goal and institutional commitments in ways which lead to persistence and/or to varying forms of dropout" (Tinto 1975, 94).

Under Tinto's (1975) proposed model, a student's likelihood to persist is based in part on how well they integrate into both the social and academic spheres of the campus. Starting with work by Elbow (1968) and Murray (1969), composition studies has a long history of connecting students socially and academically to the university through pedagogies involving group work and conferencing individually with students. At one of the focal institutions in my study as well as elsewhere (Barnhouse and Smith 2006), FYC classes have increasingly been part of learning communities, which promote student involvement in various academic and social activities (Tinto 1993, 1997). Composition teachers and researchers have long recognized tacitly that "choices of curriculum structure and pedagogy invariably shape both learning and persistence on campus, because they serve to alter both the degree to which and manner in which students become involved in the academic and social life of the institution" (Tinto 1997, 620).

Despite the popularity of Tinto's work, especially his retention model, he has not been without critics. Some have noted that his work might not be applicable for minority and non-traditional student populations. For instance, one study found that social integration does not predict the success of Latina/o students (Torres and Solberg 2001). Other researchers (Cabrera, Stampen, and Hansen 1990; Cabrera, Nora, and Castaneda 1993) noted that Tinto's model did not sufficiently account for external factors such as the ability to pay and that an integrated model combining Tinto's model with a greater consideration of external factors resulted in a "a more comprehensive understanding of the complex interplay among individual, environmental, and institutional factors" (Cabrera, Nora, and Castaneda 1993, 135).
   A recent and important contribution to retention scholarship from composition studies is the work of Powell (2009; 2014), who has taken a critical stance on some of the retention literature and has advised composition teachers and scholars to look at the push to raise retention rates with a critical eye. In particular, she noted that colleges and universities need to undergo more radical changes than currently being envisioned to support student success and that in composition classes we should consider teaching students with the realization that not every student is going to finish their college degree. Nonetheless, as Powell (2014) emphasized, writing instructors are in a unique position because they work with the majority of incoming students in relatively small classes.
   Another exception to composition studies' absence from broader conversations on first-year student success and engagement has been the CWPA partnership with the National Survey of Student Engagement (NSSE). This partnership led to the creation of 27 questions informed by current research in composition that have been added to the NSSE. Because this survey is being administered at 584 colleges and universities in 2012 alone, this partnership promotes the importance of writing in the first year of college while providing invaluable data concerning students' writing experiences and its role in promoting engagement and success. The creator of the NSSE, George Kuh, has focused extensively on student engagement in the first year of college and some of his work is particularly salient to the study presented in this book.
   Using two other surveys he created, the College Student Expectations Questionnaire and the College Student Experiences Questionnaire, Kuh evaluated whether or not students' first-year experiences matched their expectations. This analysis resulted in a rather depressing conclusion: "Students' expectations for college often surpass the academic demands they are presented. That is, students typically study less, write

less, and read less than they come to college expecting to do. The gap between expectations and experiences also extends to life beyond the classroom" (Kuh 2005, 106). While 87 percent of students say they will use support services like writing centers, only 56 percent have done so by end of the first year (92). These numbers reveal that students often come to college with high expectations and for a variety of reasons, these expectations are consistently not met.

Shilling and Shilling (2005) confirmed these findings about expectations, writing that students come to college expecting to work harder than they actually do, but work less than they initially expect. In a study focused on limited learning taking place at college, Arum and Roksa (2011, 69) found that 37 percent of college students report spending five hours or less per week on studying and class preparation. Only 42 percent of students reported substantial reading and writing assignments.[4] Students in my study came to college with expectations for much more work than high school and the reading demands in particular exceeded their expectations.[5] On the other hand, outside of their FYC and history classes, students generally were assigned much less writing than anticipated.

Astin's (1997) *What Matters in College: Four Critical Years Revisited* provides a number of findings that detail student and faculty traits and practices that promote student engagement and success. Drawing on data from more than 20,000 students, 25,000 faculty members, and 200 institutions, Astin found that students were more successful when they lived on campus and were taught by faculty at institutions with a teaching orientation. In addition, he found that student-student, faculty-student interactions, time spent socializing with friends, talking with faculty outside of class, and being invited to a professor's home were all positively correlated with success. Of some of the most negative involvement factors, working full-time as a student, which many LM students do, and working even part-time off-campus, were seen as having negative effects on student retention. From the review of these various factors, Astin (1997, 197) concluded, "Practically all the involvement variables showing positive associations with retention suggest high involvement with faculty, with fellow students, or with academic work. Most of the involvement measures showing negative effects (working full-time, working off campus, commuting, reading for pleasure) represent involvements that take time and energy away from the academic experience."

As I argue more fully in my concluding comments, the writing classroom is a small but important part of most students' first-year experiences and a site with great potential to promote student engagement. By exploring research like Astin's (1997), Kuh's (2005), more critical takes like Powell's (2014), and conducting studies like the one presented in this book, composition researchers can begin to shape writing programs and classrooms to better serve students on campus who struggle in adapting to college. These students may no longer match the traditional profile of a college student as a "primarily middle class, eighteen years old, single, fresh out of high school, studying full time, enrolled in a four-year college, living away from home for the first time, meeting traditional standards of academic preparedness, and graduating in four years" (Ishler 2005, 15). Instead, they may come to college with limited high school preparation, have to work part or full time to support their studies, struggle with aspects of academic English, or have a dependent or two to care for.

As noted by other researchers (e.g., Hrabowski 2005; Leki 2007; Merisotis and McCarthy 2005; Sternglass 1997; Suárez-Orozco, Suárez-Orozco, and Todorova 2008; Valdés 2001), and present in the case studies throughout this book, it is clear that LM students face a number of challenges outside the classroom that impact the writing they do in and for the classroom. Too many institutions and teachers, writing teachers included, operate from a monocultural, mainstream US point of view, which means students' home lives, cultures, and languages are often ignored in the actual university classroom (Canagarajah 2006; Horner and Trimbur 2002; Matsuda 2006; Stage and Manning 1992; Schroeder 2011). The focal institutions in this study are no exception in this regard, as the vast majority of instruction occurs in English and, as will be discussed later, assignments rarely build on students' multilingual competencies. As a field, we have come a long way in realizing that our FYC students are not a "homogeneous" group (Matsuda 2006), but still have much work to do in transforming our practices and institutions into spaces ready for the twenty-first century student.

## THE STUDY
### Community Context
The study presented in this book was conducted in El Paso, Texas, a major metropolitan area on the US/Mexico border and home to approximately 700,000 people. The partner city, Ciudad Juárez, is right across the border in Mexico and home to around 1.3 million people. The two cities have been closely connected throughout history, as citizens from both have regularly crossed the border to work, shop, seek educational opportunities, and enjoy the nightlife. This exchange of people has been increasingly limited over the past several years due to the militarization of the border as evidenced by the construction of the border wall through

El Paso; as well as the increasing drug violence in Mexico. Because of the violence in Ciudad Juárez during the time of this study, many people from El Paso stopped crossing regularly unless necessary to visit family or attend to business. On the other hand, people who live in Ciudad Juárez, including one student in this study, regularly crossed into El Paso to shop, study, and visit relatives, some having emigrated there for safety.

According to data provided by Borderlands Community College (BCC), 82 percent of El Paso is Latina/o and 61 percent of the businesses are Latina/o-owned, which is well above the national averages. However, the median household income is $35,637 and almost a quarter of all families are below poverty level. 18.4 percent of El Paso citizens have less than a ninth grade education, a rate three times higher than the national average of 6.4 percent. About 25 percent of citizens have some sort of degree from higher education (an associate, bachelor's, or graduate degree), which again, is below the national average of 35 percent. In response to these low education levels, the postsecondary institutions in this study have worked hard to serve the local community and foster educational attainment.

El Paso has a unique linguistic situation compared to non-border US cities of similar size, and most inhabitants are bilingual to some extent, some Spanish dominant and some English dominant. Knowledge of both Spanish and English is commonly expected of job applicants where people work directly with customers or clients, such as in banking, law, and more service-oriented jobs. While the majority of homes are Spanish dominant (US Census Bureau 2009), English, Spanish, and Spanglish are commonly heard in public spaces. The neighborhood where the high school was situated was very Spanish dominant.

### Academic Contexts

The first part of this study was conducted at Samson High School (SHS), which was an overwhelmingly Latina/o, low-income school of approximately 1,300 students, including a high percentage of limited English proficiency (LEP) students (see Table 1.1).[6] In classes, students generally used Spanish to communicate with each other when they worked in groups; however, as was common at this particular school, they would often switch between English and Spanish during their conversations. Teachers used English for the vast majority of instruction, only sometimes saying words in Spanish to help or connect with students. The English teacher who taught all the mainstream senior English classes did not know Spanish beyond a few basic words.

Table 1.1. Characteristics of Samson High School

| Student Characteristics | Percent of students |
|---|---|
| Minority (overwhelmingly Latina/o) | 99.5 |
| Economically Disadvantaged | 93.1 |
| Limited English Proficiency | 38.2 |
| Immigrant | 8.1 |
| Migrant | 4.5 |
| At-risk[7] | 80.1 |

Students, teachers, and administrators all felt extreme pressure due to state and national mandated testing, which came in the form of the Texas Assessment of Knowledge and Skills (TAKS), a test that every student needed to pass in order to graduate.[8] Because SHS had a high number of LEP students, they faced a particularly acute challenge in preparing students to pass since the instructions and problems for the test were all in English.

Borderlands University (BU), where four of the students from this study began college, was a publically funded institution with just over 21,000 students during the time of this study. Around 19,000 were undergraduate and 3,600 were graduate students, with the latter number increasing as the university strived to be a top research university. BU drew mainly local students, with 83 percent of the student body coming from El Paso County. An additional 8 percent of students were from Mexico, with these students primarily coming from Ciudad Juárez, just across the border. BU was overwhelmingly Latina/o, with 76 percent of students identifying as Hispanic and an additional 6.7 percent as Mexican nationals. Given that BU drew students largely from the local area, it is unsurprising that 40 percent of the students were enrolled part time as they maintained full or part time jobs while attending school. Also, the average age of undergraduates was twenty-three. When the students profiled in this study entered college, tuition and fees at BU were about three times those of Borderlands Community College (BCC), approximately $2,600 for twelve credit hours.

BCC, where three students from this study began college, served approximately 30,000 students on five different campuses. All students attended the Colorado campus, which had about 4,500 credit-enrolled students. BCC's credit student enrollment was over 85 percent Latina/o, which was a slightly higher percentage than the university's Latina/o population. While breakdowns for individual campuses were not available, faculty interviews confirmed percentage variances between campuses. For instance, the Colorado campus served many students from downtown neighborhoods, which were overwhelmingly Latina/o and low income. The tuition and fees at the College were much lower than at the university, approximately $800 for twelve credit hours.

**Study Design**

This study began its development about a year before collecting data, when I entered SHS as a volunteer through a college readiness program with a desire to conduct a study focused on students transitioning to college. Over the course of that first year, I came once or twice weekly as a volunteer—first in ESL classes and then in senior English classes, meeting students and teachers who later became part of the study. While taking part in various classes and having informal interactions with teachers and students, I refined research questions and developed interview protocols that would later be used in the more formal data collection stage. After spending a semester and a half at the school, I extended invitations to all students in SHS's senior English classes to join this study, explaining that the main criteria for inclusion was a strong intention to begin college locally the following fall. I then began to actively collect data from participants at the beginning of the spring semester, following students their final semester at high school and through their first year at college. I conducted follow up interviews with five of the seven participants at the end of their second year at college in order to see if their paths had changed since the conclusion of the larger study.

In conducting this study, I took an ethnographic case study approach, in which I immersed myself as fully as possible in the high school culture for an extended period of time while focusing on individual agents within that community. The ethnographic approach enabled me to develop a broader understanding of the educational environments students inhabited as it involved going beyond individual students to gain the perspectives provided by teachers, administrators, and institutional documentation. Combining this with case studies enabled me to look at the participants as individuals with different abilities and different sets of struggles connected with larger environments they inhabited, a focus that becomes prominent as I move into presenting their case studies.

A key element of ethnographic research is taking the stance of a participant observer in order to become more fully connected with the culture one is learning from. Action research has a long history in rhetoric and composition, with researchers recognizing the value of being more integrated in a community (Faber 2002; Heath 1983; Moss 1992) as well as the ethical issues of traditional research in that it tends to benefit the researcher more than the researched (Bleich 1993; Brueggermann 1996; Cook 1998; Faber 2002). In the book *Community Action and Organizational Change*, Faber (2002, 13) criticized the traditional university/outside world, researcher/participant dichotomies, arguing that the researcher needs to play a more active, interested role in the community they are studying in order to understand it better: "I found that in order to fully understand change, I needed to play a self-conscious, direct role in change and fully experience the consequences, successes, and risks associated with change."

As an action researcher, I did not passively observe the classes I attended, but circulated separately from the teacher, supporting his efforts in giving individual students feedback on various writing assignments. I occasionally led activities, especially those building up to an analytical essay on *Lord of the Flies*. Being in this role helped me witness the constant challenges bombarding teachers at SHS: constant last-minute interruptions to class schedules for events such as pep-rallies, laptop carts where only half the computers worked, and a lack of books necessitating that students do all their reading in class. When occupied with helping students during class time, I would record observation notes between classes. Outside the classroom, I helped the study participants with scholarship essays and, in one case, wrote a recommendation letter for a scholarship. In college, I kept in touch with students via text messaging, MySpace, Facebook, and email. I exchanged texts with one participant on Friday nights as she was trying to figure out a thesis for an essay and with another one who was at the records and registration office struggling to register for her classes. I met with some students regularly at their request to give feedback on their essays. In one instance, I edited an essay last minute to help a participant avoid the wrath of a teacher obsessed with grammatical correctness. I kept in touch with the students who never started college, Facebook messaging them or texting them to see when they planned to go back and how I could help.

### Participants

Although attending the same high school, the students in this study came to college with differing abilities and resources to support their transitions. While some had low B averages, others were in the top 10 percent of their high school class. While a few lived in the United States all their lives, others came to the States as late as eighth grade. While most identified Spanish as their first language, one learned Spanish in high school. See Table 1.2 for an overview of participants.

Here, I will introduce each student briefly in anticipation of the detailed case studies featured in chapters 3–6.

### *Bianca*

Although Bianca spent her whole life in the United States, she lived in a Spanish-speaking household and attended bilingual classes until about sixth grade. Bianca had exceptional challenges in her home life. Her mother was arrested and deported her junior year in high school, leaving Bianca to care for her younger siblings. As a result, Bianca was responsible for three children as she graduated from high school with a B average and transitioned into college, where she was supported by a scholarship program for children of migrant workers. As will be explored in her case study, Bianca was also a very active member of a non-denominational Christian church, which was a very important source of support in her life.

### *Carolina*

Carolina was born just across the border from El Paso and lived there until the beginning of eighth grade when she moved to the United States with her mother after her parents separated. Carolina reported attending ESL classes along with a few other classes in English in eighth and ninth grades. Because she had not learned any English in her classes in Mexico, this was a difficult time for her and she reported understanding nothing in her classes at first. Although Carolina lacked confidence in her English and was very quiet when I met her at the beginning of senior year in high school, she was an exceptionally dedicated student. This dedication helped her learn English in a few years, graduate a year early from high school in the top 10 percent of her class, and have a very successful first year of college at BU.

### *Daniel*

Daniel spent his whole life in the United States and was the only student in the larger study to identify English as his first language. Although his grandmother only spoke Spanish and his father was a native Spanish speaker, he did not really develop his knowledge of Spanish until high school. There, he felt pressure to learn in order to fit in with the dominant student culture. Daniel attended a middle school where he

Table 1.2. Overview of study participants*

| Participant | Years in US (start of study) | Family status | HS Senior English | HS GPA | FYC 1 | FYC 2 | College GPA 1st /2nd semester |
|---|---|---|---|---|---|---|---|
| Bianca | Entire life | Guardian of 3 siblings, lives in US | B- | B | C | B | 2.57/not reported |
| Carolina | 4 | Lived with mother and siblings in US | A | A+ | A | A | 3.42/3.75 |
| Daniel | Entire life | Lived with grand-mother in US, parents separated | A | B- | B (dev.) | Dropped | 0.0/0.0 |
| Joanne | Entire life | Lived with cousin in US, then with parents in Mexico | B | Not reported | No writing class | No writing class | 0.0/0.0 |
| Mauricio | 0 | Lived with parents in Mexico | A+ | A | B | A | 3.0/4.0 |
| Paola | 11 (always attended school in US) | Lived with parents, later with b/f in Mexico | A | Not reported | A | Dropped | 4.0/0.0 |
| Yesenia | 9 | Lived in US with mother and siblings | B | B+ | B (dev.) | B | 2.66/2.57 |

\* *Due to IRB restrictions, this information was self-reported by the participants.*

remembered speaking English all the time, which also had a lower percentage of immigrant students than the middle school that Carolina, Paola, and many other students at SHS attended. Daniel was different in other ways as he was the only non-first generation college student in the study, with his father working as a teacher and pursuing a master's in Education. Nonetheless, he struggled throughout the latter part of high school and especially during his first year of college at BCC.

### Joanne

Joanne was a quiet, hard-working student when I met her in high school. Although she spent her whole life in US schools, she spent her early years living with her parents in Ciudad Juárez. In order for her to easily attend US schools she lived with different family members on the United States side of the border. In high school, she lived with a boyfriend for a while with whom she had a child her junior year, but they separated and she moved in with her cousin who was attending community college. She started college at BCC and struggled to balance her dual lives of parent and student, dropping or failing most classes.

### Mauricio

Of the students in this study, Mauricio came from the most affluent background. He had spent his whole life in Ciudad Juárez and continued to live there while he transitioned into the US school system in the first year of high school. He explained that he had come with no knowledge of English except for the alphabet, which his mother had taught him, even though neither she nor Mauricio's father knew English. While he reported having an English class in elementary or middle school, he said it was more like a free period and thus he did not learn much English there. Due to his language abilities, his grades suffered his first year at high school but he ended up graduating in the top 10 percent of his class. This remarkable achievement stems in part from his close relationship with his sophomore year ESL teacher, which went way beyond the classroom, as well as his parents, who aggressively pushed him to succeed academically. In general, he had a successful first year at college, but did not get the 4.0 GPA he hoped for.

### Paola

Paola came to the United States in first grade with parents who immigrated seeking better opportunities for their children. She was in a bilingual program until fifth grade; however, like other students, she reported a tough transition into mainstream classes as the bilingual program was mostly in Spanish. Paola and Joanne were close friends, always sitting together in their senior English classes and helping each other with class activities. In high school, Paola was a bit of a hippie, carrying a hemp bag emblazoned with a marijuana leaf and wearing more casual and baggy clothes than the other female students in her class. She spoke English very well and was a strong writer, something likely supported by her deep thinking personality. She started college at BCC and earned a 4.0 GPA her first semester, but stopped out[9] her second semester as she became more involved in a relationship with a boyfriend across the border.

### Yesenia

Yesenia had one of the most active social lives of the students in the study (i.e., she liked to party), regularly bringing friends to interviews and talking about going out on the weekends. She came to the United States in fourth grade with her mother and older brother. She said she did not have a father, which may be taken to mean she did not know or remember him. After a failed attempt to settle in Denver, Yesenia's family returned to Ciudad Juárez before settling in El Paso. Compared to other students in this study, Yesenia faced more education-related challenges, possibly because she transitioned to the US educational system later than some of the others. She was in an ESL program from fourth through seventh grade, and transitioned to mainstream English in eighth grade. She graduated high school with a B average and was placed in developmental writing classes upon starting at BU.

### Data Collection

The primary and most important source of data came from interviews with the student participants in this study, which were held three times a semester. These interviews were semi-structured, guided by six questionnaires (see Appendix A for student survey and interview guides). I asked students questions that focused on their background and home lives, their favorite and least favorite writing teachers and practices, the writing experiences they had in high school and college, their attitudes and experiences with standardized testing, and successes and challenges they faced both inside and outside school. Before each interview, previous interview transcripts were reviewed in order to modify questions or, if necessary, formulate follow up questions. Student interviews provided the most personal view into the students' lives and helped examine how they view their development and how they reacted to the numerous contextual factors influencing their development as writers. The personal contact afforded by these interviews gave me an opportunity to build trust with participants that was essential in obtaining meaningful, honest, and helpful responses from them.

In addition to student interviews, interviews were conducted with the participants' writing teachers and, at the college level, a few other relevant teachers and administrators. During high school, I interviewed the senior English teacher I worked with, Mr. Robertson, as well as most of the English teachers at the school. At the college level, I interviewed the students' writing instructors, or in the case that a student did not have a writing instructor, an instructor from a class where they were likely to do more writing such as a first-year seminar. Teacher interviews focused on pedagogical practices, types of assignments, hindrances to providing good writing instruction, use of technology, and opinions of the participant/s they taught.

Other interviews at the college level were conducted with the head of a scholarship program one student was involved in, history professors, and administrators who focused on improving students' first-year experiences. Administrator interviews centered on their experiences promoting student success and the history professor interviews focused on how and why they focused so much on writing in their classes. Protocols for teacher and administrator interviews are found in Appendix B.

Another important source of data came from classroom observations. As mentioned earlier, I took a more active role in the classroom at the high school level. For the students' last semester at college, I attended classes twice a week, alternating classes each week due to the block scheduling used at the school. Because of the nature of action research, observation notes were taken during down times in class or between classes, which led to fewer notes than I normally would have taken. At the college level, I took a traditional researcher stance in the classroom because of my familiarity with the perspective of a college instructor. Here, I focused on observing participants' writing classes and, in the case that they did not have a writing class, a related class where they did writing such as their first-year seminar. I observed three classes for each student each semester, and interviewed the teachers of these classes. These observations focused on what the teacher and my focal students said or did during the classes since the other students in the classes were not involved in this study.

I collected writing samples from students as they were willing to share them. With permission, I made copies of their senior English portfolios; however, some students had full portfolios while others had barely anything in them, preferring to keep work at home because of concerns that other students would take their work. I also made copies of at least two major senior year assignments for their English class. At the college level, some students actively came to me for feedback, emailing essays from not only their English classes but also their history class. In other cases, where students did not send me writing for feedback, I collected at least one sample a semester from students or their teachers, usually more.

Because of our close relationship, the high school teacher shared much of his teaching materials and lesson plans. For the college level English classes, I collected syllabi, and when students or teachers shared them, individual assignment prompts for essays. Since the BU

FYC curriculum was standardized, information about the assignment prompts were taken from the program guide. In addition to having FYC class assignments, a few BU students shared their history assignments as well (the BCC students did not write in history classes). In addition to class-related documentation, I collected materials such as school newspapers, announcements distributed in class, and other items that were relevant in better understanding the study sites.

### Theoretical Framework and Analysis

A number of researchers have critiqued how traditional academic research focuses too intently on the classroom, ignoring the importance of students' lives outside the classroom in determining their success (Arispe y Acevedo 2008; Cummins 2000; Leki 2007; Rendón, Jalomo, and Nora 2000). While what occurs in the classroom is important, data consistently show that characteristics such as family income level, parents' educational background, employment while attending school, and social connections on campus are correlated with success. Understanding that students' transitions to college—and their success in writing classes—are situated in a much larger context, I designed this study to examine both students' curricular and extracurricular lives and argue throughout that both need to be considered by researchers in studies on college transition and writing development. Bourdieu's theories of habitus, capital, and field[10] along with Yosso's (2005) theory of community cultural wealth, a reinterpretation of Bourdieu's theory of capital informed by Critical Race Theory (CRT), provided a theoretical framework that moved data collection and analysis beyond the classroom to help me situate the institutions and writing classrooms students passed through in a broader context.

Throughout the case studies, I include figures based on Yosso's (2005) theory of community cultural wealth. Traditional research has often used Bourdieu's theories of habitus and capital to focus on how LM students lack the habitus and capital necessary to succeed in schools (Oropeza, Varghese, and Kanno 2010; Yosso 2005). Understanding that Bourdieu's theories were being used unjustly (and, as I argue in chapter 7, inaccurately), Yosso (2005, 74) used a CRT framework to reinterpret Bourdieu's theories, which she said "refutes dominant ideology and White privilege while validating and centering the experiences of People of Color." Instead of perpetuating the deficit mindset, Yosso began with the premise that minority communities possess cultural wealth. In her study, she identified six types of community cultural wealth:

- aspirational capital—high aspirations possessed by community members for a child's future
- linguistic capital—"the intellectual and social skills attained through communication experiences in more than one language and/or style" (2005, 78)
- familial capital—extended family network, including immediate family, extended family, and close friends
- social capital—"networks of people and community resources" (79)
- navigational capital—the ability, with help of the social and familial network, to negotiate unfamiliar institutions
- resistant capital—"oppositional behavior that challenges inequality" (80)

In readapting Yosso's model, I included challenges that the study participants faced in making successful transitions to college, understanding that it is important to account for these while avoiding the "deficit" mindset that Yosso criticized. The figures presented leave out resistant capital, since it was not a common theme among the participants.

As is typical for longitudinal studies like this one, data were analyzed recursively throughout the collection process. All interviews were transcribed, read recursively, and coded as the study progressed. Codes were developed inductively from the data, and separate sets of codes were developed for the instructor and student participants. Student codes identified attitudes toward teachers, fellow students, challenges and sources of support, and reading and writing assignments, among other items. Teacher codes identified themes such as philosophies about teaching, types of assignments given, and attitudes toward multilingual students as well as students in this study. I began to write the case studies while collecting data, revisiting previous data, incoming data, and the case study drafts, refining them through and beyond the data collection process. Data were triangulated throughout this process, with student and teacher interview data being compared with observational data. This triangulation helped me move beyond the bias inherent in participants selectively remembering experiences or wishing to construct a particular image of themselves and those around them.[11]

## PLAN OF THE BOOK

The next chapter begins by exploring why students decided to pursue a college degree and how they chose between attending a two-year or four-year institution. The remainder focuses on exploring writing instruction at the different institutions involved in this study in more detail, drawing on institutional and observational data along with the interviews conducted with teachers at the high school and college levels.

Chapters 3–6 turn to student case studies that are grouped by how smoothly students transitioned into college. Like Leki (2007), I utilize secondary sources minimally in these chapters in order to focus on the students' stories. The case studies are all similarly structured, starting by detailing the students' backgrounds as well as the challenges and sources of support they found within school and outside of school. Joanne's and Daniel's stories are shared in the third chapter, "Struggling Transitions." The next chapter, "Difficult but Successful Transitions," focuses on Bianca and Yesenia who overcame great odds to have successful first years at college. Chapter 5, "Smooth Transitions," discusses the experiences of Maricio and Carolina, who excelled in high school and transitioned to college with relative ease. The sixth chapter, "An Unpredictable Transition," features Paola, who started out strong her first semester but dropped out early in her second semester because of personal choices.

Chapter 7 revisits the case studies in light of two theoretical frameworks, Bourdieu's analytical tools of habitus, capital, and field as well as Yosso's theory of community cultural wealth, and explores how students formed robust networks of capital to facilitate transitions to college. This is followed by a discussion that moves the discourse of student success away from student failures to a focus on how students are failed by institutional and other factors.

The final chapter concludes the book by offering ways that writing administrators, teachers, and researchers can facilitate institutional and societal transformations to more effectively support LM students as they write across institutions. I explore how teachers and administrators can assess student needs and redesign program and classroom curricula to engage and support the success of LM student populations. I suggest ways that writing administrators and teachers work toward curriculum alignment across institutions while developing stronger community engagement in writing programs. Finally, I call on researchers to rethink composition studies' processes of disciplinary knowledge construction in order to gain more credibility with institutional leaders and policy makers.

The book concludes with an epilogue based on interviews with five of the seven students at the end of their second year in college. It depicts how their stories are continually being formed and emphasizes the multitude of factors that come into play as students transition into and through college, explaining that while the first year is important in determining student success, much can happen beyond the first year.

## Notes

1. Institution names and all participant names are pseudonyms.
2. I use a few different terms to refer to diverse student populations throughout this book. The most prominent one is Latina/o. I prefer this term over Hispanic because of the politicized nature the latter has acquired through being an official census and institutional term. In using Latina/o, it is important to be aware of the work of Hall Kells (1999) and others who have explored the problematic nature surrounding the broadness of a label which treats first, second, and third generation immigrants who originally came from a wide number of different countries as a homogeneous group. In order to be more specific, I use Mexican American when talking only about the students in this study. In expanding the discussion to include multilingual non-Latina/o minorities, I refer to linguistic minority students, which Kanno and Harklau (2012, 2) define as "multilingual individuals who speak a non-English language at home." Daniel is the only student who does not quite fit under this label, as he did not really learn Spanish until high school and speaks mostly English at home; however, Spanish was an important part of his home life, especially in communicating with his grandmother.
3. Throughout this manuscript, I prefer the term retention over persistence even though the latter is more commonly used among retention researchers like Tinto (1993). Retention focuses on the need for an institution to take action to help make students successful, while persistence places the onus on individual students to succeed. Consequently, as I focus on the need for institutional change in order to avoid upholding the tradition of looking at students through a deficit lens (i.e. they fail to persist), I prefer retention in this manuscript. In doing so, I do recognize a sense of mutual responsibility and that the primary goal of retention initiatives should be to help students persist towards graduation, not simply boost institutional retention rates. Similarly, I recognize Adelman's (2006, 107) point that overemphasizing institutional agency has the risk of treating students as deficient and passive receptors of institutional interventions.
4. Arum and Roksa (2011, 71) defined substantial as twenty plus pages of writing in a class over the course of the semester and a weekly average of forty plus pages of reading. These expectations could be met in different classes.
5. As will be discussed later, even the highest achieving students in this study did not complete all the reading they were assigned, often choosing to skim the reading or not do it at all when they knew it would be lectured through in class. On the other end of the spectrum, some students did little to no reading assigned to them, in part because they were not held accountable for it.
6. Enrollment and, where relevant, tuition data for the three institutions were collected from district and/or institutional websites.
7. In 1988, the Texas legislature created an official definition for at risk students, which was defined as a student meeting one or more of the following conditions: "The student had been retained one or more times in Grades 1–6 based on academic achievement and remained unable to master the Essential Elements at the current grade level; the student was two or more years below grade level in reading or mathematics; the student had failed at least two courses in one or more semesters and was not expected to graduate within four years of entering ninth grade; the student had failed one or more of the reading, writing, or mathematics sections of the Texas Educational Assessment of Minimum Skills (TEAMS), beginning with the seventh grade" (TEA, 2006, 102). Interestingly, in the report from which this information was taken, the authors repeatedly grouped "at risk" with "immigrant," "limited English proficiency," and "migrant" when referring to "other student characteristics" (50).

8. The TAKS was the assessment used by Texas since 2003 but has recently been phased out, replaced for the 2011–2012 school year by the State of Texas Assessments of Academic Readiness (STAAR). The new test requires students to write two essays rather than one (TEA 2011b), so it may lead to better writing instruction as long as those two essays are from different genres.
9. Stop out is an alternative to drop out, as the latter and more commonly recognized term indicates that one is perpetually out of higher education after a moment of departure. Stop out on the other hand indicates that some students come and go for reasons such as saving money to pay for tuition, and that it does not mean they have given up on pursuing higher education. I prefer the term stop out to drop out throughout this book, because it is normal for non-traditional students to go in and out of college.
10. For those unfamiliar with Bourdieu's framework, field is the encompassing framework where habitus and capital are developed, and one can inhabit multiple fields. In this study, I considered the participants' home and educational settings as different fields and broke down the educational field by institution: high school, community college, and university. This was further broken down to the classroom level. Because this study was conducted on the border, I considered, along with the local contexts in both countries, the state and national context in the United States. One develops certain dispositions or habitus, based on the fields they inhabit. This habitus may be better aligned for success and capital acquisition in certain fields while not as useful in a different field or fields. Capital can refer both to economic and cultural capital, with certain ways of being and acquisition of tangible or intangible objects valued in different ways in different fields. Looking at the high school to college transitions of students requires one to consider how the habitus they developed in high school (and the associated capital that brought them to a particular high school and supported or failed to support their studies within) facilitates or hinders their transition to college.
11. This was particularly the case with Mauricio. For instance, he told me he would never speak Spanish in his English class, but observations revealed this to be different. He brutally chastised some of his first-year college instructors, and observations confirmed some of these critiques while dispelling others.

# 2
# COLLEGE DECISIONS AND INSTITUTIONAL DISPARITIES

**MAKING DECISIONS ABOUT COLLEGE**

With the decline of the well-paying manufacturing jobs and inexpensive agricultural lands, education is the new form of entry into US society for students from immigrant families like those featured in this study (Suárez-Orozco and Suárez-Orozco 2001; Perez 2008). Apodaca (2008, 59) has claimed that education is the single most important asset to "ensure personal and professional growth and to become a more productive member of the community." The desire for a more successful future is strong among all the students who took part in my study, and it is clear they identify education as a key element of this future. However, not only the choice of going to college is important, but also the choice of where.

A major challenge facing the success of Latina/o students is that they often receive limited information about college. They commonly depend on information from family and friends, many of whom may not have attended college (Department of Education 2006; Person and Rosenbaum 2006). Persistent financial barriers and family members unfamiliar with navigating the complex processes of applying for financial aid and scholarships are also a problem (Department of Education 2006; St. John and Musoba 2010). Because of these factors, along with a desire to be close to family, Latinas/os have a tendency to attend a much less competitive institution than they might otherwise be admitted to (Kurlaender 2006; Nuñez and Sparks 2012; Ortiz and Santos 2009).

### Why Attend College?

At the beginning of this study, I asked students why they wanted to go to college. Here are their responses as originally written:[1]

### Desire for a Better Life
Yesenia: "I want to go to college because i want to have a good life."

Daniel: "I would go to college to get a degree in something so I can not have to worry about financial and other problems."

Mauricio: "Day to day life gets harder and harder, and the only way ohaving a little chance of succesing its by having a college education."

Carolina: "I want to go to college because i know that that's the only way I can have a better future."

### Desire for a Better Life for Family
Bianca: "Well i want to attend collage because i want to be a succesful person in life and i want to buy a house for my mother and little brothers . . ."

Mercedes (did not matriculate to college): "I would like a better future for my future family and I."

### Achieving Personal Goals
Cecilia (did not matriculate to college): "I want to go to college because I want to be a better person, more trained and skilled."

Andrea (did not matriculate to college): "I would like to go to college because i want to do something with my life."

Joanne: "to study what i want to be"

### Feeling of Obligation
Paola: "I am trying to figure out if i want college but i think i need it in order to survive but i dont want to go i dislike this feeling of obligation."

With the exception of Mauricio, most of the students came from families that sometimes struggled to make ends meet, whether this meant having enough food on the table or paying for medicine or medical care when a family member became ill. Elaborating on her survey response in an interview, Yesenia stated that she wanted a better life than her mother had been able to provide: "I don't want to live like my mom, like the day and day, I want to have good money, a good house, and a good car. And for that I need education and stuff." Carolina similarly connected the lack of college degrees in her family to their life of struggle.

The second group above contains students who did not explicitly reference a better financial situation, but the desire to be a "better person," to achieve personal career goals, and to do something valuable with their life. As will be discussed later, Joanne's idea of what she wanted to be was still unformulated at this time, and constantly changed throughout her first year at college. While unfinished, Andrea's story is particularly upsetting. In discussing her response on the initial survey, she shared some details about her family: "My sister was gonna go to college but she didn't. She had a baby [at] 16, 2 years before she graduated from high school. And she graduated and she was living with her boyfriend and they separated and now she went with her current boyfriend to Atlanta and she's living over there, but she's not going to college, she's working. And then my mother never went, my dad didn't went my, nobody from my family went."

Andrea kept repeating a desire to get out of town as quickly as possible. While she had aspirations to go to the state flagship university, she eventually settled on a small state college several hundred miles away. Unfortunately, she became pregnant over the summer before college and was too overwhelmed with working out ways to provide for her future child to consider college at the time.

### In Town or Out of Town?

After deciding whether or not to go to college, students make the choice to attend a local institution or conduct a statewide or national search and application process. For the "traditional" middle or upper class college student, moving out of town and becoming independent is part of the "college experience." However, for many of the students in this study, financing an out-of-town education was ultimately out of the question, and, for those with sufficient access to scholarship money to leave town, leaving their families was too difficult.

For several of the students, like Mauricio and Andrea, the state flagship university was one of the major out of town options. Because of a state law that stipulates the top 10 percent of high school graduates have to be admitted to any school in the state university system (see Rodríguez 2012), Mauricio and Carolina would not have had a problem getting admitted. Mauricio applied and was admitted to the flagship school, but he ultimately decided to stay in town and attend BU with the rationale being his family: "My family. I'm really attached to them. It's not real good, right but I am attached to my parents and brothers and everything here. I think that leaving would make things way hard. Harder than it would be here."

Carolina and Bianca also considered out of town colleges, and actually applied to them, but ultimately decided to stay in town for their families. Carolina had gone on a campus visit to a Catholic college in San Antonio, applied, and was accepted. However, she felt it would be hard to move away because of her connection to family and her desire to help with their difficult financial situation.

Bianca thought about going out of town as well, albeit to a university 45 minutes from El Paso. She planned to apply for a scholarship program for children of migrant workers, the College Assistance Migrant Program (CAMP), that would help cover the costs. However, because she had custody of her siblings, this was a priority in making a college decision. She explained, "Yes, I have [thought about leaving town] but it's really in my family. My brothers [siblings]. I don't want to leave them . . . There's nobody that can take care of them like me." She decided to stay in town.

Yesenia also demonstrated serious interest in leaving El Paso, albeit for different reasons than the others. She initially planned to attend a state university or the local community college in San Antonio that her boyfriend attended. Outside of going for her boyfriend, she gave other reasons such as there were more fun things to do there and it would help her experience the world beyond El Paso. The traditional idea of becoming more independent of her family also played into her mind: "Well, I think it's good because I can become more independent and try to do stuff by myself. Because here like your mom is gonna be like oh *mi hija* do you want help or something and I don't want to be like that, I want to be independent." Like the others, Yesenia stayed in town. She realized that living with her boyfriend would put her under more financial hardship, and was influenced by the fact that her mom promised to help buy her a car if she stayed: "I was like if I stay here I'm going to have a new car and have more money to spend, clothes and everything. If I move I'm not going to have a lot of money."

**Community College or University?[2]**

Given the propensity for the participants to stay in town, the biggest choice they had to make was whether to start at the local community college or the university. This choice was by no means simple for many of the students, who went back and forth and considered factors ranging from class size, confidence, and cost in their decision-making process. Nonetheless, students like those profiled in this study continue to be overrepresented at community college and underrepresented at four-year colleges and universities (Cohen and Brawer 2008, 55–56). In 2010, 46 percent of Latina/o college students were at two-year colleges, compared to 37 percent of African American, 27 percent of white, and 22 percent of Asian students (Redden 2011). Although most students going to a two-year college attend with the goal to transfer to a four-year institution, the reality is that only about 25 percent of them actually do (Cohen and Brawer 2008, 60–65).

As noted in Table 2.1, an initial preference for a university, whether local or out of town, generally translated to a student ultimately beginning at BU. Similarly, if a student was set on BCC or wavering between the two at the beginning, they typically ended up at the community college. This consistency of preference aligns with the findings of a study of thousands of students in Indiana (Hossler, Schmit, and Vesper 1999).

Of the students, Daniel was set on BCC from the beginning, while the highest achieving students, Mauricio and Carolina, were strongly committed to BU. Daniel was a continual advocate for the community college first, describing it as a "step stool" and preferring it because he knew the classes would be smaller. In one interview, he commented that it would be "just like high school." As indicated in the following exchange, Daniel was largely following family members and his parents' preferences, even though they would not be contributing financially to his education:

> *Todd:* Why did you decide Community over BU or going out of town?
>
> *Daniel:* Well, it's kind a late to go out of town. BU I got accepted and everything but I'm just following my family, how they went to Community first and then make up my mind, what I want to do and my career and just go from there.
>
> *Todd:* So your family members also started at Community? Did they tell you why or did they make that recommendation for you?
>
> *Daniel:* Cause that's what our parents wanted. They wanted us to go to Community first. Or if we had the chance to go out of town to go but like . . . my family's not that smart so it's kind a hard to do that.

Even though Daniel had a precedent at BCC as his sisters were attending when this study began, they soon either dropped out or were suspended. Another consideration that was common among the students who chose the community college was cost. As Daniel noted, doing the "basics" at BCC was much cheaper, about a third the cost of BU.

For a time, Bianca was leaning toward BCC because, even though BU had a CAMP scholarship program too, she understood that she would have to live on campus her whole first year at college, something that would be impossible with her siblings. In rationalizing her decision to go to BCC, Bianca echoed BCC's advertising slogan "The best place to start," saying, "I know BU is a better quality college but BCC is the best place to start." Similarly, Paola commented, "Because I think it's a good way to start. You can just move up to BU." As with Daniel, finances were

Table 2.1. Student college preferences

| Student | Initial preference | Final choice |
|---|---|---|
| Bianca | Other University | BU |
| Carolina | BU | BU |
| Daniel | BCC | BCC |
| Joanne | BU/BCC | BCC |
| Mauricio | BU | BU |
| Paola | BU/BCC | BCC |
| Yesenia | Other University | BU |

an important concern for these students, and Bianca recalled a friend's advice: "Well this friend of mine told me it's better to go to BCC first and then transfer to BU because she went straight to BU and she told me it was harder and she had to pay a lot. She already finished. She already has her bachelor's degree but she has lots of loans and stuff like that. And I don't think she had any scholarships and stuff so she told me no, it's better to start at BCC because it's the same, the basics."[3] Without scholarship help, BU is more expensive and many of its students go to school on and off to avoid student loans, working in between to save money for tuition. However, just because both schools provide the "basics" does not mean that they are "the same," just as both offered very different writing experiences from those students experienced at SHS.

## WRITING INSTRUCTION ACROSS INSTITUTIONS

While volunteering, working, or researching in the three different institutional contexts of this study, it became readily apparent that students' experiences varied widely between them. In this next section, I explore these differences and their causes, discussing how high-stakes testing at the high school level, resource disparities at the postsecondary level, and other factors actively shaped students' literacy experiences as they transitioned from high school to college, helping construct a hierarchy of readiness for college and beyond.

At SHS, we see how political meddling in the K–12 system plays an important role in the persistent divide between high school and college, as universities have traditionally been "untouchable" in this regard (Kirst and Venezia 2001, 93). Turning to BCC, we learn how overworked and underpaid faculty members contribute to the existence of a very traditional writing program. Finally, examining BU, we learn how increased financial and knowledge resources contributed to the development of a writing program more situated in current disciplinary practice.[4]

**SAMSON HIGH SCHOOL**

Like many high schools serving high percentages of minority and low income students, SHS was no stranger to negative impacts from outside political forces. As the United States-Mexico border was increasingly militarized in the early 1990s, the border patrol began to harass students and faculty members. According to court records, the border patrol had a "regular, consistent, and prominent presence" (citation omitted for anonymity) on and around campus. The football coach was held at gunpoint and students were subjected to unauthorized searches and often forced to show evidence of citizenship.

Via a successful legal challenge, SHS overcame the negative and intrusive presence of the border patrol on and around campus. However, the first decade of the twenty-first century brought No Child Left Behind (NCLB), the most prominent example of political interference in K–12 schools in recent memory, going so far according to Suskind (2007, 450) as to govern "the nature of every school-age child's daily transactions with print." Researchers have extensively documented NCLB's negative impact on such schools and their students (Abedi 2004; Abedi, Hofstetter, and Lord 2004; Ambrosio 2004; Causey-Bush 2005; Lee and Wong 2004; Paul 2004; Stringfield and Yakimowski-Srebnick 2005; Jiménez 2003).

With this increased focus on standardized assessment at both the state and national levels, SHS had a new external challenge to contend with and increasingly faced the danger of being shut down because of low test scores. The school had its first year of low performance in the 1997–1998 school year and gradually progressed through stages of reform, reaching stage 5, around the time I began visiting the school. According to the "Title I School Improvement: Stage 5" document published by the Texas Education Agency (n.d.), a stage 5 school is defined as "A Title I, Part A campus identified for Stage 4 School Improvement in the previous school year that subsequently misses AYP [Adequate Yearly Progress] for the same indicator for the sixth consecutive year." A school at this stage is required to restructure, a process that "requires major changes in a campus' operation. The Local Education Agency (LEA) oversees the implementation of the campus' restructuring plan for alternative governance that was developed during Stage 4. The LEA must continue it's [sic][5] increased oversight and responsibility of the campus' reform efforts." The requirement for "alternative governance" can be met in a number of ways: (1) reopening the school as a charter school, (2) replace most or all of the school staff responsible for not meeting AYP, (3) bring in a private management company to run the school, (4) turn over operations to the state educational agency, or (5) "Any other major restructuring of school governance arrangement that makes fundamental reforms."

In general, teachers at schools like SHS are monitored more heavily and limited in terms of what and how they can teach (McCarthey 2008), something illustrated in the following discussion of literacy instruction at SHS. With these monitoring regimes, schools like SHS are increasingly under pressure to think in terms of a "sterile management imperative," pushing out students who drag down test scores (Booher-Jennings 2005). To maintain control over the school and ensure that teachers keep their jobs, the biggest priority within SHS was ensuring that students pass the TAKS. Consequently, test preparation completely dominated the literacy instruction that occurred in the majority of SHS classrooms. In the words of one teacher, "This is a TAKS academy; it's not a high school."

**Culture of Testing**

Preparing students for the TAKS assessment occupied much teaching time from freshman through junior year, with junior year being the year in which students took the exit level exam. Test preparation materials were found everywhere in the school, filling most of the bookshelves in classrooms and ending up in stacks several feet high in teacher lounges. When I volunteered with an ESL teacher during my first semester at SHS, virtually every class period was devoted to test preparation exercises such as multiple choice sentence correction, activities that were repetitive and uninteresting for both the teacher and the students.

One can understand the typical literacy tasks used in SHS classrooms by learning about the structure of the TAKS. The English section of the test began with a few short readings, totaling about seven pages. They were generally short narrative pieces, such as "My Father Sits in the Dark" by Jerome Weidman and "Going to America" by Nicholas Gage, both found in an April 2006 test packet. These were followed by a visual one-page text. Then students would be asked to answer multiple choice comprehension questions on the two stories, with a few questions expecting them to consider both stories together. After that, they answered three short answer questions, with two focusing on the readings separately and one asking students to consider them together (e.g., "What do the narrators learn about their fathers in 'My Father Sits in the Dark' and 'Going to America'? Explain your answer and support it with evidence from both selections."). This was followed by an essay with a prompt that built off of a theme in the stories. The English section concluded with a revising and editing section that asked students to demonstrate their ability to correct errors via multiple-choice items.

In contrast to the expository writing encouraged by the short answer questions, the essay encouraged more of a narrative. One prompt read, "Write an essay explaining the value of the small, everyday elements of life." As Beck and Jeffery (2007) demonstrated, there was a disconnect between prompts asking for an explanatory genre and benchmark papers consistently providing narrative examples. This disagreement on the genre expected for the TAKS essay existed among English teachers at SHS.

Ms. Carrera, who typically taught junior level students, recalled being told when she came to the high school a few years previously that she needed to focus almost exclusively on the narrative essay. Another junior teacher, Ms. Padilla, similarly felt pressure to teach the narrative, despite the repetitive nature of doing this type of writing all the time. In discussing this focus on the narrative, Ms. Padilla lamented the fact that teachers would help produce a "whole generation of crappy writers" because they would not know the other types of writing out there.

However, other teachers felt that the TAKS allowed for other types of writing, and that it was the teachers' fault for not teaching them. For instance, the sophomore year teacher Ms. Morgan, who often worked with ESL students, said she taught the narrative essay because that was the easiest type of essay for students to write. Over the course of the year, she brought students up to a passing score, a two, and expected junior level teachers to take them beyond this level by teaching expository writing.

In addition to teaching toward the test, teachers were expected to navigate and teach to state standards; however, multiple teachers noted that the TAKS did not align with these standards. For instance, the state English III curriculum expected students to read various literary, persuasive, and procedural texts (Texas Education Agency 2008). Similarly, students were expected to do different types of writing: creative, expository and procedural, and persuasive (Texas Education Agency 2008, section 110.31). A sophomore level teacher, Ms. Ortega, described the lack of alignment: "The focus is on TAKS . . . No one asks us for our lesson plans or asks us what we're doing to meet curriculum requirements. Because the curriculum is aligned to college writing. But no one is asking us to be accountable or responsible for that curriculum." As Ms. Ortega indicated, there was some understanding of the expectations of college-level writing in the state standards, but the goals set by the curriculum are negated by the design of the TAKS and the pressures associated with passing this test.

It has been well documented that LM students often have limited college preparation in high school due to a lack of advanced coursework or being steered into vocational tracks (Callahan and Shifrer 2012; Kirst and Venezia 2001; Mosqueda 2012). With this in mind, it is perhaps unsurprising that AP classroom experiences were very different from the mainstream ones, especially in terms of preparing students for college. Ms. Ortega explained that AP classes at SHS aligned closer to the actual state curriculum. As a result, AP students would write persuasive essays, analyses, syntheses, and other types of writing that mainstream students at SHS would likely not experience until college. Mr. Cordero, who exclusively taught senior dual credit and AP classes, explained that he did not feel pressure by the administration to teach a certain way: "As far as the pressure that's placed on me and the pressure I feel from administration, there's virtually none. I feel very confident in what I do and the students I have." This comment contrasted sharply with that of a mainstream teacher like Ms. Padilla, who explained that she was repeatedly disciplined and told to teach a certain way, even though it did not align with what she had learned in her teaching certification program.

Outside of AP courses, there was one other context in which teachers had relative freedom: senior year. This is the year I am most familiar with, having spent a year with Mr. Robertson in his classes, which included all of the mainstream senior English students. The two major essays during the year of this study were on *Beowulf* and *Lord of the Flies*. In addition, students read *Macbeth*, but did not have time to write an essay on it. Despite freedom from the TAKS, it was still a struggle to complete the readings in the class, and students were not able to finish *Lord of the Flies* or *Macbeth* but did finish the abridged version of *Beowulf* in their textbooks. This resulted from a number of factors, including a culture of no homework and the lack of books for students to take home, even if attempts were made to assign homework. Besides these problems, there were constant interruptions to class schedules. These interruptions included visits from college recruiters, visits to the computer lab to work on applications and financial aid, absences for basketball games, and shortened schedules for pep rallies. While understanding the importance of college-related activities, Mr. Robertson felt the interruptions were excessive and I witnessed firsthand how difficult it became to set and meet teaching goals.

Outside of these major writing assignments, senior mainstream students did have a few in-class writing assignments that were reminiscent of the TAKS. These writing assignments were part of another assessment mechanism, the Texas English Language Proficiency Assessment System (TELPAS), which was used to test students out of the Limited English Proficiency (LEP) classification. Like the TAKS, they encouraged personal narratives, albeit more explicitly. For this assessment, most teachers, including Mr. Robertson, had all students write essays to avoid singling anyone out. Students in the classes I observed responded to these three prompts:

- Write about a time you learned a powerful lesson about trust or loyalty, either because you were betrayed or supported.
- Write about a time you made up your mind about something and swore to yourself it would never change, no matter what.
- Write about a time you did a lot of thinking about doing something you knew was wrong, and then you did it, and then you wished you hadn't. When were you "guilty?" During your thinking? Or only after you acted?

Interviewed students generally had no idea why they were writing these assignments, consistently reported learning nothing through completing them, and did not receive any feedback from Mr. Robertson. It appeared that they were simply one of the many assessment hoops students were required to complete while at SHS, hoops that were designed without real consideration of student learning.

### BORDERLANDS COMMUNITY COLLEGE

Three of the seven focal students of this study began college at the same BCC campus, Colorado. As depicted in this section, students at BCC generally engaged in very different types of writing than those at both SHS and BU. While BCC did not face the political meddling that SHS did, it was constrained in ways that differentiated it from BU. For instance, while a four-year college has a specific mission oriented toward graduating students with undergraduate or graduate degrees, community colleges serve a variety of often disparate functions, including academic transfer, vocational-technical, continuing education, and community service tracks (Cohen and Brawer 2008, 22–26). Perhaps a more important driver are the systemic resource disparities typically found between two- and four-year institutions in overall funding and in specific areas like the amount of tenure-track lines (Klausman 2010) and technology access and support (Cohen and Brawer 2008).

### First-Year Composition

The FYC program at BCC was a two-semester sequence, ENG 1301 and ENG 1302, with the first-semester class taking an EDNA-style (expository, descriptive, narrative, and analytical) modes-based approach and the second-semester course being a combination of topic-based research and literary analysis. The official ENG 1301 syllabus revealed a traditional pedagogy, mentioning the usage of "modes of expression for writing assignments," understanding "Standard Written English in terms of grammatical sentence structure, spelling, punctuation, mechanics, and usage." Students were expected to "Draft [at least five major] essays of approximately 700–1000 words that focus on a thesis statement, with introduction, multiple body paragraphs which develop the major points indicated in the organizational plan of each essay, and an appropriate conclusion."

The EDNA modes dominated in the BCC ENG 1301 classes, with all four writing teachers interviewed for this study referencing this model when mentioning their classes. Paola's professor Dr. Thompson, who taught at the college for thirty-five years and had received his PhD in Rhetoric and Composition from a major Southwestern research university, explained his adherence to the modes approach: "I generally take . . . a rhetorical mode approach to the class, I'm not sure it's the best one, but when they write essays they tend to write classification, definition, comparison contrast, those kind of old chestnuts . . ." As Dr. Thompson explained, and this was echoed by others, his desire to innovate was limited by time. With a full-time teaching load at five courses a semester, which typically involved a minimum of three different class preparations, it is unsurprising that he described the papers as a "millstone" around his neck at times. While Dr. Thompson had the knowledge from his doctoral work and exposure to various composition journals, he simply did not have the time to implement new ideas unless he wanted to give up any semblance of a personal life.

Dr. Thompson's syllabus followed the modes model set forth by the standardized syllabus with four major essays: a personal narrative, definition, comparison/contrast, and cause/effect argumentative essay. He would also have students complete an in-class mini essay responding to an art museum exhibit and a final in-class essay, as a final exam was required by the department. From my observations, it became clear that Dr. Thompson required his students to do a lot of freewriting, even more so than other teachers observed/interviewed at the college.

There was some variation to the generic modes standard at BCC. For instance, I observed a learning community course, which paired ENG 1301 with an introductory sociology course and was taught by Ms. Warner, who had master's degrees in both creative writing and sociology. While students in this class tended to follow the modes taught in other courses, they were more fully integrated with sociology; for example, on the process essay, Ms. Warner had students write about food while including concepts about family and culture. The major essay of the semester, which counted toward the final grade in both classes, built on the process essay and had students research the culture surrounding the food with some sort of primary research.

BCC's second-semester FYC class, ENG 1302, focused half on writing a major research paper and half on analyzing and writing about literature. According to the course syllabus, some of the course objectives including expanding the knowledge learned in ENG 1301, having students "Follow an objective, logical, step-by-step process of research but demonstrate enough flexibility to revise plans as new insights emerge," and write one long or two shorter research papers. For the literary part of the class, students were expected to "use literary terminology," "Demonstrate analytical insight and appreciation of two literary types (short stories, poetry, drama, or film)," and write at least two essays with an interpretive/analytical emphasis.

Instructors typically went with the longer version of the research paper, which was typically in the eight to ten page range. One instructor, Ms. Flores, typically had students write fifteen pages and required them to submit forty-five pages of handwritten notes as part of their process. Ms. Flores said ENG 1302 was one of the most dropped courses at BCC and attributed this to the research paper: "Everyone has to take 1302. Like you cannot graduate, you cannot go on to BU or wherever until you take 1302. So, so many people get overwhelmed. I mean, not just my class. This is across the board, you know, with the paper. Like they get overwhelmed that they can't do it and they drop or they stop coming. But there's—it's like Dante getting out of hell. I mean, they still have to do it at one point in their life or else they're not going to finish." Ms. Flores connected students' difficulty with the research paper with the emphasis on testing in high school.

After the research essay, students at BCC would spend the latter half of the semester reading and commenting on literature, ranging from poems to short stories, as the teachers usually did not have students read novels. Interviewed BCC instructors generally valued and defended the literature portion. Ms. Flores said it was difficult to focus on research the whole semester, and that students are generally relieved to turn to literature after the drier research essay. A developmental writing instructor that one BCC student had, Ms. Mariscal, explained how literary analysis would be different at college: "I tell them you have probably read these stories in high school already, but very superficially because that's what was required of you, but now we're gonna read them very analytically." During the last ENG 1302 class session I observed, Ms. Flores led her students in analyses of sonnets by Shakespeare, Steve Smith, and e e cummings. As a creative writer, it was clear she took great pleasure from teaching students how to analyze and write about literature. However, not everyone agreed with this approach. A developmental teacher at BU criticized this focus on literature, explaining how high school teachers and college instructors loved teaching literature and felt they earned it. As a result, they would be reluctant to remove literature components from their class, even if they were limiting students from practicing research and other types of writing that would better prepare them to write in a variety of genres.

**Developmental Writing**[6]

As will be discussed in his case study, Daniel was placed into ENG 0309, which was the first developmental class, a paragraph-based writing class. According to the catalog description, this course "Provides intensive development in basic writing skills, including work in sentence structure, vocabulary, punctuation, and paragraph development." Daniel's first-semester teacher Ms. Mariscal described this as a paragraph-level writing course and explained that the course was based on the ENG 1301 essay modes but focused more on learning the differences between the styles of writing than ENG 1301 did. Ms. Mariscal valued this mode-based approach because, as she said, it is pretty much "standard written English" because "you're either comparing or contrasting something, or cause and effect, or persuading . . ." In the semester I observed her class, Ms. Mariscal found that there were a number of stronger writers like Daniel, so she encouraged them to write longer compositions.

Daniel's second-semester developmental writing teacher, Mr. Madison, seemed to emphasize much more the grammar component when teaching ENG 0309, teaching students basic English grammar and preparing them for the department's end of semester grammar quiz. In contrast, the second-semester developmental writing class aimed at bringing students up to writing short essays, requiring three in-class essays and three take home essays. In part because it was his first time teaching the course, Mr. Madison found these goals difficult. He compared the writing done by students in ENG 0310 to high school level standardized test writing: "What I've noticed about this class is it's basically, it's almost like TAKS writing, except it's not personal narrative . . . If I can get them to write paragraphs about one thing with some support . . . we've succeeded." He initially planned to have students write topics based on readings in the course textbook, having them write an essay on holiday traditions for instance; however, he found this was not working and soon moved to more extended short answer responses, showing them short videos or quotes and having them write about it. For instance, in one class, he projected a quote from Gandhi on the board, discussed it with the class, and then had students write in response to the following prompt: "According to Gandhi, why may you have to stand alone against the world?" Assignments like this appeared to be an improvement on TAKS writing because, as Mr. Madison noted, it required students to think more analytically and consider an external source, albeit in a limited sense.

### Writing across the Curriculum

Students at BCC were unlikely to engage in writing across the curriculum and, when they did, these assignments were generally fairly simple. None of the students reported doing much writing outside of their English and first-year seminars, with the exception of short answers on exams in government and psychology classes. Exams in students' history courses were generally multiple choice and no research essays were required during the course. One exception was the first-year seminar where students generally had a major writing assignment for the semester, assignments that will be detailed in the case studies presented later.

### BORDERLANDS UNIVERSITY

The literacy experiences of students at BU were very different from those at both SHS and BCC. As will be discussed in this section, writing instruction at BU, especially in the FYC program, had been affected in part by strong graduate programs in rhetoric and composition and associated faculty. The FYC program had recently undergone a radical redesign, shifting from a decades-old modes orientation to one focused on disciplinary concepts such as discourse communities and a much greater integration of technology in instruction.

### First-Year Composition

With the arrival of an ambitious new director and a $55,000 redesign grant from the Texas Higher Education Coordinating Board, BU's FYC program underwent a broad transformation a few years before this study. The new director aligned the program curriculum with the recently revised "Writing Program Administrator's Outcomes Statement" that described "the common knowledge, skills, and attitudes sought by first-year composition programs in American postsecondary education" (Council of Writing Program Administrators 2008). Among other things, the statement recommended teaching students a more complex understanding of rhetorical situations and the discourse conventions of different genres. The program design was also influenced by Beaufort's (2007) work on situated literacies, in which she critiqued traditional FYC courses for not creating a rhetorical context beyond the classroom. Here, Beaufort developed a theory of discourse communities, in which she placed knowledge about discourse communities as the overarching domain of knowledge supported by writing process, subject matter, rhetorical, and genre knowledge. Finally, another influential component of the WPA outcomes statement was its emphasis on composing in electronic environments, encouraging instructors to have students "Use electronic environments for drafting, reviewing, revising, editing, and sharing texts" and "Understand and exploit the differences in the rhetorical strategies and in the affordances available for both print and electronic composing processes and texts" (Beaufort 2007, 3).

The influence of the outcomes statement and Beaufort's (2007) work was evident in the revised *BU Guide to First-Year Composition*, which explained that the goals of the first-semester course (ENG 1311) included asking students to "Understand a theory of discourse communities," "Address the specific, immediate rhetorical situations of individual communicative acts," and "Develop technological literacies as they pertain to researching and composing in the 21st century." Teachers began ENG 1311 with an introduction to the concept of discourse communities by having students create discourse community maps. The course took a community orientation with students writing an agency discourse observation memo; a rhetorical/visual analysis paper, which often focused on analyzing an organization website; an annotated bibliography; and a community problem report. Students also created a website or blog where they could post their work and interact with peers. Towards the end of the semester, students would compose opinion pieces and a multimedia project, which could be a video public service announcement, a brochure, or poster.

The second-semester course, ENG 1312, was a hybrid course in which students had one face-to-face (F2F) day a week, with the other class day being conducted online. This decision was made in part to ensure that all FYC classes could be in computer classrooms, since technology was an integral part of the classes. ENG 1312 aimed to deepen students' researching skills while also expanding their rhetorical knowledge. As the assignments tended to be more complex, there were fewer major assignments than in ENG 1311. For ENG 1312 students began by writing a genre analysis in which they chose two texts, videos, or pictures from different genres but on the same topic, and analyzed how the genres communicated in different ways. The next assignment was the largest assignment of the semester, a literature review and primary research report. For this assignment, students conducted both primary and secondary research to write a report that had some similarities to the IMRAD (introduction, methods, results, and discussion) genre common in scientific disciplines. In the latter part of the course, students composed extensively in digital environments, advocating policy change through a video documentary, an online opinion piece, and a website. A unique part of the redesigned ENG 1312 was a distributed assessment model in which teaching assistants, not students' instructors, graded and gave feedback on final essay drafts. These TAs met in regular norming sessions to ensure consistency in grading across the program.

Overall, the revised FYC curriculum was different in many ways from the previous one as well as the curriculum taught at BCC. For instance, the only citation style taught in the program was APA, with the rationale that this style is more common across the disciplines and would better serve students as they transfer their knowledge to new writing tasks in college. The BU curriculum was also situated more strongly in contemporary rhetoric and composition scholarship, which focused in part on the importance of increasing awareness of discourse communities and genre conventions in order to teach writing in a way that the knowledge is transferrable to other tasks and situations. Finally, the program was in line with contemporary scholarship (Selfe, 1999; Yancey, 2004; 2009) as well as the WPA outcomes statement (Council of Writing Program Administrators 2008) with its focus on developing technological literacies.

### Developmental Writing

One of the students in this study, Yesenia, enrolled in a developmental writing course at BU. According to the instructor of that course, who was also the director of the program, the class had been recently redesigned so that it would better prepare students for literacy experiences in ENG 1311. Students in the developmental course learned about discourse communities, wrote a memo on a discourse community along with constructing an application for a study abroad program, and wrote a review of a restaurant, movie, or other entertainment venue. Like the FYC classes, the developmental courses were held in computer classrooms, so that students would have ready access to computers for researching and writing.

### Writing across the Curriculum

As will be revealed in more detail in the student case studies, students at BU wrote more extensively and had more complex assignments across the curriculum than their counterparts at BCC. By far, students did the most non-FYC writing in their history classes, writing multiple two- to three-page essays each semester in addition to shorter response essays and written responses on exams. While the history courses tended to be large, with 100–200 students or more, the professors of these courses benefited from having graduate TAs who read, graded, and provided feedback on students' writing. Essays for history classes varied: reading summaries, comparison/contrast of accounts of historical events, and expository essays in which students developed a thesis and made an argument about a book or textbook reading.

Interviews with two first-year history professors helped reveal why writing was an important part of their classes. Both felt that writing had an inherent value, with one commenting that it is "something that can be used in every other class that they take in college and in their careers" and the other explaining that "I think it forces them to kind of think—I'm not sure if it's working anymore, but the reason why I still like [to] have them write essays and exams is because I want them to think broadly." In articulating the value of writing, one professor referenced its centrality to work in their discipline.

Like at BCC, writing at BU was common in first-year seminar classes, albeit at a more complex level. Within other courses such as sociology and art history, students typically did less writing, but regularly had essay exams and often an essay or two for the semester. However, feedback provided in classes outside FYC was generally limited. Students shared graded history essays with me that were evaluated via rubrics with very little written commentary.

## CONCLUSION

As noted in chapter 1, SHS served a predominately lower-income student body, with parents who often could not afford to live in more expensive neighborhoods with more rigorous schools. When it came to college, students ostensibly had more choice, with some seriously considering going out of town and many weighing the pros and cons of starting at BCC or BU. Nonetheless, their choices ultimately came down largely to extracurricular considerations, primarily cost and familial influences. Ortiz and Santos (2009), Kurlaender (2006) and others have noted the importance of family in Latina/o students' lives and the common desire among Latina/o students to be close to their families while at college. Person and Rosenbaum (2006) have also pointed out, as is apparent in Daniel's case, that Latinas/os may be more likely to rely on families and friends to make decisions about college. While this can be helpful when a first-generation college student is unfamiliar with institutions of higher education, it can also be limiting in that a student like Daniel may not consider other options that could serve him better.

The institutional profiles shared in the latter half of this chapter illustrated a point documented by a variety of scholars: the educational institution students choose to attend can make an important difference in the types of literacy experiences they face (e.g., Allison 2009; McCarthey 2008; Ruecker 2014; Weisberger 2005). As repeatedly noted by students, SHS offered very different opportunities for students than other schools around the city. Moreover, despite impressions by Daniel and others that the "basics" at BCC and BU were the same, the reality was very different. Factors such as state and national educational policies, resource disparities, faculty expectations and qualifications, among others, came in to play to shape the way students wrote across institutions, an issue we return to in chapter 7. For now, let us turn to the individual student journeys through these various institutions.

### Notes

1. Note that I included responses from students who have since dropped out of the study or did not start college. While most student quotes in this book are from interviews, these were typed on a beginning of study survey and are presented in their original form.
2. Given that BU is largely an open-access institution, with the exception that some students might enter on probation, students' decisions primarily revolved around the cost difference between the two institutions and not on their ability to be admitted.
3. It is interesting that the focus of this statement is on the loans that came with the degree as opposed to recognizing the fact that she had received her degree. Even

though it may be less likely that a student receives a degree by starting at community college (Pascarella and Terenzini 1991), cost tended to be the primary motivator in decision making.
4. See Ruecker (2014) for more on writing instruction across these three institutions, including the professional development options available and the impact of disciplinary expertise.
5. I have only used [sic] in the context of secondary sources such as this one in order to respect student and other voices contained within this book.
6. Commonly referred to as basic writing (e.g., *The Journal of Basic Writing*), developmental writing is the term used in Texas public postsecondary institutions.

# 3
# STRUGGLING TRANSITIONS

This chapter details the stories of two students who were not enthusiastic about college but began in part because it was expected of them. They both started at the local community college and ended up doing very little writing their first year. Although Daniel had relatively strong writing ability and was a former pre-AP student, he ended up in a developmental writing class; the second student, Joanne, did not have any writing class her first year. Despite some factors working in their favor, both dropped out of college their second semester.

## DANIEL: A QUESTION OF MOTIVATION

> *"I put that off like crazy. Like, I'd go home and I'd be like, 'Eh, I don't wanna do it.' And then just time passed and you needed to study for a test, and you didn't do good in it."*
> 
> —Daniel on studying

> *"When he was there, he was present. But he seemed like one of those kind of when I'm not here, I'm not thinking about this. I'm not going to do anything more than what's bare minimum kind of. What I'll do, I'll try to do well. But I'm not going to break my back necessarily to do it."*
> 
> —Daniel's second-semester developmental writing teacher

### Background and Defining Characteristics and Experiences

Daniel possessed many markers of a successful student. English was his first language, something that resulted from his immigrant grandparents' push to teach his father English and his parents' decision to raise him in an English-speaking household. He did not really learn Spanish until high school, where he saw learning Spanish as a way to integrate himself into the student community. Although Daniel's mother dropped out of college when she became pregnant, his father was a teacher who recently finished a Master's in Education. Daniel felt pressure to attend college from his parents, his uncle, his sisters, and cousin, who had either graduated from college or were currently attending college when I first met Daniel. Daniel had been in advanced classes in middle school and pre-AP courses his first two years of high school. In growing to know the reticent Daniel more closely, I learned about some of the challenges that may have limited his success.

Daniel attended a different middle school from most of the study students, which had a high percentage of minority students, but about half the immigrant students that the other school did. Similarly, while the school where most study participants attended had over half of the students labeled as LEP, less than a third were labeled as such at Daniel's middle school. Due to these circumstances, it is perhaps unsurprising that Daniel reported speaking English "all the time" in middle school. Home to his favorite writing teacher, Daniel's middle school appeared to serve him well. He described her as one of the few teachers who made him work: "We'd have to write in her class, that was the only time I had to write when I went to school . . . and then she'd check it and write like notes and stuff and then she'll give you a chance to fix it and then we'd eventually just pick up the habits." In comparison to that class and other writing he had to do in middle school, Daniel reported that his high school was very different: "It's mostly about book work and TAKS until I guess my senior year . . ."

The impact of minimal high school demands particularly affected Daniel because he was a student who would complete his work diligently, but not go beyond what was asked of him. He tended to choose the path of least resistance because he was adverse to stressful situations. When asked why he was no longer in the AP or dual-credit track, he explained that he did not take the test to place into AP because he was stressed at the thought of writing long essays: "I think it would have been too much 'cause they had to turn in a twenty-five-page essay and if they didn't turn it in they would have failed the semester. I guess it's really stressful. I was like, I don't need that yet." Thus, after the more advanced literacy demands of middle school and early high school years, Daniel chose a less stressful option that never required him to write more than a two- or three-page essay. By the time he entered college, he was placed in the developmental writing track—and did nothing to resist that placement—despite the fact that he (and I) felt his writing abilities were beyond the class. At college, his path of least resistance mentality led to him missing class when his car would not start or there was construction work blocking his normal path to campus. When his printer cable broke, he handwrote all his essays for the semester instead of seeking out a replacement cable or printing his work at the school library.

The perceived family support mentioned in the introduction diminished as I delved deeper into Daniel's life. Daniel's educated father was largely absent since he divorced and integrated himself into another family. He did not have much of an interest in supporting Daniel as he pursued a college degree, telling Daniel that he needed to work as he was not going to support him financially in any way. During high school, Daniel was taken to court and required to pay a $1,000 fine for excessive absences. He began skipping school because it was so easy: his mom left for work at 6 am and did not return until 6 pm. The two older sisters who were in college when Daniel began this study dropped out by the time he started college, one saying that she simply did not like school and the other having failed out.

Nonetheless, Daniel had some supportive family members helping him succeed. After the attendance incident, his uncle began taking him to school to ensure he went. He also began living with his grandmother, who was around more often to take care of him. Daniel had a cousin at the community college as well, who helped him navigate the registration process and occasionally helped him with homework. However, the benefits of living with his grandmother dissipated during his first semester at college when he began missing a number of classes in order to take her to the doctor. Like other study students, Daniel placed great importance on family even if it would interfere with his schooling, saying, "I'd rather deal with my grandma than go to school and have her sick at home, you know what I mean?"

Another factor that seemed to negatively influence Daniel's success was his quiet personality. In high school this may have resulted from his limited knowledge of Spanish in comparison with his peers, as the vast majority of students outside of AP classes always interacted in Spanish. During his first semester at college, his writing teacher saw him as a "loner" who did not seem to have many friends in the class, much less at the college. She expressed these concerns to me: "He doesn't have a support group outside of the classroom and I'm not really sure how many students he knows in the classroom, he doesn't seem to speak to other people in the class so, when I do see him on the outside, I see him by himself, so that worries me, that might be a deterring factor that may not allow him to persist if he doesn't have a support system." Daniel explained why he found it difficult to find friends at college: "Yeah, cause I mean, they're focused on school, they'd rather get that done than make new friends. I mean you still have a lot of time to make friends after college." Daniel seemed to value independence, finding that the responsibility to learn was on the individual and that if one did not do well, it was their fault.

Despite these challenges, Daniel had high aspirations for college and hoped to get a degree so he would not have to deal with the financial uncertainty his parents had previously faced. Early in the study he expressed an interest in being an engineer or, if that did not work out because of the difficulty of the curriculum, to be an elementary school teacher. As he transitioned to college, his major interest switched to biomedical engineering, as he found the science/healing connection interesting.

### High School Literacy Experiences

Daniel had a variety of literacy experiences in high school. He was in a pre-AP class his sophomore year where he did more reading and writing than students in mainstream classes. Students in the sophomore year pre-AP class read *Lord of the Flies*, something that Daniel's senior English class read. However, his sophomore year was interrupted as he transferred to another high school where the attendance problems started. He did not like the new high school but recalled that when he went, there was a lot more learning going on than at SHS: "They give you a little bit of work [here] but over there, everyday there was something new. And if you didn't show up for one day it's like missing a whole week. So I guess that helped them a lot. They made us like fall behind [at SHS]. You know what I mean?" In contrast to more demanding literacy experiences at the other high school and at his middle school, Daniel recalled his high school English classes at SHS focusing mainly on TAKS preparation and "book work." By "book work," Daniel meant reading a book or a story and answering questions about it, without having any real discussions or writing an essay about it.

Daniel felt that senior year did more to prepare him for college than the first three years of high school as the writing demands were increased. In addition to writing more in English, Daniel wrote papers for his government, economics, and theater classes. His theater essay was one of his favorites, as it asked him to read a play and write a summary report on it, and he found the play interesting and the assignment overall "pretty cool." In government and economics, he would often write short answer responses, but reported doing a few essays as well.

Like the other students in this study, Daniel's major senior year writing projects were the personal statement and essays on *Beowulf* and *Lord of the Flies.* He found the *Beowulf* essay different from most of the previous high school writing he did, with the exception of the sophomore year pre-AP *Lord of the Flies* essay he completed. In writing the *Beowulf* essay, he learned how to develop a thesis and how to "to add examples from the text . . . into your writing to make it better," skills that were previously unfamiliar to him. In contrast to much of his previous high school writing, the *Beowulf* essay required him to read a book and write about it, instead of writing on a generic topic assigned for test preparation. In talking about his essay, Daniel said his thesis was his favorite part. It read, "By demolishing Grendel, a demon that tortured the Danes, Beowulf shows that the Anglo-Saxons were the type that don't run away, but would fight vigorously until the end." While the thesis was fairly complex, the essay did not develop the thesis as it could have. The three short body paragraphs were overwhelmed by quotations, without much contextual information or explanation of how they supported the thesis. Daniel's limited practice in writing this type of essay hindered his success on the assignment.

For the final senior essay on *Lord of the Flies*, Daniel wrote about the different desires for power between the two main characters of the novel, Ralph and Jack. While more awkward than the previous thesis, this one still indicated a clear purpose: "Power is a thing that separates Ralph, a person that is for the better of the rest of the kids and Jack only wants power to be supreme." For the first several paragraphs, Daniel focused relatively well on his thesis, making points such as Jack losing two elections and then seeking other ways to steal power from Ralph. In another paragraph he explained how Jack bribed the others to leave with him. Despite these early successes, the latter half of the essay lost momentum and focus, possibly due to the required length of three to four pages, which was longer than the one- to two-page essays previously required of Daniel. His essay ultimately ended up at two and a half pages.

In contrast to the difficulties in writing these two essays, Daniel had no problem writing a TELPAS essay (described in chapter 2). He had to write personal narratives for this assignment, with one prompt being "Write about a time you did something you know was wrong." In response he wrote a short, focused essay on the time he had attendance problems at high school. Daniel clearly felt more comfortable with this type of writing, and indicated multiple times in interviews that he did not like to be hindered by a prompt, but wanted to be free to choose what he wrote about.

On the TELPAS essay, like most other essays he wrote senior year and throughout high school, Daniel did not receive any feedback. He felt ambivalent about this, saying that "If you write a certain way and somebody tells you to not write that way it's gonna be harder for you to write." However, he also recognized that if one does not receive feedback they do not know what to fix. Daniel understood that Mr. Robertson could not give too much feedback because he had so many students. Even if Daniel's teachers had taken time to give him feedback, it appeared that it would not have been overly useful unless Daniel was required to revise. Otherwise, he said, "I'd probably just throw it away. I got a grade for it already so . . ." While Daniel did not receive much written feedback on his final essays senior year, Mr. Robertson was always moving around the class while students were drafting to give them advice and suggestions.

Overall, Daniel's high school literacy experiences were relatively limited. He read no more than a few books and wrote no essay longer than a few pages, with the vast majority of essays focused on test preparation. Due to different factors including a lack of self-motivation, transferring between schools, and the attendance issue, Daniel fell out of the AP track and into the mainstream English track. After graduation many of Daniel's friends in the higher tracks, or in his words, "way up there," were going out of town to various colleges and universities. In contrast, Daniel was going to the local community college where he would begin in a paragraph-level developmental writing course.

### Literacy and Learning in the First Year of College

#### First Semester

In the first interview with Daniel after he started college, he had already recognized that he was one of the better writers in his developmental writing class. When asked if the course was helpful, he explained, "It's like half and half. Cause like, they're trying to get students to write paragraphs, but I already know how to write essays. And so I mean, with the grammar and stuff like that, I still have to learn that cause I really mess up, other than that, it's really boring." Fortunately for Daniel, his instructor Ms. Mariscal recognized that students in her class exhibited different abilities and she pushed the more advanced writers to write short essays, while understanding that some students were not at that stage yet.

Daniel was required to write regularly for this first semester writing course, producing eight essays, four personal reflections on selected textbook stories, and a final exam paragraph/essay written during class time (see Daniel's first-year writing experiences detailed in Table 3.1). The course did have a technology element, which involved completing

Table 3.1. Daniel's first-year writing experiences

| Fall Semester Classes | Writing Assignments |
|---|---|
| Writing (Developmental) | Eight paragraph/essay length compositions under a page |
|  | Narration, description, process, definition, classification, comparison and contrast, cause and effect, and argument |
|  | Four short reflections on textbook stories |
| History | Short answer responses |
| Reading (Developmental) | No writing |
| Education | 2–3 page career essay with sources |
| Spring Semester Classes | Writing Assignments |
| Art Appreciation | No writing |
| Writing (Developmental) | Three take home essays |
|  | Three in-class essays |
| Math | No writing |
| History | No writing |

hours in the PLATO tutoring lab, a drill-based grammar program that had also been used in remedial education at SHS. Essays in this course were largely modeled after those in the mainstream college writing class, albeit shorter, and included process, classification, and narrative essays, among others. Daniel's process essay, which he turned in late, explained how to make chocolate covered strawberries. For the definition essay, Daniel was asked to define one of the following topics: a miracle, a spoiled child, a (insert adjective) police, bling bling, mind games, a slacker, a fashionista, a hacker, or a groupie. Ironically, Daniel chose slackers, writing that they usually learn their behavior from family members and that they avoid work by "any means necessary."

Daniel was required to give examples for these essays but was not obliged to give any sort of textual evidence. As a result, it appears that the type of writing asked of him was a step back from the type of writing he was doing at the end of high school, at least in regard to preparation for later college source-based writing. Daniel noticed this, explaining that the writing he was doing at college did not seem any more difficult than high school, but he soon expected it to be worse.

Daniel was the only study student who was not typing his essay assignments the first semester of college. Ms. Mariscal recommended typing but allowed for handwritten essays if the handwriting was clear. Overall, Ms. Mariscal was more attentive to the diverse needs and complex family

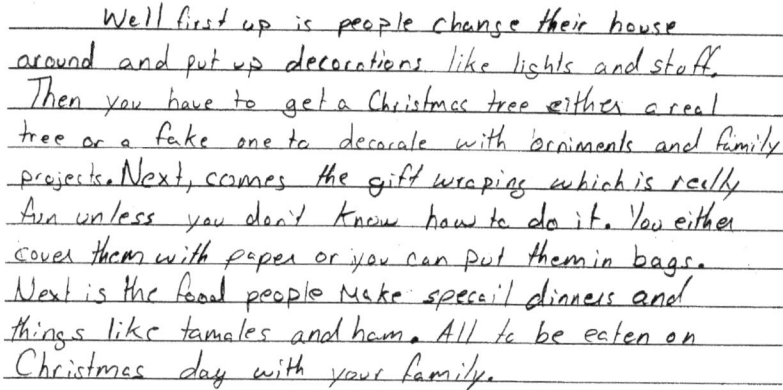

Figure 3.1. An excerpt from Daniel's handwritten Christmas narrative essay.

situations of her students than other interviewed instructors at both BCC and BU, making accommodations such as allowing handwritten essays and going out of her way to ask Daniel what was going on when he missed class, which he frequently did. This appeared to help Daniel and harm him at the same time, and he noted that he was surprised how little most of his college instructors cared about him coming to class or completing the work. Daniel ended up receiving a B for the class despite the fact that, according to Ms. Mariscal at one point, he "was not doing very much at all." In another course, he may have failed or dropped out, and Ms. Mariscal thought that a higher writing placement could have done this to him: "Had he been put, placed into a higher level English, I don't think probably he would persist, so I think that Daniel is doing the best he can and he's doing a good job in this class . . ." On the other hand, this supportiveness caused laziness, which Daniel admitted. It made it easier to miss class and allowed him to handwrite his papers, which he found more comfortable, even though he would be required to type all his later work at college.

Outside of the writing class, Daniel's writing experiences his first semester were limited. For his first-year seminar, which he ultimately dropped because he was going to fail, he wrote an essay about a career he was interested in. This essay focused on archaeology even though he never mentioned it to me as a career interest. Outside of that assignment, Daniel wrote short answer responses to readings in his history class and did not write at all in his developmental reading class, where he mostly read short pieces and answered multiple-choice questions. His reading class was his favorite because it was easy and he liked the teacher.

Overall, Daniel felt mixed emotions about his first semester at college. He regretted failing his first-year seminar, which he planned to retake in the summer with his reading teacher, but was confident that he could learn from each mistake. He also regretted not going away for school, saying "I know I could have gone somewhere else, you know what I mean, like, if I really would have pushed instead of messing up in high school, I could have been somewhere like UT [Austin] right now." However, on the social and family fronts, things were looking up, as Daniel reported meeting more friends and his grandmother was feeling better, so he would not have to miss class to take her to the doctor anymore.

### Second Semester

As Daniel began his second semester, two of his four classes, history and math, were online. Thinking back to his first-semester teacher Ms. Mariscal's comments about him being a "loner" without a support network, I was concerned about this setup because Daniel seemed to do best with a supportive teacher pushing him to do well. My concerns were confirmed when Daniel did not even remember what one of his online courses was when interviewed about a month into the semester, as he had not logged into the class for a week since he had been sick. The decision to take online courses stemmed from problems with lateness the previous semester. Daniel felt that having online courses would limit his troubles getting to school and also allow him to do work on his own time, so that he could postpone things when he did not feel like working.

Another surprising piece of news that came out of the first second-semester interview was that Daniel had a major shift in his future educational plans, saying, "I don't want to be a biomedical engineer anymore. I want to be more of a car mechanic, 'cause I don't know, I like cars a lot. My cousins work on cars like on the weekend, like just something that always happens to one of the family's cars, and they always bring it to us, we'll figure out how to fix it. I think it's fun, and I think that's what I want to do, it's pretty cool." This decision appeared to stem from Daniel's disappointing first semester: while receiving an A and a B in his non-credit developmental reading and writing classes, he failed his two non-developmental courses. He explained that he did not want to go to school for the amount of time it would take to be a biomedical engineer and that he preferred a more fulfilling path even if it meant a minimum wage job. He hinted that he would like to return to school later for a degree in biomedical engineering, as he would like to have multiple careers to choose from.

As the semester progressed, Daniel fell further and further behind. By early April, he dropped all his classes, with his struggles in the online classes being the primary driver: "I had already failed two last semester. So—and now with the math, I didn't understand it at all. So I was gonna fail that one and that was gonna put me on probation. And then I knew I was failing history. So that was gonna put me on suspension. So I dropped them all because I was like, 'Well if I'm on suspension, why am I gonna work my butt off to get nothing?' You know what I mean?"

Daniel's rationale for dropping appeared to be a combination of pragmatism and his inclination to take the least difficult path. As the counselor advised him, it was smart to drop the online classes before he received Fs for them on his transcript; however, he did not necessarily need to drop the art history and developmental writing classes where he was receiving passing grades. As we discussed the situation that led up to the decision to drop, Daniel admitted that taking online classes was a mistake for two reasons. First, he never got in a habit of studying at home, and once outside the class, generally forgot about schoolwork. In an earlier interview, he recalled forgetting what was due because he did not take his backpack out of the car. Thus, he was not spending the time doing the online coursework that he needed to. Second, and this was particularly a problem in math, when he needed help with something he would go online, but there was no one to whom he could ask questions. He failed to make it past the first few chapters in his math book and did not have anyone checking his comprehension.

Although he dropped it along with the other classes, Daniel's second-semester writing class was his favorite of the year, largely because he had a few friends there he met in high school. He explained the value of this: "Instead of gettin' in the class where you know nobody and I mean you have to start knowing people. But I mean, it's better to know somebody than start all over, you know what I mean?"

Daniel reported no writing assignments outside his writing class. For history and art appreciation, his homework was mainly reading, which he tried to do at first, but it was simply too boring for him with the art history book "just talking about paintings and things like that." According to Daniel's writing teachers, he would generally turn in all the required essays, although sometimes late. However, as indicated by his comments here, Daniel found it particularly difficult to sit down and read, and his reluctance to read and study seemed to be his ultimate downfall. He identified studying as his biggest challenge in succeeding, saying, "I put that off like crazy. Like, I'd go home and I'd be like, 'Eh, I don't wanna do it.' And then just time passed and you needed to study for a test, and you didn't do good in it."

## Conclusion

As mentioned in chapter 1, I am including maps of student networks of capital to accompany each case study. Figure 3.2 is the first of such figures presented in this book and depicts some of the challenges Daniel faced in transitioning to college as well as the network of capital he developed to overcome or protect himself against those challenges. On first glance, it appears that he had a fairly developed network; however, a closer look reveals gaps.

As indicated in the beginning, Daniel had positive indicators for success on the surface; however, these largely fell away as one took a closer look at his life. To be successful he knew he had to "Actually put time into studying and do my work" and felt that this was his responsibility and not that of his teachers or school. While Daniel's lack of motivation to work was partly to blame, there were other factors at work. For instance, Daniel's high school preparation was lacking in some important areas. He explained that he was not required to write source-based essays in high school, but this was not his primary reason for dropping. Rather, high school failed him because, as he explained, "it didn't teach me, like, how to do things by a certain date and all that. And like how important it is to do good and study, you know what I mean." Teachers at Daniel's high school were actually discouraged from giving homework given the "unique" background of the school's students. While this policy may have helped the students in the short term, it appears to have harmed Daniel in the long term by not preparing him for the more independent work required at college.

Another factor that could have influenced Daniel's success at the college level were teachers who reached out and supported him. Daniel had expectations of college being more independent, but was surprised about how little the instructors cared about him as a student. The only two teachers he interacted with outside of class were his first-semester reading and writing teachers. His writing teacher Ms. Mariscal checked up on him when he was missing class to take his grandmother to the hospital. Most other teachers interviewed at both BCC and BU said they expected the students to contact them if there was a problem, and not the other way around. Either due to his own fault, his instructors, or a combination, Daniel had difficulties communicating with instructors in

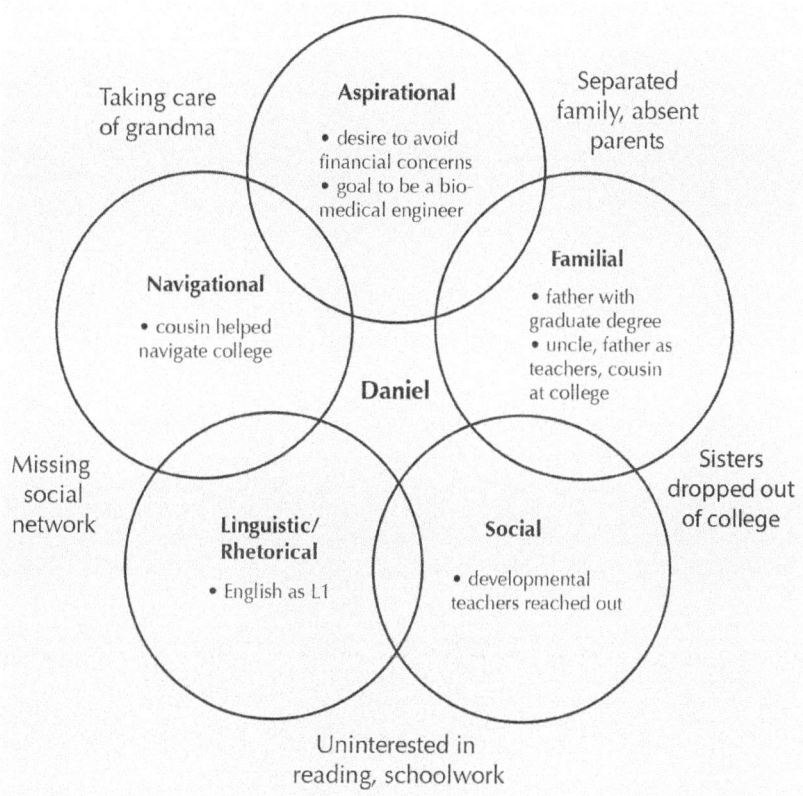

Figure 3.2. Daniel's sources of capital and challenge.

his online courses, which limited his success especially when he struggled in understanding the content.

Finally, Daniel could have benefited from a stronger network of friends at the college. As indicated above, he liked his second-semester writing class because he knew some people there, and did not have that feeling of going into it alone. With a friend to study with, share notes in the case of a missed class, or ask if they are absent, a student like Daniel may be more likely to succeed.

By the end of the semester in which he had dropped out, Daniel changed his mind about switching to a mechanics program and set a goal to finish his basics even though he would have to pay for his classes because of financial aid suspension. While he certainly would have liked his first year to go better, he felt that he could graduate from college, albeit at a slower pace. In discussing this, he referenced his father, saying, "my dad, like, he did the same thing. Like, he stopped for a while and it took him forever but he got to where he wanted to be. And I don't know, I guess that's how it is with us." While off to a rough start, Daniel was interested in continuing school, encouraged by upset family members who wanted him to achieve his initial goals of finishing college and being an engineer.

## JOANNE: BALANCING LIFE AS A MOTHER AND A STUDENT

> "... in school, it probably would be like studying because I don't study much ... I just think, 'Oh I have to study,' and I get the book or the notes, and I try to start to study, but then ... I don't like to study. It gets real boring."
>
> —Joanne on her biggest challenge in college

> "At this point she won't do well, she will not be successful but if she is willing to get busy, get back on track, and realize what she needs to do, she'll do okay. In my class if she would attend and do the best ... she would pass. That will happen, so far no one has ever failed this class just because of low grades because I give them so many opportunities to make good grades."
>
> —Joanne's first-year seminar teacher

### Background and Defining Characteristics and Experiences

My first impression of Joanne was a quiet, hard-working student who had fairly strong English skills compared to her classmates. She always sat next to Paola, another student in this study, in her classes. They always worked together, helping each other out with various assignments, although Joanne felt Paola generally helped more. Like Paola at times, Joanne was never particularly enthusiastic about going to college. This may have stemmed from various challenges that Joanne faced throughout her life, which were not readily apparent.

Joanne had been in US schools all her life, attending a bilingual program until sixth grade and ESL classes in seventh. She was disappointed with the program, saying that it was mostly in Spanish. She could not understand anything when she transitioned to mainstream English classes and consequently received low grades. However, these difficulties may have stemmed from other factors, as Joanne reported moving schools every year during middle school, attending various schools around town before starting high school at SHS.

In addition to moving schools, Joanne's living situation appears to have altered as well. When growing up, she lived with her aunt in El Paso so she could attend US schools more easily while her parents continued to live in Juárez. Midway through high school, she moved into an apartment with her boyfriend, presumably so that she could get to school easier. She became pregnant while living with her boyfriend and had a child her first semester senior year. She was living with her cousin at the beginning of this study as she and her boyfriend split up because he had been cheating on her. Despite the challenges that this event brought her, Joanne did not mention it too openly as a problem during high school, just casually mentioning that she had to take a month off of school when she had her daughter.

The difficulties in raising a child and attending school were not as visible during high school as Joanne, like other students at SHS, rarely had homework. However, once she started college, with shorter class hours and higher homework loads, the difficulties started. Joanne dropped three of her four classes her first semester because of fear of giving speeches in speech class and failing grades in the others. She failed her first-year seminar, the only class that she did not drop. Joanne struggled to balance the duties of being a college student and a mother: "It's hard cause like I have to take care of her and then like I said I have to read or do like homework, I don't know, like something about school, and at the same time I have to be with her, you know." Because of these difficulties and the limited amount of support her cousin could provide, Joanne moved back in with her parents across the border in Juárez at the end of her first semester, with hopes that they would help with her daughter while she attended school.

Joanne's cousin was an important source of information and support when Joanne started college, as she had been attending community college herself. She helped Joanne navigate the registration process, encouraged her to find a work-study job, and in general encouraged her to pursue a college education. Nonetheless, Joanne fell behind in her coursework her first semester, and, after a realistic assessment of her possibilities, decided to change to a shorter program of study to be an assistant physical therapist. This decision was made in context of the desire to be with her young daughter: "If I go study more, I'm not gonna be, like have time to be with her." Also, given that she struggled so much during her first semester of college, Joanne felt that four or more years of that kind of work would be too much.

## High School Literacy Experiences

It was difficult to get many details from Joanne throughout the study. She was a quiet person who did not talk much during interviews, responding to my questions with a one-word response or a couple of sentences. This was compounded by the fact that she was never fully engaged with school, reporting that art and lunch were her favorite classes. She described her senior English class concisely: "Sometimes it's interesting and sometimes I don't like it."

Joanne struggled as she made the transition from a bilingual program to ESL to mainstream English, and she ended up failing the TAKS her sophomore year. Although others put a lot of negative pressure on her for failing, Joanne did not feel too badly about this, as she knew her junior TAKS, which she passed, was the one that counted. After failing, she spent junior year in tutoring, for which she was pulled out of various content classes. She said most of her writing for the first three years focused on the exam, and that she did not like it largely because she was required to read a lot and she did not like reading.

After a bit of coaxing, Joanne admitted to having one stand out English teacher, the strict Mr. Sanchez referenced by other participants. She described him as "mean," but valued the fact that he was demanding of them, and, especially as she started college, wished that she had been pushed more by other high school teachers. In contrast, she never felt especially pushed by her other English teachers, including Mr. Robertson.

Joanne reported writing a little for science and history senior year, which consisted of short responses to questions. Unfortunately, she did not receive feedback on how to improve her responses or her writing, but just marks if her answers were right or wrong. However, she similarly reported that she did not receive feedback from her English teachers as well, with the exception of Mr. Sanchez.

Mr. Robertson was concerned about the struggles that Joanne faced as a mother; however, he felt her writing ability was high in comparison to other students in the class. An examination of Joanne's major senior essays confirms this. In interviews, Joanne felt that the *Beowulf* essay was more difficult than the *Lord of the Flies* one because it required her to focus on analyzing one character, Beowulf, instead of comparing two characters, as in the other essay. Joanne clearly struggled with the *Beowulf* essay as it was very different than the TAKS essays that dominated her first three years of high school. Guided by Mr. Robertson, Joanne created a strong thesis which read, "Beowulf manifests his aggressive nature that benefits the Danes by killing Grendel, which reveals that

Anglo-Saxon strongly believes in protesting themselves with the use of force." Unfortunately, the rest of the essay, while strong in terms of English fluency, was largely a summary instead of an analysis. The conclusion was short, undeveloped, and did not connect the story with a larger societal issue as the teacher requested.

The *Lord of the Flies* essay was more successful, although with its share of problems. The thesis in the short opening paragraph appears somewhat confused, focusing both on how power shifts in the novel and the different types of power used by the characters. In the first two body paragraphs, Joanne jumped far into the story, telling the ending before analyzing much of the book. Nonetheless, there were some strong points of analysis, such as "Ralph and Jack want the power for many different reasons. Ralph wants to have the power so everybody can be together and to fight together so they can be rescued. And on my opinion the reasons of Ralph are for good of them. On the other side, Jack wants power only to kill and hunt." Unlike the *Beowulf* essay, Joanne used quotations as evidence throughout, and even drew fairly successfully from a questionable outside source (*SparkNotes*) in supporting her analysis, which she cited.

Like most students, Joanne finished high school without feeling prepared for college. Her cousin had warned her that the writing demands at college would be much greater. From teachers Joanne got the impression that she would need to use bigger, more complex words in college writings. When asked how she would cope with moving from writing one-page essays to writing three pages or longer, Joanne said she would simply add more details.

### Literacy and Learning in the First Year of College

#### First Semester

As discussed earlier, students at the community college rarely wrote outside of their English classes and, as evident by the table below, Joanne was no exception. She did not do much writing at all, with the exception of a career portfolio in her first-year seminar and some short answers on history and government exams (see Table 3.2 for a list of Joanne's first-year writing experiences). Her first semester at college can hardly be considered successful, with Joanne dropping or failing all her classes. She dropped her speech class first because she was nervous about presenting in front of others.

For the first-year seminar, Joanne was required to create a career portfolio. She chose photography, one of multiple career interests for her

Table 3.2. Joanne's first-year writing experiences

| Fall Semester Classes | Writing Assignments |
|---|---|
| Speech | Speech outlines |
| Government | No writing |
| History | No writing |
| Education | 10-page career portfolio |
| *Spring Semester Classes* | *Writing Assignments* |
| Speech | Speech outlines |
| Government | 4 exams with essay component (choice of 3 questions) |
| History | No writing |
| Psychology | 5 one-paragraph profiles on famous psychologists (make up for missing exams) |

over the course of the study (psychologist, assistant physical therapist, and border patrol officer were others). For the portfolio students had to provide the following sections, enclosed in a three-ring binder: title page, table of contents, introduction, contents, conclusion, and a bibliography. They were required to have at least six sources, including a book, an Internet source, and an article, that they needed to cite in APA or MLA style. The instructor required students to turn in a draft, a task that Joanne, starting this project late, did not complete.

Despite the promising nature of this assignment, it was limited in that the instructor told me multiple times that she was not the English teacher, and as such, was not responsible for teaching students writing. She referred to the project as a "cut and paste affair" when talking with me and told the students during an observed class that she would not be able to tell the difference if they mixed up APA and MLA style. Despite a slow start, Joanne quickly stepped up to work harder on this project, meeting with me to get feedback since she missed the draft deadline. With photography as her career choice, Joanne began her advantage section like this: "They are many advantages to being a photographer, including doing something creative that you can enjoy, and being able to concentrate on what you like to do. Being a photographer is a chance to meet plenty of people and travel. One of the major advantage to working as photographer is having the opportunity to work with credibility and showing the artistic passion."

The only other writing Joanne reported her first semester were short answer questions on her government exams. She failed all the exams, getting a 16/100 on one of them. She explained that she could not answer these questions because she did not complete the "boring" reading. On the other hand, Joanne was doing the reading in history, as she found the subject and the reading more interesting; however, she similarly reported failing reading quizzes there, and ultimately dropped this class as well.

Joanne reported none of her instructors reached out to inquire about her difficulties, unlike Ms. Mariscal reaching out to Daniel. Joanne's first-year seminar instructor noticed that Joanne was having attendance problems, but did not approach her to find out what was going on. This instructor did allow students to make up missed tests, and Joanne went up to her after one observed class to make arrangements to do so. However, because she did not study before the make-up date, Joanne skipped the make-up appointment, further solidifying her poor reputation with her instructor and lowering the chances of passing any first-semester class.

### Second Semester

Joanne's struggles and limited writing experiences continued the second semester. She began with the same schedule she had in the fall: history, government, speech, and psychology. She stopped going to two of them, history and speech, in early April without formally dropping them. Her primary reason for not attending speech was her nervousness speaking in front of others. She initially did okay when Paola was in the class with her at the beginning of the semester. However, Paola stopped attending the class, removing the little support Joanne had. In dropping history, Joanne explained that the instructor made this potentially interesting topic boring. Beyond the speech outlines, Joanne reported no writing tasks in either class.

As indicated in Table 3.2, Joanne did some writing in her psychology and government class, albeit in limited amounts. For instance, the government exams, like the previous semester, were half multiple choice and half essay. Students were given three questions and had to answer one of them. A look at three responses showed her writing about the House of Representatives and the Senate, constitutional amendments connected to civil liberties, and the US news media. Joanne's essays were about one half to one unlined handwritten page, and consisted mainly of descriptive commentary such as, "The congress is organized by two groups, those of Representative and Senate. The members that participate in the Congress have specific rules to follow." However, the news media response ended with a more analytical comment that read,

"Public Opinion can be very important to public/governers/politics because they can know what the people think and say about things around/what is happening to the government." Joanne's grades for the three essays ranged from a thirty-two to a thirty-six out of fifty. The instructor's comments were generally brief and difficult to read (Joanne could not make sense of them), including a few positive words along with a request for more specifics.

The only other writing Joanne did her second semester was for psychology when she was given the opportunity to make up missed exams by writing profiles on the famous psychologists B. F. Skinner, Ivan Pavlov, Solomon Ash, as well as on theories of classical conditioning. Joanne found this writing interesting, as she did her psychology class in general. While she used an entry from Wikipedia in writing these profiles, she based the rest of her writing on class notes and the textbook. Her profiles commented on why a particular figure was important to psychology and included a description of their famous experiment or experiments. For example, her description of Pavlov began, "Ivan Pavlov is a Russian psychologist of digestion. The most famous and original example of his experiments is the one of the classical conditioning which involved the salivary conditioning of dogs." A quick Google search shows that Joanne took the second sentence almost word for word from Wikipedia. Given her lack of experience with source based writing, this is not particularly surprising.

One other writing opportunity that Joanne had, but did not participate in despite showing strong interest, was to write a two-page extra credit essay for her history class for Black History Month. For this assignment students were requested to write an essay "discussing an African American who has had a positive influence in your life" that would be entered in the Black History Month essay contest.

### Conclusion

When asked at the end of her first year how she would describe the difference between high school and college to seniors at her high school, Joanne replied: "That in college, you are more independent by yourself, that it's based on you if you want to do your work or not. And then in high school . . . the teachers are like there and there and there, telling you what to do or what not to do." Like most of the other study students, she noticed the increased independence at college, something that most students anticipated. However, unlike most of the BU-bound students, Joanne struggled with this independence and, as a result, had a disappointing first year, dropping or failing most of her classes.

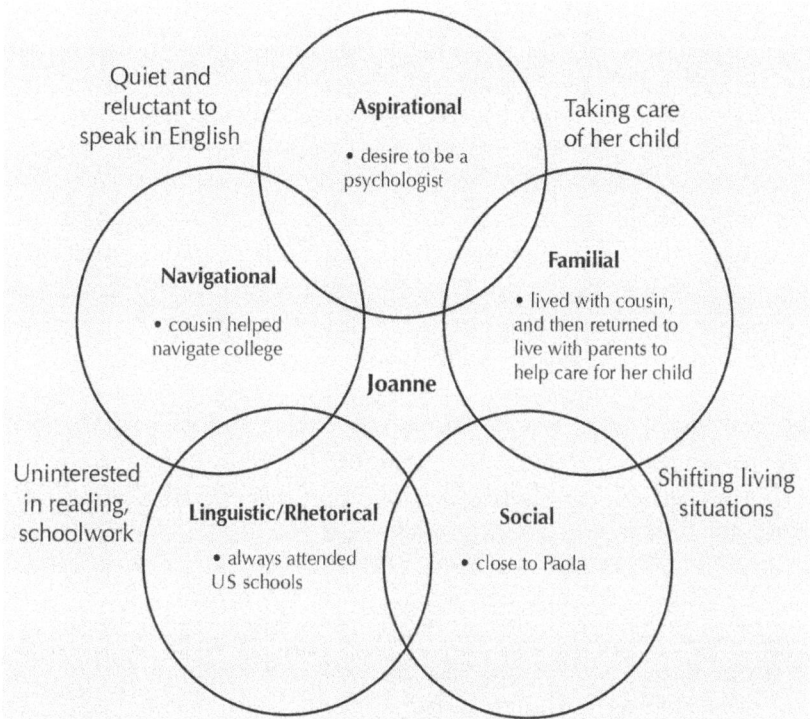

*Figure 3.3. Joanne's sources of capital and challenge.*

Joanne's difficulty adjusting to college appeared to stem from two areas. First, she had the challenge of being a mother with no support from her child's father, limiting the time she could devote to studying outside school. Drawing on her family capital, she returned to living with her parents so that they could help out more, allowing her to focus on school tasks. Nonetheless, living in Juárez would bring its own set of challenges, as it would take much longer to get to school every day and living on the other side of the border could further distance Joanne from the college community. Joanne's second challenge concerned her lack of interest in studying, which she failed to do more of even with the time that living with her parents gave her to focus on schoolwork. She identified studying as her biggest challenge in succeeding at college. She reported limited interest in it and rarely studied or completed her reading for school because she found it "boring" and was not self-motivated. No teacher reached out to Joanne and asked why she was not doing well while she was failing or dropping classes. As with Daniel, she did not expect them to: "Because like I know that what I'm doing, I know what I'm missing and all that, so I think it depends on me, more on me than the teachers." However, as seen in the case with Ms. Mariscal and Daniel, a teacher reaching out can make a huge difference.

Like both Daniel and her friend Paola, Joanne's attitudes toward college shifted over time. At the beginning of the second semester, she indicated a clear desire to drop out and pursue a career in border patrol or another career where she could finish more quickly and have more time to spend with her daughter in her formative years. She seemed destined for this path as she stopped going to two of her four classes. However, she indicated in the final interview that she wanted to finish her basics and then decide what career/degree path to pursue from there. Given that she was planning to work full time while pursuing this goal, and now in the position of paying for the classes herself, this path would likely take more than the two years that the basic college requirements typically take (she had lost her financial aid from dropping and failing too many classes). From the high school senior only slightly interested in college, to the first-semester college student excited about possibilities, to one resigned to a more vocational path, to an end of first year college student with a goal to finish her basics and go from there, Joanne's story, like others shared in this book, is unique, unpredictable, and yet unfinished.

# 4
# DIFFICULT BUT SUCCESSFUL TRANSITIONS

The two students in this chapter faced academic and non-academic challenges as they finished high school and transitioned to college. They both had to care extensively for younger siblings, drawing time away from their studies and limiting their ability to participate in extracurricular activities. While both were generally underprepared for college like the other students in the study, Yesenia started with perhaps the lowest writing ability of the participants. Nonetheless, Bianca and Yesenia sought and found sponsorship from a variety of individuals both in and beyond the institution, working extra hours to balance school responsibilities with often extensive extracurricular demands on their time. Their stories illustrate the value of self-efficacy, literacy sponsorship, and the role of community and academic organizations in promoting student success.

## BIANCA: OVERCOMING CHALLENGES WITH VALUABLE SOURCES OF SUPPORT

> *"when you come to college, it's like topics that you have to look for information that will help you or will make like a point. An idea or something. And in high school, you just have to write like the clouds were red."*
>
> —Bianca on the differences between high school and college writing

> *". . . she's a very good student she always, she's very outgoing, eager, confident too. I think she'll do well, she's very focused also . . . And she's outgoing and friendly and I think, you know those kind of students will have a better chance of doing well cause you know, they'll reach out for help."*
>
> —Bianca's junior English teacher

### Background and Defining Characteristics and Experiences

Although she had lived in the United States all her life, Bianca had perhaps the most challenging extracurricular life of all the study participants. In a scholarship essay she wrote in senior year she recalled "hard times [when] we lived in poverty struggling day by day for needs such as bills and the rent" and remembered hearing her mother cry every night when she was about ten years old. While most of the students in this study were no strangers to poverty, Bianca had an additional experience that separated her from the rest, something that she wrote about in her personal statement for college:

> It all started one afternoon when I was in my room watching TV. I had just arrived from the Holocaust Museum when I heard somebody yelling, "get down, get down," from outside my house. I jumped out of bed and I ran to the living room and suddenly I saw a bunch of men coming into my house and yelling. As I threw myself to the floor, I noticed that these men came after my mother.
>
> It was chaos all over the house. My younger brothers and sisters were crying and I was just thinking how to control the situation. With my mother getting mistreated by these men and my siblings scared and crying what I was supposed to do, I felt a lot of pressure and wondered whether to cry or to keep strong for my family. I was only seventeen years old and I had to keep mighty like a mother for my siblings and be strong like a good daughter for my mother. They had come to take my mother to jail because she was in the U.S. illegally. However, I believe that a document shouldn't determine or be an excuse to mistreat a human being.

With her mother arrested and eventually deported and her father out of her life, Bianca became the legal guardian for her three siblings, aged five, seven, and thirteen, when she was a junior in high school and only seventeen years old.

Having responsibility for her siblings meant that Bianca had to take them to school and pick them up afterwards, find a new place for them to live, cook, clean, and read to them at night, all while completing high school. As she explained, Bianca could no longer participate in extracurricular activities as her life outside of school was no longer hers. While she lamented the fact that her teachers did not push her enough, she admitted that not having any homework in high school made her newly acquired parental responsibilities easier. She took charge of her siblings' education by helping them with homework and moving her younger brother to a new school when she realized he was not learning enough at the old one.

Despite the challenges that came with being a guardian of three children, it appeared to be helpful in some ways for Bianca as she matured rapidly with the new responsibilities. Her English teacher for both junior and senior year, Mr. Robertson, noticed a big change and recalled that Bianca had often been "loud" and "obnoxious" the previous year but that she "grew up quick" and developed into a quieter and harder working student.

As she made plans for college, Bianca constantly talked about applying for the College Assistance Migrant Program (CAMP), a program that aims to "assists students who are migratory or seasonal farmworkers (or children of such workers) enrolled in their first year of undergraduate studies at an [institution of higher education]" (Department of Education 2014). Both BU and another state university about forty-five miles from El Paso, offered this program. However, concern for her siblings constantly factored into Bianca's college decision-making. She initially wanted to go to the other state university, but quickly realized that moving out of town was not an option because, as she said in reference to her siblings, "There's nobody that can take care of them like me."

While the CAMP program was available at BU, Bianca began leaning toward BCC for a variety of reasons, largely because she expected she would have to live on campus as part of the program. By the end of senior year, she resigned herself to the community college: "I know it's better for my family. I don't have to look just for myself. I have to look for them. And I believe that it doesn't matter where you go to college. Just go." She mentioned a friend told her that the community college was "A better place to start" because it was cheaper and easier while being essentially the same. I urged Bianca to work something out with the CAMP director at BU, telling her that he would understand her situation and work with her. I pushed her in this direction because it seemed clear that the extra academic and financial support provided by the scholarship program would greatly increase Bianca's chances of success at college.

Ultimately, Bianca was accepted into the CAMP program and began college at BU. As part of the program, she took summer classes and lived on campus for a month. During the summer session, she recalled being required to go to tutoring every day until ten at night and sometimes until two in the morning. By living with fellow CAMP participants in the dorm, Bianca formed friendships that sustained her throughout her first year at college. Not only did they participate in events on campus such as a lip-syncing contest but they helped each other with homework that provided Bianca with support beyond the daily tutoring required at the CAMP program office. Bianca felt the program gave her an advantage in multiple ways. By attending summer classes where she was pushed to achieve high grades, Bianca felt much more ready for regular work because it was less intense than summer classes. The program helped change her procrastinating habits, requiring her to have work drafted in advance and meet with peer leaders for feedback.

Other areas of support beyond CAMP helped Bianca overcome the challenges she encountered. Certain family members were not particularly supportive. Bianca recalled feeling abandoned by extended family members when her mother was in jail and she lacked the financial means to support the family. However, her aunt stood out during this time. While Bianca attended summer classes, her siblings lived with her aunt. During college, her aunt regularly came over to help cook and clean, sometimes spending the night. While Bianca's mother was now forced to stay just across the border in Mexico, Bianca talked to her every day and visited on weekends. Bianca's mother was proud she was going to college, and Bianca held strong dreams of moving up the social ladder and providing for the family that was so important to her: "I want something like a social worker to work with people, like more, I want to master in something, a good paying job . . . when I finish college, I want to buy a house for my mom and my brothers [siblings]."

Church also played a huge role in Bianca's life. She went to meetings at a nondenominational Christian church in downtown El Paso four to five times a week, usually bringing her siblings as well. When discussing the difficulties she had faced in her family, she always took a positive attitude, saying that God was with her to support her. Beyond the spiritual support provided by church members, Bianca explained that some members helped support her financially, with one member regularly filling her gas tank. She also learned about college through members at church, and was pushed to attend and succeed at college by them as much as by her mom.

**High School Literacy Experiences**

Bianca clearly had a favorite high school English teacher and was generally unsatisfied with other teachers, as she felt they were too relaxed or did not push students enough. Her freshman-year teacher Mr. Sanchez was known among students for being very strict. Bianca recalled that Mr. Sanchez pushed students to work in class and required students to read and write outside of class (almost unheard of at the school due to a no-homework culture pushed by administration). For Mr. Sanchez's class, Bianca typically wrote two-page essays, which she described as five paragraph essays. She said that this was the first class she ever typed an essay and lamented the fact that she wrote more her freshman year than during the rest of high school.

Bianca's sophomore year writing teacher was largely unmemorable, as she did not push the students much. For her junior year, she had the same teacher as she did senior year, Mr. Robertson, whom she also felt was too relaxed with students. For the most part, Bianca said her first three years in English class were dominated by practicing for the TAKS, which she always passed, typically earning three on a four point scale: "Practicing for the TAKS, that's what we do mainly here. Practice for the TAKS." There were occasional exceptions to this, especially in Mr. Sanchez's class, where Bianca recalled writing an opinion essay about criminalizing teen possession of permanent markers.

Bianca had more diverse writing experiences outside her normal English class than the other study students her senior year, as she took film and a creative writing course with another English teacher. In addition she had a college prep class where she wrote extensively, especially in preparing for the ACT. She also had an anatomy and physiology class where they regularly had to complete PowerPoint presentations and for which she wrote her most interesting paper at SHS, a paper on chlamydia. Bianca found the essay on chlamydia both interesting and important because she learned a lot and was able to provide valuable information to the students in her class. Her ACT prep class may have been a little too late, as she recalled having a horrible time on her ACT. Because of time limitations, she did not finish many of the questions and felt very pressed for time on the essay. She was still outlining when she was told she had five minutes left.

Bianca's film and creative writing courses required fairly extensive writing, and I had the opportunity to observe a few of these classes. The teacher highly valued personal expression, and had the students journal several times a class in response to songs, videos, and other types of media. For her creative writing class, Bianca recalled writing an eight-source research paper on global warming; however, all the sources were from the Internet and the paper was only a few pages long.

In addition to writing for other classes, Bianca wrote a few major essays and a personal statement in her senior English class. Some of this writing, such as her personal statement, journals, and a scholarship essay based off of the statement, were very personal. Because of the emotions raised by writing about the experience with her mother, Bianca felt that the scholarship essay was the most difficult writing she did senior year. Helping with a draft of her scholarship essay showed me that Bianca was able to write an interesting narrative in English, but needed support with surface features and expressing herself more vividly.

As most of her writing experiences in high school centered on personal narratives, it is unsurprising that Bianca's major senior year source-based analytical essays, on *Beowulf* and *Lord of the Flies*, were less successful. Her thesis for the *Beowulf* essay was fairly simple: "Beowulf's aggressive nature reflects the bravery of Anglo-Saxon society." Although Bianca did provide required textual evidence for each paragraph, quotes were always placed right at the beginning of the paragraphs without any kind of signal phrase. Despite this, she did cite the line numbers for each quote and, especially in the first body paragraph, provided some insightful commentary on the quote. The latter half of the essay, including her extended discussion connecting Grendel to a well-known Mexican drug lord in the concluding paragraph, did not effectively connect back to her thesis.

Bianca's *Lord of the Flies* essay had similar problems, starting off strong but losing steam about halfway through. For this essay, she focused on the different uses of power by the main characters: "Ralph and Jack often fighting for the respect and power, which lets us know that power, can be use in two different ways. Power is use so much in this story because both Jack and Ralph want the respect and power from the others." In evaluating this essay, Mr. Robertson noted that citations were lacking throughout, with only one quote including a page number. Even more disturbingly, there were multiple paragraphs lifted verbatim from *SparkNotes* in the latter half of the essay. While the first body paragraph wandered a bit, there were moments of strong insight and overall the paragraph supported Bianca's thesis. For instance, she wrote, "Unquestionably, Ralph wants the civilization and productive leadership while the others want to be playing around so this tells us who really wants the good for the group." Unfortunately, this and other insightful statements were partially lifted from the *SparkNotes* character analyses. This revealed that Bianca could find sources that discussed her topic; however, she was unsure about evaluating and citing these sources and inexperienced in providing these insights on her own. It revealed her struggle with writing a very different type of essay that was significantly longer than previous texts she produced in high school. While Bianca's tendency to procrastinate may have hindered her less other times during her high school career, learning a new genre of writing takes time, time she may not have had due to procrastination with this essay. Also, given her situation at home, she certainly had other things on her mind. The practice of copying was clearly atypical for Bianca, as Mr. Robertson was surprised and disappointed but suspected her challenges at home might have played a role.

Overall, Bianca was disappointed with high school literacy experiences and did not feel prepared for college. Her favorite teachers were those who expected a lot of students. While Bianca acknowledged she had extra demands that would limit her ability to complete homework, she still repeatedly wished that Mr. Robertson would work them harder. As she transitioned to college, she thought her biggest shortcoming was vocabulary, expecting to need "more extensive . . . bigger words" for college writing tasks.

### Literacy and Learning in the First Year of College
#### First Semester

Bianca's transition to college went differently than the transitions of the other students in this study as she was in the CAMP program. As mentioned above, she was required to take summer courses and attend regular tutoring and study hours in the CAMP office. She had a special orientation and the program took care of registration, ensuring that CAMP participants would be in learning communities together.

Having never read a complete book in high school, Bianca was shocked by the amount of reading she was expected to do for college classes, identifying it as her biggest challenge and much higher than anticipated. In the beginning of the semester she said she spent about three hours a day reading, with most of it for sociology and history. Looking back at high school, she felt that a key area where they could have improved was in requiring students to read more often and more difficult works: "I think the books that we read in high school, they were really easy compared to the ones we're reading now so they should have difficulter books to get us prepared for university." Like other study students, Bianca quickly found ways to manage all this reading. Her strategy consisted of skimming the reading and skipping a lot of pages, knowing that her professor would discuss the readings in class.

For her first-semester writing course, Bianca had the same projects that other students taking BU's ENG 1311 class had: a memo about a community agency, an annotated bibliography and an associated research paper, a blog, and other projects (see Table 4.1 for a list of Bianca's first-year writing assignments). Her instructor, Ms. Perry, themed the course around peace studies, a choice that influenced several of Bianca's projects.

Bianca's first project for the class, a peace blog, was to be an ongoing project, but she ended up only posting one entry focused on what came to mind when she thought of peace. The first few lines read: "When I

Table 4.1. Bianca's first-year writing experiences

| Fall Semester Classes | Writing Assignments |
| --- | --- |
| Art | No writing |
| FYC | Homepage portfolio |
| | 2–3-page agency discourse memo |
| | 3–5-page rhetorical/visual analysis |
| | 7–10-source annotated bibliography |
| | 4–6-page community problem report |
| History | 2–3-page analysis essay on *Pocahontas and the Powhatan Dilemma* |
| | Essay exam |
| | 2–3-page argument/analysis essay on *Incidents in the Life of a Slave Girl* |
| Sociology | Essay exam—Three essays, each 1 page |
| *Spring Semester Classes* | *Writing Assignments* |
| Art | No writing |
| Criminal Justice | 8-page essay on DNA exonerations |
| FYC | 4–6-page genre analysis |
| | 7–10-page literature review/primary research report |
| | 5–6-minute documentary (group project) |
| | 2-page online opinion piece |
| | Advocacy website |
| Political Science | 1-page opinion/background essay on the third party and César Chávez |
| | Unspecified essay |

think of peace different things come to mind first of all peace in the world no wars love amoung countries a dream that is far from happening. Another point that comes to mind how do we expect to have peace in the world if their is not such thing in the country amoung one another." Because Bianca did not finish the blog, Ms. Perry ended up giving a low grade for this assignment, despite a comment on this first posting that the "peace blog looks good!"

Bianca's other projects for the course seemed stronger. For instance, Bianca wrote a memo about a community agency that helps pregnant women. Bianca reported drawing information about this agency via its newsletter, which she cited at the end of her memo, and a friend who had used their services. Bianca's inexperience in referencing outside sources was apparent in the fact that she posted just a weblink under the heading "Sitations." Her spelling was better than in the blog posting and challenges with subject-verb agreement were only occasional: "[Name omitted for anonymity] organization consist of many purposes and one of the main purposes is to grant better opportunity to the families living in the shelter. This is a place for women who have been through family violence. This organization provides everything for the women such as food, shelter, and clothing." Ms. Perry, like many mainstream writing teachers working with L2 students, did not provide any feedback on language issues; instead, she was mostly positive, making just a brief comment on formatting: "You did a really nice job on your memo. It's well organized, detailed, and well-written! The bullets and indented margins shouldn't be there. Otherwise, great job!"

Bianca's annotated bibliography and subsequent research paper were about Nelson Mandela and Tom Fox, and she was asked to compare their lives and activism. Bianca felt the annotated bibliography was the hardest assignment of the semester, as it was an unfamiliar genre and she had trouble meeting the eight-source requirement. Her CAMP peer leader helped her, showing her how to evaluate sources and helping with the citations. This tutoring benefited Bianca, as she had a good variety of sources, including academic books and articles, and provided concise yet informative annotations for each of them. Her APA style reference entries were generally formatted correctly and the spelling and subject-verb agreement issues that were relatively frequent in previous writing were mostly absent.

The research paper based on the annotated bibliography seemed a bit less successful and, as her teacher noted, was a page short of the four page minimum requirement. While Ms. Perry praised Bianca for the introduction and the organization of the paper, she noted that it was missing an abstract and in-text citations while having some issues with propositions. Ms. Perry, however, realized that this may have been the first such assignment for Bianca, and wrote, "Writing a research-based paper for the first time is challenging. Good job on your first try. Each time you'll improve. I recommend that you get help along the way from the University Writing Center." As seen in the discussion of Bianca's earlier writing, she was not familiar with using citations in her writing. While the references listed in her annotated bibliography generally conformed to APA format, she did not cite these in her research paper nor include a reference list. Her comments in one interview indicate that she had not learned APA research paper conventions by the time she was required to write the research paper. It is also interesting that this is the first time Ms. Perry made mention of language issues in Bianca's writing; however, she did not point out specifics but simply directed her to the writing center for help.

Outside of English, Bianca wrote a paper in sociology that required her to talk to her parents about where they were during important societal events and how they experienced these events. However, like the other first-semester students at BU, Bianca did the most writing outside of FYC in her history class, where she was required to write a couple two- to three-page essays that were worth 35 percent of the final course grade. In addition, she had to write short answers and essays for her mid-term exam, which ended up being one of her most negative experiences of the semester, as she failed: "I felt really stressed, I was trying to put all the information and like I think I did it really fast, but then I, we didn't even have enough time so." This experience hearkened back to her ACT essay experience, and reveals the problem of timed writing for students like Bianca, who could likely perform much better on these types of assignments if having sufficient time to develop, organize, and write their ideas.

Despite the setback of the mid-term exam, Bianca was encouraged after meeting with her TA, who explained that she could still get a B for the course. Her essays for the course were much more successful, and she received a B for the first one and an A for the second. In reading the two essays, the first one seemed more developed, as if she put more time into it. This essay asked Bianca to evaluate the credibility of Camila Townsend's interpretation of Pocahontas in *Pocahontas and the Powhatan Dilemma*. In this essay she gave multiple examples that she cited parenthetically using MLA style, and drew connections with the Disney version of Pocahontas. For this essay, Bianca was graded via a rubric, which included title, introduction, thesis, evidence, conclusion, organization, and style and grammar. The amount of written feedback consisted of, "Overall, well done! You effectively answered one of the two paper topic questions. Your thesis argument became apparent early in the paper, and you progressively argued for this thesis through the remainder of the paper. You just need [to] analyze more evidences [sic] from the book." Despite some issues with sentence structure and referring to the biography as a "bibliography," Bianca received an "Excellent" for "style and grammar," with no comments on improving her writing in this area.

For the second history essay, Bianca responded to the prompt, "Is Harriet Jacobs correct when she argues that slavery was far more horrible for women?" This essay was significantly shorter than the previous, coming in just under the two-page minimum requirement. Nonetheless, this essay showed Bianca becoming more confident in incorporating and citing textual evidence, as evident by this example: "Women where easier to take advantage of as Harriet Jacobs states, 'This poor women endured many cruelties from her master and mistress: sometimes she was locked up, away from her nursing baby for a whole day and night' (15). As said the owners of the slave would do cruel things as such just to make slave women suffer this is one of the cruelties made toward women." Bianca was now able to incorporate textual evidence and comment on it in a more complex way, revealing that she had progressed since writing the *Beowulf* essay discussed earlier. Nonetheless, as evident by misspellings such as "where" for "were," subject-verb agreement problems, and a number of awkward sentence structures, this essay seemed less polished than the previous one. Nonetheless, Bianca received an A and did not recall receiving any feedback on "style and grammar."

In the interviews, Bianca noted that she was required to do much more on the computer in college than in high school, saying, "here everything's in the computer. It's really different. The grades, you have to submit your work, so it's really different." For her FYC class, she worked on a blog, analyzed websites, and created a movie. Most of the work for that class, as well as for her other classes, was submitted via the course management system, Blackboard. While keeping everything digitally has its advantages, it can be problematic in one way. Her first-semester FYC instructor noted that she no longer provided in-text comments on student writing, because of the difficulty downloading the individual papers, using the comment feature, saving them differently, and re-uploading them. Instead, she, like Bianca's history TAs, used rubrics and provided summative comments. As a result, Bianca did not appear to be getting the support she may have benefited from in regards to persistent issues with sentence structure, prepositions, spelling, and other stylistic features.

Overall, Bianca's first semester at college was less successful than she hoped, and she ended up with a 2.57 GPA, failing her art history class and receiving a low C in her English class. Ms. Perry explained that Bianca's grades in the course declined over the course of the semester, and her attendance dropped a bit as well. Her final course grade was particularly hurt by failure to complete the blogging assignment, and she received a zero on participation as she did not comment on other classmate's blogs. Bianca explained that she kind of blew off these requirements, not feeling that they were enough to bring her grade down. She had trouble accessing the blog after she forgot her password, and did not take the necessary steps to recover the password or create a new blogging account, because of the belief that it was not a big deal.

### Second Semester

By the beginning of the second semester, Bianca was confident what field she wanted to study, but was unsure how to go about declaring a major, something she figured out as the semester progressed. She was set on majoring in criminal justice and minoring in psychology and explained her choice: "Because like in the criminal justice rank I want to work with kids like involved in situations. Like if their parents were put to jail and stuff like that. I want to work with the kids, so that's why—that's the reason I got like psychology and criminal justice." Her choice was largely based on her own situation where she took care of her siblings in the aftermath of her mother's deportation.

As depicted in Table 4.1, Bianca continued to write in most of her classes her second semester, although most of the writing still occurred in FYC. As described in chapter 2, the second-semester FYC class at BU was a hybrid course, which Bianca was a bit concerned about at first. She noted that it would be harder because she would have to be more self-motivated, doing things on her own time, and that she would not have the same connection with the instructor that she had in traditional classes. Nonetheless, when the class did meet face to face, she valued the structure of the class, in that it was more discussion and group work as opposed to lecture oriented, commenting that "everyone's talking, giving opinions and we learn."

Bianca felt the FYC class was the hardest of the semester, because she was always having to "read and summarize and stuff like that," posting to the course Wiki every week. In addition, her instructor had adopted a writing-about-writing approach to the course so students read rhetoric and composition disciplinary articles almost every week (see Downs and Wardle 2007). In addition to these weekly readings and postings, Bianca had a few major essay assignments, a video documentary, and an online opinion piece. She liked how the assignments built on each other as students were asked to focus on a particular topic throughout the semester. Bianca focused on teen pregnancy.

While Bianca did very well on the documentary, which she worked on in a larger group, she struggled more with the traditional essay assignments, receiving a low B on her genre analysis and a C on her literature review/primary research report. Her literature review fell short of the assignment requirements, as she only had three secondary sources, two of them low quality, when she was expected to have at least seven. This may have stemmed from the confusion of whether or not her primary sources counted toward the total, as she cited a total of four interviews in the reference list. As the grader noted, her primary research was of high quality, but really overtook any secondary research she offered, which was the primary focus of the assignment. Bianca's shortcomings on this assignment likely stemmed from a few areas. She found it hard to stay engaged in longer assignments and got bored during the researching and writing process. She also explained that she already knew a lot about teenage pregnancy from friends and family members, so likely felt less compelled to utilize secondary sources.

Bianca's genre analysis was overall a more successful assignment, albeit a simpler one as it required her to compare and contrast two sources on teenage pregnancy from different genres. As her grader noted, Bianca could have done more by including specific details from the genres, such as quotes. Nonetheless, she got an A on focus and generally stayed focused on analysis of the genres as opposed to the topics, one place where students commonly errored. One problematic element of Bianca's grades for both assignments was her writing fluency grade as she received a C for one and a D for the other with no elaboration except what was provided by the automated rubric. The rubric characterized a C as "Demonstrates adequate writing fluency, exhibiting a fair number of mechanical errors." The D read similarly with "adequate" swapped for "minimal" and "fair number" for "numerous." While Bianca may have gotten some feedback on this aspect of her writing from mentors in the CAMP program, it appears that localized feedback within her classes was limited. A look at her writing for the literature review/primary research assignment revealed she struggled with the language necessary to write a research paper, resulting in awkward sentences like this: "In the third question it's going to be discussing the parent's involvement in the child's life how is the child affected physically, mentally and emotionally." Her genre analysis writing was stronger overall and both papers were stronger in terms of subject-verb agreement and spelling than Bianca's first-semester papers.

Bianca's most interesting writing for the semester was an eight-page essay for her criminal justice class in which she wrote about DNA exoneration. Not only was it the longest essay Bianca had ever written, but it required her to do more research than ever before. She noted that having to look up lots of articles was tiring. While most of the sources she used were Internet sources, a few came from the library databases, but no library books. Being interested in the topic contributed greatly to her level of motivation in this assignment, and she received a 90 percent.

Bianca also completed a few writing assignments for her political science class, with an extra credit essay on César Chávez and third party movements as well as a three-page essay on one's favorite public servant, for whom Bianca picked Michelle Obama. The public servant essay had four paragraphs, focusing on the position of importance, historical outline, political interaction and media coverage, and self-reflection. At the end, Bianca included a list of three references (from biography.com, fruitsandveggiesmorematters.org, and the *Huffington Post*) under the heading "Citing and References." A look at Bianca's essay revealed a strong focus, with her achieving the goals of giving background information on Michelle Obama, critiquing media coverage of her, and expressing support for her campaign against obesity. However, language problems persisted, making it difficult to understand at times. For instance, one sentence read, "Throughout time presidents wife have been on the look and the media coverage has been negative than positive even thought they do affords to do good to society." Despite the presence of sentences like this throughout the essay, Bianca reported getting a 95 percent, only losing points for citations.

Outside of school, Bianca's life stayed mostly on track her second semester, and she did not report many major problems. Money continued to be a concern as she, like most students in this study, struggled to find a job. For a while, not having Internet access at home was making it difficult to keep up with the work in her hybrid English classes and she would often bring her computer to church to access Internet provided by the city. After I helped her secure home Internet access, she had another technology-related struggle in that her computer only had Microsoft Works, which saved files in a format incompatible with Microsoft Word.

### Conclusion

As revealed throughout the discussion of Bianca's experiences and depicted in Figure 4.1 below, Bianca overcame major challenges in developing a robust network of capital that helped her succeed.

For Bianca—and most of the other study students—college was a very different experience from high school. In general, she explained the difference in these words: "First you have to read a lot. You have to read a lot, like a lot. And then you have to write a lot. Then you have to study a lot. Then you have to wake up early a lot." While for some students, college may mean waking up later, Bianca often had 7:30 am classes in addition to the responsibilities of making sure her siblings got to school, so she had no time to sleep in. Balancing early mornings at school with raising a family was the biggest challenge: "The fact that I

*Difficult but Successful Transitions* 79

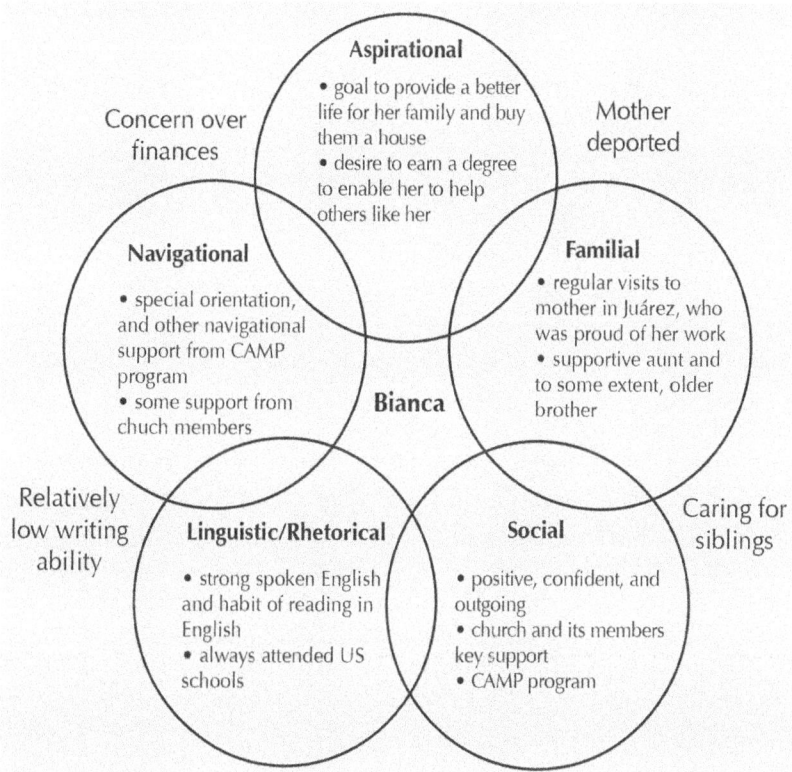

*Figure 4.1. Bianca's sources of capital and challenge.*

had to come to school early, and you know that I need to take the kids to school, so I had a lot of trouble. So this lady helps, but there were days she couldn't help, and I had to give her money for gas. And so that's the biggest challenge in my life—in my family stuff. But it affected like school also." Bianca's family situation also made evenings difficult as she could not focus on studying when at home. She would look at books for hours without learning anything, and often stayed up well after her siblings were asleep. Consequently, she always tried to complete as much work as possible at school.

Bianca consistently wished that her high school teachers had made her read and write more, and talked in detail about the differences between high school and college writing in our last interview. Her struggles with both the content and language in her research-based papers such as the literature review and her DNA exoneration essay likely stemmed from a lack of practice at the high school level: "In high school, we used to write papers but not like this type of papers, you know? Long and research. Like in high school, we didn't have to research like all, a lot of articles. And cite work, reference page. That's really different. I think high school should start teaching that . . . we used to do a lot of three-page essays, but like really basic. Just like, they only focus like on the thesis statement. I don't know. Just like the little things. Just like TAKS type of essays. It's not like focus like on the really important subject. It's just like a little topic and you have to just write about it." In comparison to TAKS essays which asked Bianca to write about topics such as, in her words, "what would you do if you had found like a treasure," her first year of college had her writing about issues like teenage pregnancy, DNA exoneration, and the value of having a viable third political party.

Despite various challenges present in Bianca's life working against her being a successful college student, she had numerous sources of capital that contributed to her first-year success. God was her most important source of support, and it is apparent that her involvement in church activities gave her a sense of confidence and optimism that was lacking in some of the study students who struggled. In addition, members of her church clearly supported her in various ways, ranging from a woman who would regularly buy her gas and another person who would take her siblings to school many mornings.

Academically, Bianca's most important source of support was the CAMP program that provided her with both financial support and structure necessary to complete the majority of her work and be successful at college. According to the program director, CAMP provided Bianca and other students with a number of advantages: "We remove all obstacles, all barriers, for not only her, but for all students, and that's so they focus on their classes only. And with her, it's allowed her to spend more time with her family." In addition, the program provided structure to Bianca's academic life, ranging from requiring her to meet with her instructors to have them complete evaluation forms to meeting a certain amount of tutoring hours every week. Thus, Bianca ended up meeting with her instructors more often than other students in this study, and was likely helped because they all knew about the CAMP program and the type of students it served. She also developed a habit of doing most of her work in the CAMP office, and would always have peer leaders and other tutors read her work, quiz her on the readings, and ensure she was completing the necessary assignments.

When asked if she anticipated any challenges standing between her and graduation, Bianca was confident in her ability to stay focused and finish college as quickly as possible. Unlike most other students in this study who expressed reluctance to take out loans, Bianca did not anticipate money standing in her way: "I don't think I'll ever quit because of money. I'm going to have to get loans or whatever. I don't care. I just want to finish." Bianca's family was always foremost in her mind, with her loan money going to support them and her desire to graduate intimately connected with providing a better future for them. The director of the CAMP program was constantly amazed by Bianca's ability to balance school and family life, and noted that she was more motivated than the typical student in the program: "She realizes that she needs to provide a better life for herself and her family. She needs to have an education to get a better paying job. It's easy for her to go work at Wal-Mart or work somewhere else, get a job, and have an income coming in. But she's chosen to invest in a four-year dream and try and graduate as soon as possible so she can help the family out." Despite the fact that she was exhausted by a first year at college in which she always had to balance family, school, and church, Bianca planned to take as many summer courses as she could to make her dream of a degree and ability to better support her family happen a bit sooner.

## YESENIA: BALANCING SOCIAL AND SCHOOL LIVES

> *"They say they're preparing you for college but really what they're teaching you is that they're not preparing you for college at all. So I think [high school students] should like read more in their own time, their free time, and like pressure the teachers to like write more papers . . . in high school you don't have to do anything, just who cares, high school. And right now, it's just, you struggle a lot. Cause you don't know how to read a book, you don't know how to like write a ten-page research paper, so yeah it's really hard."*
> —Yesenia on how high school prepared her for college

> *"When I saw her writing, I was scared . . . Yesenia is one of those success stories from here, she loves me after all the hard times I gave her, I called her coach and I, you know she's not doing her work, I called her mom, and it got to where the point like she just loved me, she did all her work and her work, her hard work paid off, every day she would do revising and editing and every day she was there participating. Dramatic, dramatic improvement on her test scores from her sophomore year to her junior year, she passed."*
> —Yesenia's junior English teacher

### Background and Defining Characteristics and Experiences

Yesenia liked to party. Our post-summer vacation interview was filled with stories of bus trips to Denver, a camping trip with friends where they got drunk and looked for bears, and a trip to Mexico that was supposed to be three days, but ended up lasting three weeks. She was an admitted procrastinator, saying that she would look for any reason to avoid finishing her homework at home, whether it be a trip to Wal-Mart, a bowling excursion, or a fly buzzing around the room. Nonetheless, Yesenia evolved into one of the hardest working students in this study, with her desire for success driving her to actively seek help from sponsors including myself, professors, and campus services such as the writing and math tutoring centers.

Yesenia came to the United States in fourth grade with her mother and older brother. She had no memories of her father. After a failed attempt to settle in Denver, they returned to Juárez before settling in El Paso. According to Yesenia, her mother's primary motivation in immigrating to the United States was to provide better educational opportunities for her children, a motivation that drove many of the families of participants in this study to immigrate.

Of the students in this study, Yesenia probably had the most educational challenges. She attended an ESL program from fourth through seventh grade, and transitioned to mainstream English in eighth grade. However, it appeared she was not quite ready for the transition, because she failed eighth grade. She had positive comments about her eighth grade English teacher, saying she helped her get used to English and she learned how to understand English better, because she was an African-American teacher who spoke differently and more quickly from what she was used to. While this pushed Yesenia to learn, she also struggled because she did not understand. However, she did not ask the teacher to slow down out of fear of looking dumb: "I think they're gonna make fun of my accent or the way I . . . the way my English was. That's pretty much the problem."

These educational challenges continued in high school, where Yesenia failed the TAKS her sophomore year, which she blamed in part on the teacher who did not focus enough on the test that year. She overcame this obstacle junior year due to help from one of her favorite English teachers, Ms. Cecilia, who helped her practice for the test, gave extensive feedback, and made her repeatedly revise her essays. Yesenia valued Ms. Cecilia so much that she visited her occasionally when she was in college to solicit feedback on writing.

Despite passing the TAKS, Yesenia's writing was the least developed compared to the other participants at the beginning of this study.

She consistently said spelling was the greatest problem for her in writing, bluntly stating "my spelling's really bad" in the first interview. Nonetheless, as she progressed through her first year in college, she overcame some of this difficulty with practice along with learning how to use the dictionary, a translator, and a thesaurus, most often on her computer. She actively sought out help from friends, teaching assistants, the university's tutoring services, and myself. She came to me more than any other student in this study for help with writing at college, an offer I had made with all students at the beginning of the study. She lamented the fact that she did not have help from home, as her mother did not know English.

Yesenia had family responsibilities that often took her away from school and distracted her from completing schoolwork. Her mother worked in Mexico and was pursuing a college degree there. Because the return crossing to the United States typically lasted a few hours, this meant she was away from home for long hours. More importantly for Yesenia, this meant responsibility for her six-year old brother fell largely on her. She described one such experience that occurred during high school and how it affected her: "Sometimes I have to like leave school like, one time, [my brother] wasn't feeling good and so my mom called me to pick up my brother from school so I like missed the whole day. And that really affects me because if you don't pass the class, you don't get to play soccer. So I have to make up all my work in one day. It affects my attendance too." After school, Yesenia always had to rush to pick up her brother and then spend the evening helping him with his homework, feeding him, and bathing him before bed.

Although Yesenia's older brother lived with them for the first year of the study, she repeatedly emphasized how lazy he was and how he never wanted to take care of their younger brother. In fact, for a while his girlfriend and their baby were living with the family as well. Yesenia and her brother used to fight about college, as her brother had dropped out after a few weeks, saying school was not for him. She explained the difference between them as a matter of motivation and competition: "I like challenges . . . if it's a competition I'm going into the competition. I don't care if I lose or not or if I win. I don't care. I'm a competitive person and he's not."

Yesenia did not want her younger brother to end up like her older one and worked on motivating him and encouraged her mom to read to him. Yesenia even took him to the library to check books out, so that he would get in the habit of reading. To motivate her younger brother, she would use her older brother as a negative example saying things like "You better like English cause if not you're gonna suck at school like your brother."

Yesenia's relationship with her mother appeared to waver during the study. She was not happy about having so much responsibility for her brother, but understood that her mom did not have many other options. She complained about money issues and her mother fairly often as well. For example, when she decided to stay in El Paso for school, she said her mom promised to help buy her a car, which she delayed doing. However, on the other hand, Yesenia did not feel pressured by her mother to work during college and her mother provided some money for expenses. This was in part due to the fact that she was watching her little brother and really could not work because of the restrictions on her schedule.

Yesenia's mother supported her in other ways. She bought Yesenia a Spanish book titled *La Vaca*, which Yesenia described as a motivational work: "They teach you how not to stay stuck in one place and keep going with your life . . . You should want more so that's pretty much why my mom bought me the book." Also, while she did not seem overtly supportive at the beginning, Yesenia said her mother became more supportive and understanding as she continued college, likely because she was going to college as well and understood the challenges Yesenia faced.

As mentioned in the introduction, Yesenia was very socially active. In high school, she played soccer and participated in DECA, an organization focused on preparing "emerging leaders and entrepreneurs in marketing, finance, hospitality and management in high schools and colleges around the globe" (DECA 2012). At college she often brought a friend or two when she met with me, and they ended up sitting outside while we interviewed or worked on her paper for thirty minutes or more. She had one good friend in particular who paid for some of her summer trips, regularly took her to school and helped her pick up her brother, printed things out for her on his printer, revised and even wrote some writing assignments for her at college.

In addition to having friends locally, who were mostly male, Yesenia had a long-distance boyfriend for most of the study. Yesenia had met him online, and said he was helpful for her English as he did not know any Spanish. Despite speaking Spanish with many of her friends and all the time at home, she talked, texted, and chatted only in English with her boyfriend. Yesenia had initially wanted to attend college in her boyfriend's city, but ended up starting in El Paso because she knew it would be cheaper to continue living at home. However, moving away and transferring schools to live with her boyfriend continued to be a goal throughout much of her first year at college.

## High School Literacy Experiences

During the final high school interview Yesenia expressed regret in choosing SHS over a school closer to where she lived: "I decided to come [to SHS] and I think the teachers over there are more prepared than they are over here cause they're like . . . over here I don't think they really care if we learn or not. You know what I mean. There, I think they do." From talking with friends she felt students worked harder at the school closer to her house, teachers did more to motivate students, and that they had better electives. However, she did note that students at SHS may have had different needs than students at the other school: "[Mexican kids] really need good feedback because in other schools maybe nobody really speaks Spanish and stuff and they really have good English, good essays and stuff, but here it's not like that."

Yesenia did not feel well served by SHS. Her first- and second-year writing teachers were not very helpful. Her sophomore year writing teacher was her least favorite teacher because he made them write a lot without providing feedback and discussed random topics during the course. Her main issue with him seemed to be that he did not focus on teaching the TAKS, which Yesenia failed that year and, as a result, was placed into tutoring courses the following year. Yesenia's relationship with the TAKS was a love-hate relationship like most students in this study. She did not like focusing on it so much, but also saw it as an obstacle to graduation, which she could not pass if her teachers did not focus on it all the time.

Junior year, Yesenia had her favorite writing teacher, Ms. Cecilia. When asked what Ms. Cecilia did differently, Yesenia replied, "What she teaches was different and like all her attention to you and not like, she teaches everyone and when you need help, she likes explain you step by step and stuff." Yesenia's complaint about her sophomore English teacher and most of her math teachers, including those at college, was that they did not explain how to do things but simply told them to do something. In an interview, Ms. Cecilia showed a special connection to Yesenia and described her as a "success story." According to Ms. Cecilia, Yesenia came to her classroom with a lot of discipline issues and she recalled being "scared" when she saw her writing. However, she was extremely patient with Yesenia and called her mom and her coach to push her when she slacked, and in the end "totally won her over." Ms. Cecilia recalled that Yesenia eventually began doing all her work and diligently revised her essays. Yesenia began to regularly borrow Ms. Cecilia's dictionary after she told Yesenia that the dictionary was her "best friend." In the end, Yesenia showed dramatic improvement and met the TAKS graduation requirement.

By the time I met her in her senior English class, Yesenia was a dedicated student and well-liked by Mr. Robertson, her senior English teacher. Her writing abilities were still less developed compared to many classmates; however, Yesenia had a stronger work ethic than most of them. The two major assignments her first semester of senior year were a personal statement and an essay on *Beowulf*. She explained that the *Beowulf* essay was difficult at first because she did not understand the story, a feeling shared by many of the students in the class who struggled to grapple with *Beowulf's* archaic language and structure. Nonetheless, she generally liked writing the *Beowulf* essay, while admitting that she did not spend much time on it. She liked the essay because she found history interesting, and was required to write about the history of the work in the introductory paragraph. When asked how it was different from previous essays she had written at SHS, she said the major difference was that it was longer than most previous essays (500–600 words instead of 300).

Yesenia clearly benefited from having plenty of time to write the *Beowulf* essay and support by Mr. Robertson who gave them step-by-step instructions, taking time for students to develop a thesis and an outline with textual evidence. While Yesenia's introductory paragraph perhaps gave too much history on the story, she had a clearly stated focus: "This revels Anglo-Saxon use their intelligence as they use their strength to defeat their rivals." The second paragraph was one of her strongest, as she gave a clear topic sentence and introduced textual evidence that clearly supported her point. Her last paragraph was a bit awkward, making a connection between Beowulf's intelligence and the intelligence used by President Obama to get elected. Students were asked to make a connection with real life in their final paragraphs, and most, like Yesenia, found this process awkward and generally made superficial connections.

Yesenia found the *Lord of the Flies* essay difficult, wishing she had more time to complete it and saying she fell 100 words short of the 900–1200 word target. As with most students in the class, she only read part of the book, resulting in a limited understanding of the work. Unlike some other students in the class, Yesenia wrote the whole essay and did not resort to plagiarizing from outside sources to meet the length expectations. In providing feedback, Mr. Robertson noted that, while there were a "lot of language problems," Yesenia made an "obvious effort and many good points." As in the *Beowulf* essay, Yesenia had a strong thesis and supported this fairly well throughout the essay with a mixture of quotes and details from the reading.

Yesenia felt the most important writing assignments she did senior year were the personal statement and scholarship essays because they counted for more than just a grade. She did not seem as grade-driven as some other students but wanted a more concrete purpose for her writing such as getting a scholarship or being admitted to the college of her choice.

Senior year, Yesenia did not write outside of English except for an eleven-page research paper for her math class, which she really disliked. Similar to most students, she did not see the point of writing a research paper in a math class, since math focuses more on numbers than words. Since Yesenia was clearly not interested in working on this paper and did not like the teacher, she reported constructing most of the paper through copying and pasting from other sources; however, she was happy with the grade she received.

Looking back on her high school learning experiences at college, Yesenia clearly wished she had been more prepared and blamed the TAKS for this more so than other students, who often had mixed attitudes toward the test. In a long criticism of her high school academic experiences, she said:

> Like make us write uh, like more papers. You know they just concentrate on the TAKS. And they just TAKS, TAKS, TAKS, TAKS, they don't really teach you how to write a ten-page research or how to start it or how to research stuff so you can make like, have a good paper. So, I think they should focus more on that than just TAKS, TAKS, TAKS. When you're a senior you don't have nothing about the TAKS like you have free hours, like outs, and the classes are just like, instead of being in class you're always making like meetings. Senior meetings, senior graduation meeting, and senior this, and senior that. They don't, like you don't really have time to do anything. Like in Robertson we did like three papers, but it was just like two-page essays, it was just like whatever. And over here [at BU] it's just like three-page paper, four-page paper, ten-page paper. It's just hard.

Here, Yesenia criticized the emphasis on preparing for a test that bore little resemblance to her college writing experiences. According to her, when they actually had time to focus on other things, such as senior year, there were so many distractions that they never wrote as much as they should have in classes like English. However, like most students, Yesenia enjoyed these distractions and breaks from classes in her senior year. It was not until she had to suffer a rough period of adjustment to college life that she regretted not having done more in high school.

## Literacy and Learning in the First Year of College
### First Semester

Yesenia's shift from high school to college writing was difficult; however, in making this transition, Yesenia actively sought help from me, a friend, and regularly visited her professors, including a history TA who provided feedback on her writing. This willingness to work hard, seek feedback, and revise helped her overcome some of the shortcomings she had going into college.

In her first semester, Yesenia had a half-semester developmental reading and a full semester developmental writing course. Perhaps because of the developmental status of her writing course, she reported doing the most writing in her history and first-year seminar courses (see Table 4.2 for a list of Yesenia's diverse first-year writing experiences). She did not seek help from me for developmental writing, indicating that she found the assignments less difficult. Nonetheless, the writing demands for this course were substantial. As stated in the course syllabus, Yesenia had to write a paragraph about a discourse community she belonged to, a memo about a campus or community issue, an application essay for a study abroad program, an entertainment review, an opinion piece, as well as a variety of daily assignments. The fact that Yesenia did not see her writing course as difficult may have stemmed from the laid back nature of her instructor, who was consistently friendly with students and kept the atmosphere of the class fun. It also may have been that the demands of the assignments and type of writing, often involving personal opinion, was not as different from her high school writing as the writing she did for other classes.

Yesenia's developmental writing course, like many of the writing courses at the university, was held in a computer classroom. Students regularly used the computers to research and begin writing about their topics, but they also used them for drilling, a common use of technology in developmental education programs. For this semester, students were asked to subscribe to a McGraw Hill online tutoring program called *Connect Writing*, which was designed to support their textbook with grammar tutoring. However, the course instructor revealed she did not plan to use it in future semesters as many students, including Yesenia, had difficulty signing up and using the program, something I witnessed during class observation.

Throughout her first semester Yesenia continually worried about the writing assignments for her history course. Fortunately, this course was paired with Yesenia's developmental reading course, where the teacher required drafts of all the history essays, including the extra credit one,

Table 4.2. Yesenia's first-year writing experiences

| Fall Semester Classes | Writing Assignments |
|---|---|
| Writing (Developmental) | Discourse community assignment |
| | Application essay |
| | Review essay |
| | Opinion piece |
| | Regular learning journals |
| History | 2–3-page analysis essay on *Pocahontas and the Powhatan Dilemma* |
| | 2 essay exams |
| | 2–3-page argument/analysis essay on *Incidents in the Life of a Slave Girl* |
| | 2–3-page extra credit paper comparing PBS documentary with textbook |
| Reading (Developmental) | Writing assignments coordinated with history class |
| First-Year Seminar | 10-page research essay on topic of choice (she chose Mexican folklore and dance) |

| Spring Semester Classes | Writing Assignments |
|---|---|
| FYC | Homepage portfolio |
| | 2–3-page agency discourse memo |
| | 3–5-page rhetorical/visual analysis |
| | 7–10-source annotated bibliography |
| | 4–6-page community problem report |
| History | Paragraph summarizing and discussing a historical document from *Voices of Created Equal, Vol. 2* |
| | 2–3-page essay comparing and contrasting Booker T. Washington and W. E. B. DuBois views on black life |
| | Essay on *Farewell to Manzanar: A True Story of Japanese American Experience During and After the World War II Internment* |
| | 2 essay exams |
| Math | No writing |
| Sociology | 2-page essay on "A Class Divided" video |

and Yesenia found the support of this learning community very helpful. For history she had to write a few two- to three- page essays, and was encouraged to write an additional essay of the same length for extra credit. The required essays were worth a combined 35 percent of the final course grade. In general the essays required her to evaluate the quality of information in the books they read. In discussing her first history essay Yesenia explained the difference from her high school writing experiences:

> *Yesenia:* Like everything, cause in high school they didn't really teach you how. They just tell you to do the paper and they don't really give you feedback or anything, so you don't know what I did wrong. Right here, like, um, just, different.
>
> *Me:* Ok, and so it was different, you didn't get feedback in high school. Ok. And what else, was the type of writing different?
>
> *Yesenia:* Yes, because you need to use a lot of transitions, put a lot of evidence, and read the whole book . . . I don't like reading, so.

In the first history essay Yesenia had to argue whether or not the author of *Pocahontas and the Powhatan Dilemma*, Camila Townsend, used reliable and convincing evidence in writing about Pocahontas's life. Since Yesenia had not read the entire work when she was first outlining this essay she struggled to find evidence to support her points. My feedback directed her to the reference list and asked her to consider the types of sources: original documents, biographies, and academic journal articles. Using these, I suggested that she mention examples of each and explain why those types of sources were reliable or not. As she had not done this type of analytical writing during most of high school, it was clearly challenging for Yesenia. She ended up receiving a low B on this paper, with points deducted for a lack of sufficient examples, language problems, and difficulties with organization. She did receive some specific comments on her essay along with a completed rubric. Comments on the essay generally focused on the need for examples, with one comment reading "What academic journals?" next to a line that read "One of the academic journals that she uses is a research, Townsend wrote about the event of 1606 when John smith and hundred and frothy-four man set out of London to Virginia (33)." Yesenia's attempt to bring in academic journals as a piece of evidence was clearly in response to my earlier comments, but it is not clear she yet understood what an academic journal was when writing her essay. After receiving her grade, Yesenia met with the TA evaluator to better understand what she needed to do to improve; meeting with him resulted in a slightly higher grade.

Yesenia also stressed about the writing demands in her first-year seminar, especially toward the end of the semester, when she was required to write a ten-page research paper. The longest paper of her first semester, it was about seven pages longer than anything she had been asked to write before, with the exception of her copied and pasted math paper in high school. The topic of the course was music and the instructor

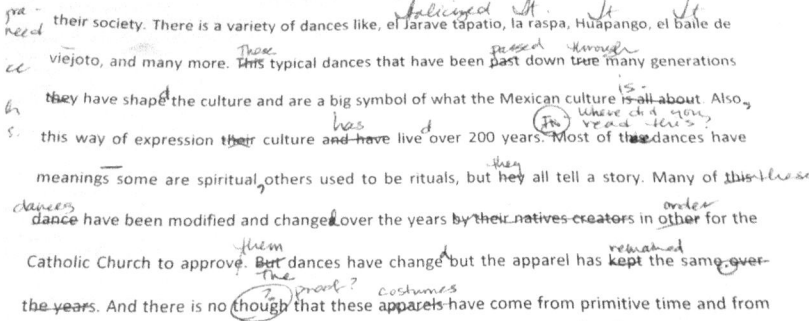

Figure 4.2. Instructor comments on Yesenia's ethnomusicology draft.

assigned a topic in ethnomusicology, the study of music in a cultural context. Yesenia chose a topic close to her, Mexican folklore music and dance. Overwhelmed by the assignment, she procrastinated and submitted her four-page draft about a week late. In one interview, she explained the struggle to fill so many pages: "It's too long, ten pages. She wants the introduction to be one page and I don't know how I'm supposed to fill out the other nine. So I guess the conclusion has to be one page too. So that leaves me with seven, yeah, huh?" Nonetheless, her instructor provided detailed feedback on this first draft, which focused on copyediting the pages she submitted (see Figure 4.2 for an excerpt).

At one point, Yesenia had put a "u" instead of "you," which elicited a very strong response: "Yesenia, you must never, ever write the letter 'u' by itself in formal writing—okay?" [emphasis in original] In the summative comments on this draft, her teacher wrote: "You have a very interesting paper. This is a wonderful look of ethnomusicology. However, your writing level is consistently low. You must take your draft (including the other pages you add) to the Writing Center in the Main Library. Please see me after class." [emphasis in original] Despite earlier concerns, Yesenia ultimately filled about nine pages, with the inclusion of images she was allowed to use. When she came to me a few hours before the final was due, she still needed help with drafting an introduction, for which I provided ideas. In addition, so that she would not be penalized excessively for grammar and mechanical issues, which were still numerous, I quickly copyedited the final draft.

### Second Semester

As Yesenia moved into and through her second semester at college, life at home began to get better after some struggles with her brother. After a fight during winter break and a bad decision to loan him some of her student loan money so he could buy a motorcycle, her brother moved out. Yesenia felt this was better for everyone because there was no longer drama at home that distracted her from focusing on school. While she was still taking care of her younger brother, Yesenia found this to be less of a problem than in high school because she did not have to miss class to pick him up and found that it kept her at home instead of out with friends. Her mom grew more supportive as well: "I think my mom's more like supportive about me, like my work and everything. She doesn't like always bug me about, 'Oh, clean this, clean that,' because now she knows I have homework and I'm really into school, so she's relaxing more than she used to." Yesenia attributed her mother's shift in part to the fact that she was attending college as well.

Midway through the second semester, Yesenia broke up with her long-distance boyfriend, which meant she would be staying in El Paso in the fall, a decision that seemed positive given her first-year success at BU. However, by the time she told me this news, she had already found an in-town boyfriend who she was spending a lot of time with, leading her to procrastinate more on her schoolwork. She knew this was a problem and that she needed to change: "It's cause after I met this guy everything was crazy. But I'm trying to get back like stop procrastinating a lot. I'm like, 'I'm not like this. I'm not like this.' So I have to go back to the way I was." For better or worse, they soon broke up and Yesenia returned to devoting more energy to school.

As she began the second semester, Yesenia was set on majoring in business, but would have to wait until fall to begin the actual coursework. She had high aspirations for the future, planning on getting an MBA and a doctorate, largely motivated by "money, a better lifestyle." She had been interested in business for a while and was involved in the DECA marketing organization in high school. She also liked organizing money-related events like fundraisers. As she received her student loan money, she made an informal business loaning money out to friends and charging interest. She clearly had assertiveness and an ability to play tough, qualities that would help in the business world. For instance, she described a group project during the second semester in which a member was not holding his own: "The basketball player, like he wasn't doing anything at all, but once I told him like, 'If you're not going to work on the project, I'm just going to take out your name and I'm gonna talk to the Miss [the instructor] so she won't give you credit for it if your name's not there.' But after that, he's like, 'Okay, just tell me what you want me to do.'"

While students are often hesitant to report on a slacking peer and just end up complaining to friends about the guilty person, Yesenia clearly did something about it, knowing that it was unfair that every member would get credit regardless of whether or not they did the work.

Table 4.2 shows how Yesenia continued to write extensively into her second semester, more than most other study students. Affirmation of her developing writing abilities was one of the most rewarding aspects of the semester: "Every time I get my grades for the essays make me happy. I think that's the greatest part ever because I put too much work and I expect a good grade, and I get a good grade." The Bs and Cs on Yesenia's first-semester writing assignments were moving up to As and Bs in the second. She continued to request meetings with me for feedback on drafts of most of her writing assignments. She also received editing help from a friend, but did not use the Writing Center after being dissatisfied with the help she received there during her only visit.

Yesenia transitioned from developmental to mainstream writing without any major problems, and was generally seen as a good student by her second-semester instructor, who described her as, "Enthusiastic, friendly, optimistic. Gets a late start sometimes. Doesn't start things quite on time. But yeah, I would say she's a good student." This instructor, the same as Bianca's, was one of the more experienced FYC instructors and had taught ENG 1311 many times. Yesenia found her nice and liked the fact that she went around helping students during the class, something more common in high school than college.

While the general theme for ENG 1311 courses was community based, Yesenia's instructor took this further, giving the class a theme focused on peace and more specifically peace activists. In the first few assignments Yesenia focused on a very local issue, immigration, as she wrote an agency discourse memo focused on the work and discourse practices of a local immigrant advocacy center. In the memo, she noted how the center helped migrants from all over the world and promoted their work and solicited donors through a strong Internet presence. She worked through multiple drafts with me, expanding and revising significantly from her first to the final. In an early draft, she wrote: "They experience rape, violence, mental abuse, all for the American dream. But not all immigrants came this far for the American dream, they are refugees from other countries that came this far to find peace in a safe country. This people need help from organizations that can help them with their migratory status and form a new life." In revising, we worked on improving aspects of her language and adding content to her memo, especially in developing a stronger focus on the topic of an organization's discourse practices. For instance, I commented on her draft: "Talk about their website, FB and Twitter pages, and their e-list in order to discuss their discourse practices—why do they need to have these pages?"

Yesenia's second major writing project was a rhetorical analysis of the *USA Today* editorial "Our View on Illegal Immigration: It Will Take More Than Fences." She came to me with a draft about half as long as it needed to be; however, her development as an analytical writer and thinker was evident from lines like this: "To further their trust, the U.S.A Today editorial board uses persuasive language to make their work credible for the audience. They do not use vulgar language or raciest words they are not trying to segregate the different races by saying 'how do you stop illegal immigration?'" Yesenia had come a long way as a writer from high school. Our discussion mostly focused on ways to expand and clarify aspects of her essay, as a number of sentences were still confusing as she continued trying on the language of an analytical essay.

For the latter half of the semester Yesenia changed topics, focusing on the increasing unrest in the Middle East. She considered the annotated bibliography and subsequent research paper some of the most important assignments of the year, as they required her to develop a few new skills: library research and APA citation style. However, having done very different types of writing throughout high school, she expressed frustration with research-based writing: "I hate writing research because you have to like search and put the sources, say where you got them, make APA style. Why can't you just like write, write, write, write, write?" Although she wrote a research paper for her first-year seminar, she said this was easier because she already knew about the topic, was more interested in it, and did not have to use library research. In contrast, Yesenia chose an unfamiliar and complex topic for her ENG 1311 research paper: explaining how Nelson Mandela's theories about peace could help Libya in its current era of unrest. A look at her annotated bibliography revealed nine mostly library sources with the exception of an online article from a Spanish-language news outlet.

The thesis for her research paper read, "Connecting Libya with Nelson Mandela even thought they do not have anything in common, is valuable because the ideologies of Mandela can really help Libya to live in peace and stop all the violence that they are going thought right now." As I worked with her to improve this essay, I explained that she needed to connect the two better, as she discussed the situation in Libya and then Mandela's ideologies but failed to make a convincing case that these ideologies were applicable in Libya's case. Nonetheless, a look at a later draft of this essay shows how far Yesenia had grown from a struggling student trying to analyze *Beowulf* or *Lord of the Flies* to a student who could integrate research from a number of sources like the US Department of State and *Al-Jazeera* in order to write an extended research essay on a completely new topic for her.

While some other students did not do as much writing in second semester history classes, Yesenia continued to write extensively, having multiple exams with essay questions as well as take home essay assignments. Her first assignment was a paragraph in which she had to choose a document from the textbook and identify the document, the author, the date it was written, and summarize different aspects of the document. Yesenia chose the Mississippi Black Codes and received a 95 percent. Later essays demanded more, as the second essay was supposed to be two or three pages. The second essay assignment required students to compare and contrast the attitudes of Booker T. Washington and W. E. B. DuBois based on texts by them in the course textbook. As with other writing assignments in the course, this one was well designed by the professor, contextualizing the issue, giving specific instructions, and telling them the main points that should be included in the essay, such as: "Compare and contrast the documents. What is similar in their observations of the African American experience in the late 19th Century? What do they propose (both directly and indirectly)? On what aspects of black life do they differ?" For this assignment, Yesenia came to me with a very strong handwritten draft. On the draft, she had crossed out "he had to pass trough a lots of stuff" and replaced it with "before in life many obstacles" indicating she was gaining the ability to self-revise in order to make her writing more formal.

The one essay that I did not see until after Yesenia submitted it was on the book, *Farewell to Manzanar*, in which students were asked to choose several themes from a list and write about them. This was one of the more difficult essays of the semester for Yesenia because her English research essay took longer than expected, so she had to stay up all night writing this one. Despite this, and not having feedback from me, she still managed an 80 percent, which she was satisfied with given the circumstances. A look at her thesis revealed a strong focus: "Even though that she was relocated to a concentration camp and her dad send to prison, and they had to go through a lot when she was only a kid and not be able to understand what was really going on at the time, by her writing this book she is letting us see the other side of war, and understanding how her childhood was, her way of living and her perception of loyalty to her country." Given that she had to write it last minute and did not have editing help, there were a fair number of errors throughout, especially with past tense verb forms, an issue that Yesenia was aware of.

Another non-English class where Yesenia did some writing was in sociology, where she had to write what she thought was the most important essay of the semester because of the topic it focused on—racism. For this essay, the class viewed a video called "A Class Divided" about an elementary school class in which students were taught lessons about racism by, for example, saying those with brown eyes were inferior. The prompt gave clear instructions on how to format the assignment and specified that papers needed to be a minimum of two pages and could follow the numbered question/answer format. The result was not really an essay, but a series of short answers to questions such as "How did the negative and positive labels placed on each group become self-fulfilling prophecies?"

Conclusion

Despite having challenges such as writing abilities and extracurricular demands on her time, Yesenia developed a fairly strong network of capital as depicted in Figure 4.3.

Yesenia entered BU through the START program, a program that provisionally admitted underprepared students. At the end of the year, she noted this as a source of support, because failing a class meant that she could not return and would have to go to community college, a serious step backward in her mind. Fortunately, through a combination of hard work, an increasingly supportive mother, and actively seeking help from others, Yesenia passed all her classes and clearly felt she was becoming a stronger reader and writer. She realized the importance of these support networks in our final interview, noting that "I think family, friends are like really important."

She did not attribute her success to high school, noting that "The transition from the way you write in high school to college is like really, really different." She was always very critical of the high school focus on testing throughout, which she felt prevented them from ever doing long research-based essays that were regularly expected of students at the college level. She also blamed high school's failure to prepare students on a culture of low expectations: "In high school we don't really do essays, like real essays. You know, in high school you just like copy-paste and they don't even care if you copy-paste. But over here, like if you copy paste, you're going to be sent to the dean's office, so you have to really like put it in your own words and that's like a really hard thing to do. . . ." As evident by this comment and my experiences at SHS, students would often copy and paste when confronted with an unfamiliar

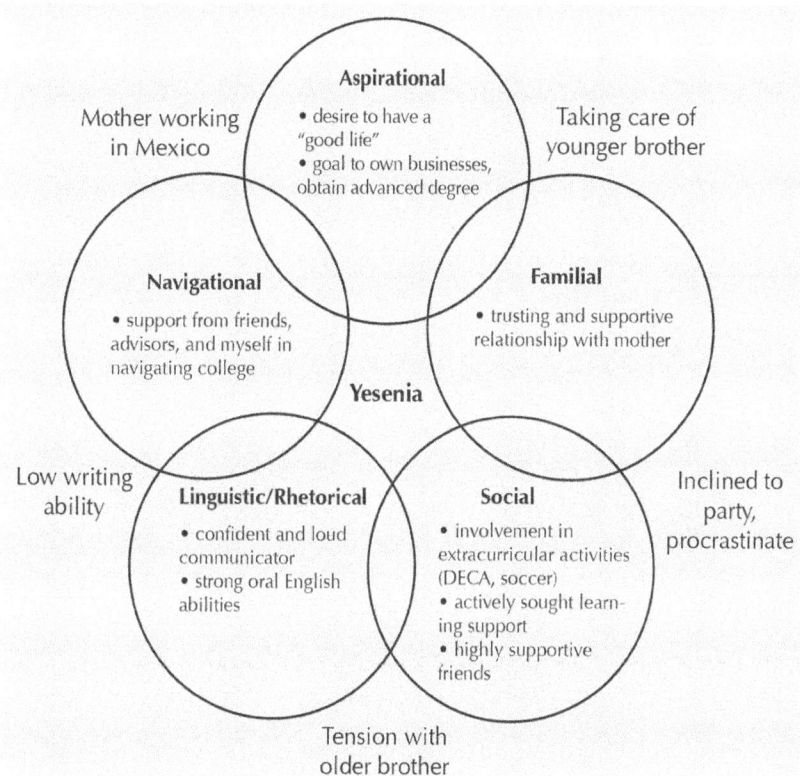

Figure 4.3. Yesenia's sources of capital and challenge.

or difficult assignment. While this may have resulted in a lower grade, teachers were not really allowed to fail students and often let this kind of behavior slide as a result.

Nonetheless, Yesenia adapted to college-level writing quite well, due to a variety of things such as the extensive practice she had and constant feedback from me. As noted elsewhere, students generally did not receive very detailed feedback on their writing from teachers, which limited their chances to improve. For instance, Yesenia's second-semester FYC teacher noted that she focused on giving summative comments after she began collecting writing electronically. This meant that Yesenia received comments to improve the overall content of her writing, but not the localized feedback necessary to improve language accuracy. In addition to practice and feedback, Yesenia noted one important way she became a better writer: "Reading. Reading and because when you read, like you catch—you learn words that, I don't know, you're like, 'Oh, this really exists,' and you know some really weird word exists and you can use it." This statement reveals how Yesenia saw a connection between reading and writing by identifying the importance of reading in expanding her vocabulary.

As noted at the beginning of her case study, Yesenia was the study participant one would most likely find at a party. Although she struggled at first balancing social and academic lives, she noted at the end of the year, "now I'm like really into my school and I know when to party and when not to party." When asked what kind of advice she would give to seniors at SHS, she replied, "Like they can go party in weekends, not during the week, because you have class. And to really like go to class and never miss the class because once you miss the class, it's going to be hard to like understand the next like time you go to class. You're not going to be on the same page as everyone. And like to read a lot." Yesenia managed to have fun, but it was clear that she was putting school first. I recall a weekend night at 10 pm when she texted me a question about one of the essays she was currently working on. In these instances, Yesenia knew that partying had to wait.

# 5
## SMOOTH TRANSITIONS

The previous few chapters brought stories of students who struggled in various ways, with some stopping out of college and some moving beyond their first year. The two students in this chapter also faced some challenges in their educational journeys, although many of these were before they came to college. Because of various personal characteristics and experiences, the two students profiled in this chapter ended up having relatively smooth transitions to college and excelled beyond many of their peers, despite having a high school education that inadequately prepared them for success.

### CAROLINA: A SUPPORTIVE FAMILY AND CONSTANT MOTIVATION

> "My mom just lets me focus on school. And many parents don't do that. And like during—I can say that they're not my support that much. I'm their support. Because they—my brother and my sister they see me as an example. So I have to be—I know that I have to succeed on college because of them . . ."
> —Carolina on family support

> "Carolina's awesome. She's the kinda student that I think any teacher would wanna have, and, yes, she's still getting better with her English skills. Carolina does in one-one-hundredth of the time what a lot of other students do as far as work, as far as improvement, so I don't know exactly where she was, say, a couple or three years ago, but I have the feeling she's come a really long way fast and I think she's gonna go a really long way fast still. So, yeah, if teachers had pets, she would definitely be one of my teacher's pets, so, yeah, I just loved having her."
> —Carolina's senior English teacher

#### Background and Defining Characteristics and Experiences

My first impressions of Carolina were of a diligent but soft-spoken and shy girl who lacked confidence in her abilities, which were quite impressive. Her high school English teacher described her as "awesome" and "the kinda student that I think any teacher would wanna have." Carolina moved to the United States from just across the border at the beginning of eighth grade with her mother and younger siblings.

Before moving, Carolina did not know any English except some basic vocabulary. Making the transition was difficult because the ESL classes were all in English and she did not understand anything at school. She attended the downtown middle school that most of the students in this study attended for one year before transitioning to SHS. At SHS, she spent another year in ESL before moving into all mainstream classes her second year. Nonetheless, she graduated from high school in three years in the top 10 percent of her class. When asked how she learned English so quickly, Carolina explained that she went out of her way to practice speaking and writing more than other students.

Over the course of the study, Carolina's motivation became a defining characteristic in her English development and general success at school. For instance, in an early interview, she mentioned that she lacked English vocabulary, to which I suggested that she read more. She borrowed *Twilight* from the library before the next interview and soon read the whole series. When her senior English teacher and I co-designed an essay for *Lord of the Flies* for the final senior essay, we asked for a three- to four-page essay, which was the longest essay most of the class had ever written and a point of contention with most students. Instead of complaining, Carolina insisted on writing a ten-page essay.

Carolina was very soft-spoken when I first met her and expressed a general lack of confidence in English. In the beginning of the study survey, she ranked her spoken and written English abilities "Not Good" but her Spanish abilities as "Very Good." While she had taken a pre-AP English class previously and started out her senior year in a dual-credit English class, she quickly became nervous and transferred into a mainstream one the first week. She initially expressed some doubt about her ability to handle university-level work, asking me if she should consider community college instead. However, as her final high school semester progressed, she increasingly grew more confident in her choice to attend BU.

Because she was the oldest in the family, there was pressure on Carolina to graduate from high school earlier and to finish college. Then she could help support her family upon graduation. Whereas other study students had to bear a number of family responsibilities, Carolina's mother made school top priority. Carolina never worked during the school year with the exception of some volunteer work. As she started college, she explained that her mom spoiled her like a baby and that she was given the time she needed to study at home, with household chores delegated to her younger siblings. Even though money was tight, Carolina explained that she had her own laptop and Internet at home, which helped her accomplish some of her college-level work more easily than if she lacked strong home computer access.

Carolina also benefited from a local Catholic community center that she regularly attended since her arrival in the United States. She went there as much as an hour or two every day during high school for homework help, reading tutoring, and computer classes. Carolina began to give back to the center senior year via volunteering with GED and citizenship classes in addition to helping special education children use the computers. She got a job at the center teaching GED and citizenship classes the summer before college. In addition to benefiting from the classes and tutoring they offered, Carolina appeared to receive college-related advice as well, with people at the center urging her to start at the university instead of the community college.

When we met a few weeks after she started college, Carolina came across as a different person from the one I knew in the spring. She was more confident and spoke much louder. When asked about her summer, she described two important experiences that contributed to this transformation. First, the above-mentioned job at the community center taught her to be more independent because she was away from her family more than normal and was required to communicate effectively with her supervisors and in the classes she taught. Second, she went to Washington, DC, with her school's DECA chapter, an organization that aims to promote future leaders for careers in "marketing, finance, hospitality, and management." In DC, Carolina explained that she learned in a week what she had not learned in two to three years of history classes. More importantly for her personal growth, she met with people from all over the world at the conference, including members of Congress. These two experiences combined to help transform Carolina from the shy, quiet girl in high school to someone who was more confident to handle the pressures of college and make connections that would support her success.

### High School Literacy Experiences

Carolina was always interested in doing extra work to improve her English, such as writing a longer essay than the rest of the class for *Lord of the Flies*. Early in the study she asked me for a college-level prompt that she could practice responding to. However, despite her dedication to improving writing, Carolina said math was her favorite subject and intended to major in engineering. When asked where English was on her list of favorite classes, she explained that she did not know because of a lack of confidence: "I think that maybe I can be better in English or language because when I was in Mexico in school the best class was Spanish because I know it and here it would be the worse class because I'm not confident in there." Her newness to English did not seem to pose a barrier in her math classes at the high school level.

Carolina desired improvement in all areas, including English. She regretted avoiding a dual-credit class her senior year, saying that she felt behind compared to her friend who took the class because students there wrote extensively while she did comparatively little writing (three two- to four-page essays). She wished her senior English teacher, Mr. Robertson, would have been stricter as the students messing around in her English class were very distracting and prevented the class from learning as much as she could. Consequently, Carolina felt she learned more English from reading the *Twilight* series her senior year.

Although she did not do as much writing as she would like in her English class, Carolina felt the writing she did was valuable. Her personal statement for college focused particularly on her parents' separation and the subsequent move to the United States with her mother and siblings. Here she recalled her early struggles learning English in vivid detail: "I confronted another obstacle. I didn't know the language. During the first weeks I used to cry everyday when I came back from school. It was frustrating being in the classroom surrounded by many people talking and can not understand a word. Everything was new to me the school, the teachers, my classmates but most important the language in which I was supposed to learned all the lessons. Together the school and my family seen to attacked me."

Despite the powerful story Carolina told in her personal statement, she felt her *Beowulf* essay was her most important piece of writing senior year because it required more from her than previous assignments. Instead of writing about a personal experience, Carolina had to, in her words, "read a book and then break it . . . to find the true meaning of the book, the true meaning of the passage. Why is the author saying that? Then you can explain it?" According to her, this would be more in line with college-level writing than the previous work she had completed for testing like TAKS and TELPAS. For this essay, Carolina wrote about how "Anglo-Saxon society is a united community that fights to defend the security of all members." Her strong writing abilities were clear throughout the essay, as she demonstrated impressive skill in making insightful analytical comments and integrating quotes with advanced signal phrases like "Courageously Beowulf accepts the risk and declares . . ." Carolina concluded by drawing on her understanding of Mexican American movements for civil rights in looking for a broader meaning to the poem. She wrote, "This poem as a whole presents a lesson to its readers, the importance of a united community" and discussed Cesar Chavez and the Chicano movement, emphasizing that their solidarity is what helped them receive the rights they demanded.

In order to gain more writing practice before college, Carolina pushed to make her final essay, based on *Lord of the Flies*, about eight to ten pages long, even though much less was required. The topic she developed focused on "The evil part that wakes up and you want power"; it was complex and required stronger analytical skills than most of the previous work she had done. Carolina chose this topic because she felt that it would allow her to make connections throughout the whole story and between all the characters in her essay rather than just focusing on a single aspect. Unfortunately, her final essay was not as successful as expected, largely because Carolina lost her flash drive on the bus and had to rewrite the latter half of the essay last minute. She provided too much background information in the first several pages of the essay, information that did not necessarily support the final point she was building. The inclusion of this information was likely connected to a desire to make the essay longer without an idea of exactly how to construct it. However, the strength of Carolina's analytical skills came out during the essay, with statements like this, that described the situation following the death of Piggy: "There was nothing to save. All reason, morality, civilization, everything was lost. The boys had actually started killing each other without any regret. Finally the savage part had dominated the civilized part."

### Literacy and Learning in the First Year of College
#### First Semester

Carolina knew that the writing demands would be different at college: "Like they expect us to tell what do we learn from, in writing. Everything is going to be in writing, that's what my teachers have told me . . . it's going to get like more . . . extended. More complicated the writing, they're going to expect more from us. Like in the history class, this paper was just a paragraph and we have to turn in one on next Thursday that's going to be two or three, no one to two pages. So it's longer." Whereas writing played a minimal role in Carolina's high school outside of her English classes, Carolina anticipated having to write more often, more quickly, and in more classes at college.

Not only would Carolina be expected to write much more than in high school, she was expected to read more as well. Her first-year seminar had the highest reading load of her classes and was consequently the hardest class. It was a learning community connected with her history class, which also had a lot of reading. The seminar teacher assigned a few academic journal articles weekly, articles that students were expected to download themselves from the databases. Carolina and her friend, also her study partner, were the only two who did this the first time around. At first, Carolina reported spending three to four hours a day just reading for her courses. However, she quickly learned that she did not have to read everything because the professors would summarize the readings in class lectures.

In FYC, Carolina had almost weekly writing assignments including an analysis of a website, discourse community map, and a memo (see Table 5.1 for a list of Carolina's first-year writing experiences). Although the official syllabus specified that the course have a community-based orientation, her instructor took a pop culture focus. Carolina built on the knowledge she had gained from her extracurricular *Twilight* reading and focused much of her work on the phenomenon surrounding the series. An early assignment structured as a memo detailed the beginning of the series and its subsequent success as it was translated into movies. Here is an excerpt from a draft she sent me for feedback: "What started as a dream now has been call a phenomenon. On June 2 2003, Stephenie Meyer had a dream that impulse her to write a vampire-romantic story[1]. Stephanie Meyer's Twilight Saga had cause a commotion primary on teenagers but also among people of all ages. Since Meyer's work was published in 2005 the Twilight series has gain followers around the world." While giving her some feedback on content, I also highlighted issues with verb tenses and prepositions. However, Carolina was doing a good job in integrating and citing secondary sources in her writing.

Carolina felt that one of the most valuable assignments in her English class was her APA-style annotated bibliography, which taught her the basics of APA style and of creating an annotated bibliography, both of which helped her complete a similar assignment in her first-year seminar. Not all of the assignments for the course were focused on *Twilight*, however, as she chose a very different topic for her visual analysis. Here,

Table 5.1. Carolina's first-year writing experiences

| Fall Semester Classes | Writing Assignments |
| --- | --- |
| FYC | Homepage portfolio |
|  | 2–3-page agency discourse memo |
|  | 3–5-page rhetorical/visual analysis |
|  | 7–10-source annotated bibliography |
|  | 4–6-page community problem report |
| History | Paragraph response |
|  | 1–2-page compare/contrast essay |
|  | 6–7-page analysis essay on the *Narrative of the Life of Frederick Douglass* |
| Math | No writing |
| First-Year Seminar | Weekly article summaries |
|  | Annotated bibliography |
|  | 7-page research paper |

| Spring Semester Classes | Writing Assignments |
| --- | --- |
| FYC | Wiki postings |
|  | 4–6-page genre analysis |
|  | 7–10-page literature review/primary research report |
|  | 5–6-minute documentary (group project) |
|  | 2-page online opinion piece |
|  | Advocacy website |
| History | Paragraph assessment |
|  | 2 essay exams (2 questions) |
| Math | No writing |
| Political Science | No writing |
| Psychology | No writing |

she focused on a Bill O'Reilly interview with the author Jacob Sullum who wrote a book titled *Saying Yes: In Defense of Drugs*. In this essay she was able to skillfully reference details from the video to support her analysis that included the commonly used rhetorical appeals ethos, pathos, and logos: "In this discussion since the beginning O'Reilly and Sullum started to use a different level of vocabulary and a higher tone of voice to try to get the leading position on the argument . . . Later as the discussion got more complicated, O'Reilly raised his tone of voice and took the discussion to an almost aggressive level. He used the words 'irresponsible' and 'libertine' to refer to Jacob Sullum." Examining arguments surrounding drug legalization became Carolina's focal topic in her second-semester FYC course, which is discussed in the next section.

In her first-year seminar course, Carolina had to write a final research paper in addition to the article analyses she wrote throughout the semester. The topic of the final paper, which she chose, was "The Virgin of Guadalupe and the Influence in Europeans in New Spain." Since much of the work on this topic was written in Spanish, Carolina's instructor explained that she could do research in Spanish as long as she translated everything to English for the final paper.

Carolina wrote several essays in her history class, each one progressively longer. The first essay asked her to compare and contrast the perspectives of two texts, the biography of a former slave and another text written by a surgeon on slave ships. Her concluding statements to this essay read: "We know that slavery was an important factor on the construction of what today is America however Falconbridge and Equiano make us realize the torment that the slaves suffered to working in the New World. This great nation, the land of the freedom, was built in part from slavery." Carolina's mid-term exam was an essay exam in which she was given two questions in advance that she could prepare outlines for. The topics were complex and asked students to synthesize information from multiple sources and perspectives. For instance, the second question cited Omi and Winant's (1993) *Racial Formation* to argue that there is "no biological basis to race" and proceeded to ask students to "write an essay that discusses how Spain and England construct ideas of race and systems that are based on these racial categories by doing the following."

Carolina felt her history writing was the most important writing first semester, especially the final essay. This assignment had students choose four from a list of eight themes to write about how the *Narrative of the Life of Frederick Douglass* "open[s] a window into the institution of slavery." The value Carolina attributed to this essay was in part because it was worth 20 percent of her final grade, but also because it was the longest essay she had written (six to seven pages), with the exception of the *Lord of the Flies* essay discussed earlier. One of the big challenges with this essay Carolina had was to choose the four themes and write about them in a way that they would be connected, as requested by her professor. In helping her on this essay, I provided ideas for making the connections between different themes, as the first draft she brought to me was largely disconnected. I also gave feedback on verb forms, something that she continued to struggle with in her drafts. These ranged from inconsistent tense when citing ("Douglass states" and "Douglass claimed") to difficulties forming the past passive ("was brutally murder").

Despite earlier concerns about not being prepared for college, Carolina excelled by the end of the first semester. She felt she was meeting the challenges of college because she was consistently getting some of the highest grades in her classes and expected all As and Bs for the semester, higher than originally expected. It also appeared that all the writing she was doing in her classes was paying off, in that she was finally getting the practice she desired to improve her writing. While some students in this study did not notice a change in their knowledge of academic English over their first semester, Carolina felt differently: "I go back to my first essay that I did at the beginning of the semester and this, this one that I missed, like way better. Like I connect in my sentences, I feel that I can express more easily than the beginning. Like my sentences were, I couldn't express what I wanted. Now it's getting more, I think." From her reading experiences outside school along with the extensive practice she was getting in her classes, Carolina was gaining the vocabulary and other knowledge necessary to express herself more fully in English.

### Second Semester

Carolina continued to excel her second semester of college and felt that the level of work was lighter than the first semester. While she still wrote extensively in FYC, writing demands declined substantially in history and were largely nonexistent in political science and psychology. She felt her English class was the most difficult: "In the other ones, it's just read and then the exam is . . . each month. So I don't have to worry until the day of the exam."

In comparison with her inexperienced first-semester FYC teacher, Carolina's second-semester teacher was one of the most experienced instructors in the program, something that was readily apparent: "We can tell from the very beginning that she knows what she's doing, what she's teaching. And then, she has all things all over the place with good information to make the assignment what she wants and she keeps a lot of information. I think I found like three papers that she wrote, aside from the guide, to help us. I think it's a good thing for her . . . for us because I think she didn't have to do that." My observations confirmed an instructor who was consistently well-prepared, confident, and who explained things very clearly to her students. She had a course wiki with pages of resources that she had developed to supplement the materials found in the program guide. In contrast, Carolina could tell that her previous semester teacher was more inexperienced, astutely noting that, as a graduate student, he was not only learning the material he was teaching but also how to teach.[1]

As noted in chapter 2, the second-semester FYC course at BU was a hybrid course, something that might have posed a problem to a less technologically savvy and intrinsically motivated student; however, Carolina liked this model, feeling that it allowed her to work on her own time. She also valued the distributed assessment aspect of the class, saying that helped remove potential teacher bias from the process. Carolina chose drug legalization for her research topic, writing a genre analysis, literature review, and an online op-ed focused on this issue in addition to creating a video documentary.

The literature review/primary research report was on par with her first-year seminar research report for being one of the hardest writing tasks for the year, largely because of the amount of research it required. Carolina's review contained nine sources including articles, academic books, and web sources, plus a survey that she conducted focused on student attitudes toward drug legalization. While she heavily qualified the small sample size of the survey in her report, she had forty-three participants, a respectable number for a FYC project. Carolina's motivation and savviness as a student was apparent in her decision to send the survey out via Blackboard in her large lecture classes to improve response rates. My comments on a draft of this report focused primarily on integrating sources and APA style as Carolina had largely overcome the verb tense difficulties present in earlier writing. She was citing not only quotes but also paraphrased information, something a lot of students overlook. She was also trying more complex sentence structures, which resulted in some confusing moments: "As Ethan Nadelmann, an important figure in the debate, explains, that drug legalization has a different meaning for every person but all of the meanings agree that it is something completely opposite to drug prohibition." Nonetheless, instances like this show that Carolina was constantly pushing herself and consequently developing as a writer.

Another major project for her FYC course was a video documentary that was generally recommended to do in groups because of the amount of work involved. However, because she did not want to give up her semester-long topic, Carolina decided to go it alone. Working on the documentary was the most stressful part of the year because of all the different aspects involved, combined with the fact that she was learning a new program and operating system, iMovie on the Mac. The night before the documentary was due, Carolina ended up staying in the lab until 10 pm, despite earlier goals of being home by 6 pm. This was one of the few times she recalled her mother being truly angry with her because of her late arrival at home. Despite the difficulties completing the assignment, she felt she learned valuable skills that would serve her well in the future.

Although Carolina entered BU with an interest in engineering, disappointing experiences in math classes diminished her confidence in pursuing this major. She consequently reconsidered her major and indicated an interest in psychology early in her second semester, as she found the introductory class interesting and liked that many things related to this topic. As the semester progressed, Carolina became more confident in this switch, and was planning to declare a major in psychology, but decided to wait until after the summer so she could research career options more to solidify her decision. While leaning toward psychology, she also considered political science either as a major or a minor, and explained her attraction to these fields of study: "They have in common that you can help others. Psychology—you can help people with their problems. Their social problems. And political science is on a higher level that you get to help problems that involve more people. Like do a lot of change—to make a change in the world." Clearly a desire to help others with problems was strong in Carolina and had been a dream for a long time: "Since I was little, I thought like I want to be someone important that can help others."

Conclusion

As depicted in Figure 5.1, Carolina had a few challenges, but developed a comprehensive network to support her success as she transitioned through school.

Reflecting on her first year at college, Carolina reported that she was required to read and write much more than she ever had to in high school, commenting that she "actually learned how to write more [this year] than any other year in English." Throughout the year, she clearly felt she was improving, becoming a better reader, writer, and communicator in English, and that her largest perceived obstacle in succeeding at college—her knowledge of English—was becoming less of a problem every day. She developed her writing skills through rewriting, noting, "I think what helps is that you can write a paper and then look at it. Not the same day. Two days later, you can see many of the errors that you did."

Carolina was truly an exceptional student. When asked what supported her success, she replied, "I think it's me. The way that I always do

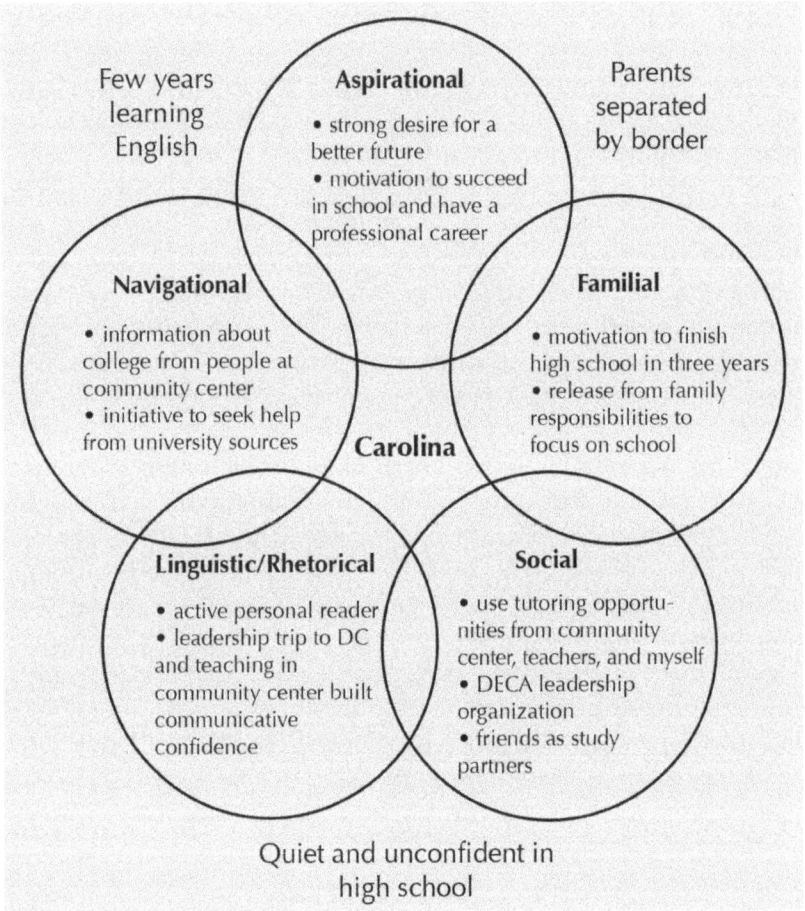

Figure 5.1. Carolina's sources of capital and challenge.

my homework and I have to spend my time like on my homework. And maybe other people, they have to work or they have some other things to do." Carolina consistently worked hard and reported spending hours every night her first-semester reading for class. She was supported by a love of learning that became evident by the way she developed various texts related to her topic in her second-semester FYC course. She was one of the few students who enjoyed reading for pleasure and the only one who reported reading books over winter break, commenting, "I always like to read. And even in high school, they didn't ask us to read or require us to read, but I did it on my own."

When asked who was her most important source of support this year, Carolina listed me as second behind her family, identifying me as one of her few sources of detailed feedback on her writing. She did not receive extensive feedback from teachers and other evaluators, merely comments simply identifying that there were grammatical issues without specifying what they were. Clearly, however, Carolina's family was an invaluable source of support in different ways, articulated in the epigraph to this case study. Unlike other students who had to take care of siblings or help in other ways around the house, Carolina's mother always told her to study first. Also, Carolina felt pressure on her being the first in the family to attend college. By graduating, she would set a strong example for her younger siblings, helping secure a better future for her whole family.

## MAURICIO: DRIVEN BY GRADES AND PARENTS TO SUCCEED

> *"I think the only reason why I go to [English] class is cause attendance counts, it's a grade . . . [writing] is important because of my grade. But, it, for me it doesn't mean anything."*
> —Mauricio on the importance of grades

> *"[Mauricio] has been one of the most motivated students in any of my classes, actually. For example, for the literature review and report, the primary research project, he created this really elaborate survey, with four different sections. And he asked me to give him feedback on it, and he was the only student who did that."*
> —Mauricio's second-semester college writing teacher

### Background and Defining Characteristics and Experiences

Like Carolina, Mauricio was a late arrival to the US school system, having studied in Juárez until his freshman year at SHS. Mauricio began school in the United States with minimal English, knowing only basic vocabulary that his mother taught him. He was an immature freshman and misbehaved into his sophomore year until his sophomore year teacher and mentor, Ms. Cooper, brought him in line with her strictness. Ms. Cooper recalled that Mauricio refused to speak English at first, screaming at her when he misunderstood that any student who did not speak English would fail. She explained that Mauricio came to her with very little English even after a year at SHS, as his freshman ESL teacher would speak Spanish most of the time.

Mauricio was the only student who lived in Mexico throughout the whole study, crossing the border every day to attend school. In high school, this meant getting up at 4 am, crossing the border, going along as his father dropped his brother off at school, and arriving at SHS around 8 am. In college, his crossing changed as he drove to a hotel his grandfather owned in downtown Juárez, walked across the border bridge, and caught a bus to the university. The increasing drug-related violence in Mauricio's city affected him in various ways during college. His parents imposed a strict 7 pm curfew that prevented him from staying at the library as late as he wanted. A family friend was kidnapped his first semester in college, resulting in Mauricio getting half credit on a major history assignment. While another professor understood this difficulty, giving him full credit for the missed assignment, Mauricio did not tell his history professor about his situation because he saw this professor as a "mean person" and who was "real closed, like, he doesn't like care about you, he just cares about you turning in the work."

While Mauricio had this additional challenge of crossing the border to go to school, he had an advantage that many other students did not: a well-off family who owned multiple businesses and parents who constantly pushed him to get very high grades in school. While Mauricio denied his family was rich, he recalled having private computer lessons when he first got a computer and had cell phones for both sides of the border, including a US iPhone. He paid cash for a four-year-old used car and briefly lent his mother several thousand dollars from his savings for a new living room set. His favorite clothing brand was Guess, a high-end mall retailer.

Mauricio described his parents as crazy as they expected him to get A+ in all his high school classes, despite not having similar expectations for his siblings. According to Ms. Cooper, Mauricio once told her a story in which he had received a failing grade in third grade and his father took him to a *maquiladora*[2] for a day, making him work alongside assembly line workers who earned low wages. His father said this would be his life if he did not do well at school, and Mauricio "got very scared and went back to school and never failed anything again." As a result of this push by his parents, Mauricio became a very grade-driven student and explained that the worst thing a teacher could do to him was threaten his grades. During his senior year, he went out of the way to type all his work for extra credit, and even fabricated an email from his parents to his teachers, which read:

> We are Mauricio's parents, and we are really concern with his grades. Lately, our son has been showing some poor and unacceptable grades that do not meet with the minimum goal that we have set for our children. We will like to know if he has been giving you any kind of respectful attitude

or if he has any issues with his attendance. Our requirements for him are to have 97's as a minimum grade in every class, but due to his last semester's grades, we are sure that in this and some other classes his lowest grade should be a 99. I would like you to please give him some extra work if possible, and we want you to know that you totally count with our authorization to keep him after school, during lunch and even before school if you think it is needed. We also understand that you you have a strict schedule to follow, so if you have problems with grading Mauricio's late or extra work please just let us know. If you have any question please feel free to contact me by email. I am totally available for "Parent Teacher Conferences." Thank you for your time and patience.

This email demonstrates Mauricio's skillful ability to communicate with others in order to promote his success. His senior English teacher Mr. Robertson did not question the authenticity of this email largely because it was in line with the parental image that Mauricio had constructed for teachers at SHS.

Largely because of parental support and pressure creating a self-driven personality, Mauricio constantly strived for the best during high school and saw that the big problem with other students at SHS was the lack of parental support. Ms. Cooper explained that Mauricio "would stand out anywhere because he has drive in him. He's gonna do well no matter where he goes because that's him. He's responsible. He wants to do [his] best." During interviews, Mauricio would regularly refer to school and life as a competition, expressing concern that he would have to be competing with students who had spoken English all their lives while studying at college. Maurico applied his perfectionist attitude to English as well, telling me in an early interview: "One of my goals is to like learn English perfectly, although it's like hard, and I know I have a really heavy accent, but I want to get rid of it and I know the way of doing it is just to practice it." While this concern over accent could have harmed a less confident student, it never seemed to affect Mauricio too negatively except to push him to constantly improve his English.

Ms. Cooper became an important mentor to Mauricio in this area. Mauricio described her role: "She taught me how to write and I think she was more like my inspiration to write because she was . . . really challenging, she was always pushing me and telling me to do this, do that. She's like a great teacher for me." He explained that the TAKS was a "huge obstacle" because he had to pass it in order to graduate, something that seemed impossible when he could barely write an English sentence upon entering his sophomore year ESL class. When she was Mauricio's teacher, Ms. Cooper recalled having other students she would require to come for tutoring before school, after school, and even on Saturdays. She recalled that Mauricio would come all the time, constantly revising his work and seeking her feedback. Because of the high standards Ms. Cooper set and the commitment she had for Mauricio's learning, Mauricio was dissatisfied with every other teacher he had during high school.

Mauricio eventually became a star student in high school, something that stemmed from not only his high grades and drive, but his self-identified ability to befriend older people with ease. As a result of this latter talent, he gained not only the trust of his teachers but also the administration. Consequently, he was asked to regularly work with the school counselors. Because they valued his work so much, they would even pull him out of class, where they knew he could catch up with ease. They even trusted him to handle the scholarship application files of other senior students. He boasted that he could essentially go to class when he wanted, because teachers trusted him and knew that he was doing a lot of work for the school administration. His work with the high school continued through his first year at college, but became more of a negative factor in his life because of having to work longer hours than the original twenty promised. During one observed college class, he stepped out to take a call from the high school, and felt that his work there contributed to a lower than desired first-semester GPA. Nonetheless, despite getting paid minimum wage for relatively high-level administrative work, he liked the responsibility and trust that went along with the job and kept it throughout his first year.

Due to the immense drive fostered by his parents and his hugely supportive sophomore year ESL teacher, Mauricio entered high school with minimal English but graduated in the top 10 percent of his class with thousands of dollars of scholarships. Although accepted to the flagship state university and pushed by Ms. Cooper to leave town for college, he decided to attend BU because of the importance of family in his life.

### High School Literacy Experiences

Mauricio showed remarkable development in his English skills during his high school years, going from knowing essentially nothing in English to being one of the best writers in his senior level English class. However, his sophomore year was by far his most important year of development. Ms. Cooper described his abilities when he arrived in her class vividly: "The first writing he did for me, the first page was one sentence. Every word was misspelled, misused. He just . . . I mean, it was very poor."

Mauricio recalled writing in sophomore English every day and having to write a TAKS practice essay every Friday. These prompts varied, but tended to be personal and creative and Mauricio invented a number of his stories. As he grew into preferring personal writing over analytical writing, which he did not really do until senior year, Mauricio thought these prompts were cool and made writing enjoyable. He said they included writing about such things as "the biggest challenge you face" or "one day you helped someone." Because he was so motivated to write for Ms. Cooper, Mauricio wrote his longest essay at SHS his sophomore year during Thanksgiving break. Over the break he was required to write five TAKS essays, one to two pages each, and he became so engaged with one of the prompts that he wrote five pages. He ended up getting the highest possible score on the TAKS writing portion after turning that into an essay for the test.

Mauricio took two English classes his junior year so that he could have enough credits to graduate in four years, since he had ESL classes his first year. These were not simply any English classes, however, but pre-AP English II and AP English III. Mauricio did not do nearly as much writing in these courses as he did for Ms. Cooper's class, finding that he would often repeat much of what he learned in her English II class. While the writing in these courses did not focus so much on the TAKS, Mauricio felt that the AP classes at SHS were like regular English classes elsewhere in the amount of work that was required of students.

After learning this history, I wondered why Mauricio was in a mainstream English class his senior year, a class he felt was easy and repeated things he learned in previous classes. Apparently, Ms. Cooper wanted him to be in a senior English AP course as opposed to the alternative dual-credit English course, as the former would hold him to national standards. However, because of low enrollment, the senior AP course was cancelled and Mauricio had not taken the test required to place into the dual-credit course. Mauricio also described his decision to be in the regular class as laziness, which seemed hard to believe.

Mauricio's major senior English writing assignments were the same as other study participants: a personal statement and essays on *Beowulf* and *Lord of the Flies*. The *Beowulf* essay was particularly difficult for him and writing it gave him a headache. This was in part because of the difficulty he had understanding the antiquated English text: "I don't like that kind of writing cause since it's Old English I can, I don't understand it totally and I have a hard time understanding normal English. The one we use usually and I think that's the reason. Cause it was Old English." It was also challenging because it required him to do something different. Instead of simply writing about himself or inventing stories, he was required to analyze a character: "I like writing stuff that I create, you know, I came out with it. If I come out with it, it will be cool. But if I have to write about something special, some character or something like that, I don't like that." Even though he did not like analytical writing, Mauricio realized that this type of writing would dominate in college.

Because of these difficulties, Mauricio's *Beowulf* essay was less successful than some of his other work. His thesis was relatively simple: "Beowulf kills the malicious creature which shows that Anglo Saxons will not hesitate to risk their lives to save their race." His first citation from the poem supported his point well, pointing out that Beowulf is willing to die in battle if not successful in killing Grendel. However, the subsequent citations ended up being confusing, such as the fragment "Bent back as Beowulf leaned up one arm" to others that did not lend support to his thesis. Mauricio's strength returned in the last paragraph, where he was encouraged to creatively connect the lessons learned from analyzing Beowulf with a real-life example. Here, he began by writing, "As far as there is life on this Earth, there will always be some Grendel or a furious dragon looking to take over of all we have," proceeding to write about the terrorist attacks on September 11, 2001, and the subsequent war on terror, which played into his teacher's conservative political sentiments.

Mauricio wrote about *Lord of the Flies* for his final essay like the other students. Despite having taken pre-AP and AP courses, he said this was the first full book he read at SHS, and, in typical Mauricio style, said his main motivation for reading the whole book (unlike most other students) was to get a good grade for the essay and the course. This essay ended up being much stronger than the *Beowulf* one. Mauricio acknowledged putting much more effort into it because he wanted to practice more serious writing to be prepared for college. He even checked out a commentary book he found in the school library that described the book in more detail and gave a different interpretation of the story.

Mauricio began his essay by again appealing to his teacher's political leanings, setting up Stalin and the Soviet Union as representative of the authoritarian character Jack and contrasting it with Ralph, who is connected to the United States' concern for the welfare of the people and democracy. While working with Mauricio on this essay, I recall him struggling a long time in trying to write the perfect introduction. I eventually pushed him to move on out of concern that he would not finish the essay on time. The rest of the essay, while having occasional lapses of focus, generally developed the thesis well, supporting the discussion with well-chosen examples from the novel. His paragraphs were grounded in strong focus sentences such as "Jack's desire to obtain total power over the island and the kids leads him to take some drastic choices." All his quotes were cited with page numbers and he included an accurately formatted works cited list at the end of the essay.

As mentioned previously, Mauricio graduated from high school in the top 10 percent of his class despite his GPA being weighed down by poor grades his first year when he struggled with English. He still feared the worst for college and felt that he was hopelessly unprepared. When asked if high school had prepared him for college, he replied, "College is beyond just a three to four-page essay and we're not even scratching the surface of college. I think I'll have a hard time in college because I'm not prepared for it. I'm not used to writing a lot and here we've had one semester reading *Lord of the Flies*. In college we'll have about a week to read a book and come out with a good essay. I don't think I'm prepared for college at all."

### Literacy and Learning in the First Year of College

#### First Semester

Despite his gloomy expectations, Mauricio went through his first semester marveling how easy college was. During a campus visit as a prospective student, he assumed everyone sleeping on couches in the library were exhausted from the work, but soon realized that "slackers" do exist at college: "I thought people like college life was gonna be like smart people everywhere and slacking wouldn't exist here. There's a lot of slackers here, lazy people. I guess with time like they'll just go away, stop college or something. But there's . . . some differences, because there are more people who actually do their work than in high school." Maruricio found the first several weeks of college especially easy. This may have led him to put less time into his schoolwork than he needed, resulting in a less than stellar first-semester GPA of 3.0.

Mauricio reported writing for most classes: first-year seminar, history, philosophy, and FYC (see Table 5.2 for a list of Mauricio's first-year writing experiences). As described earlier, the FYC curriculum at the university was very different from the type of writing students did at SHS. Instead of personal narratives, Mauricio had projects like a memo and an annotated bibliography, both of which he struggled with.

For the memo, Mauricio was asked to observe an agency in the community and write a memo informing the audience about its key characteristics, discourse practices, and the relation of the agency to an "important social or community issue." An early email to me from Mauricio revealed frustration with trying to write in a new genre: "I have

Table 5.2. Mauricio's first-year writing experiences

| Fall Semester Classes | Writing Assignments |
|---|---|
| FYC | Homepage portfolio |
| | 2–3-page agency discourse memo |
| | 3–5-page rhetorical/visual analysis |
| | 7–10-source annotated bibliography |
| | 4–6-page community problem report |
| History | Five 1-page response essays |
| | 2–3-page argument/analysis essay on *Incidents in the Life of a Slave Girl* |
| Math | No writing |
| Philosophy | Online discussion postings |
| First-Year Seminar | Online discussion postings |
| | 7-page research paper |
| *Spring Semester Classes* | *Writing Assignments* |
| FYC | 4–6-page genre analysis |
| | 7–10-page literature review/primary research report |
| | 5–6-minute documentary (group project) |
| | 2-page online opinion piece (cancelled by instructor) |
| | Advocacy website (cancelled by instructor) |
| History (in Spanish) | No writing |
| Math | No writing |
| Political Science (in Spanish) | 5 3-page essays |
| Communication | Essay exam |

no clue of what I am doing!!! This is an easy assignment, but I am having a hard time with it because of the instructions." He attached an underdeveloped and unclear draft of a memo that had a couple of paragraphs describing the basic facts about a for-profit clothing company, not a nonprofit company that he should have been focusing on. Mauricio's difficulty with this assignment may have resulted from lack of direction from his inexperienced instructor who did not seem particularly adept at explaining and scaffolding assignments. It also may have stemmed from this being a completely new type of assignment for Mauricio, unlike anything he had written in high school. Despite these difficulties, Mauricio found the memo assignment the only valuable writing he did all semester because of its real-world value: "The most valuable, well, maybe the memo because I think those are useful, but I don't see myself writing a rhetorical analysis, am I wrong? Do you really do that?"

Another FYC assignment that caused Mauricio consternation was his annotated bibliography, for which he asked my help. For this assignment he was asked to come up with a research question, create an abstract, and provide annotations of seven to eight sources that he would use in a later course assignment. Although he had an interesting research question, "Does the way we talk to babies have a future impact on their learning?" he began working on this assignment last minute and unsurprisingly struggled to find enough required sources. While giving feedback on drafts, I provided APA templates as his reference formatting was off, and recommended that his draft abstract be significantly shortened. Here is an example from his early draft:

> Thiesses D. Erick (January 2005) General format retrieved from, http://findarticles.com/p/articles/mi_m0816/is_1_22/ai_n15860801/
> This article was published in BNET.BNET it's an online magazine that along with Smart Planet are owned by CBS Interactive. In this article, Erick D. Thiesses, Ph D., the director of the Infant Language and learning Lab, directs a series of experiments where he exposes 8 month old babies to different types of speeches with the purpose to find out what kind of effect our words have upon the babies' learning. Dr. Thiesses found out that the children that were exposed to words with exaggerated sounds identified words quicker than the babies who were exposed to every day English. As a consequence of the results of his experiment, Dr. Thiesses highly recommends to parents with children of one year of age or less, to speak to them with an exaggerated intonation. The article helps us have a wider view on the techniques that help kids learn better.

The annotated bibliography ended up being the most difficult assignment of the semester for Mauricio, largely because of his unfamiliarity with APA, which he had identified as the "official" citation style of the university because it was being taught in his FYC course. Unfortunately, at the time of the assignment, his instructor had not taught any APA conventions, which did not help students like Mauricio who were unfamiliar with this style. After the assignment, the instructor spent a few weeks lecturing from PowerPoint presentations on minute details of APA style, with one observed class dedicated to every detail of alphabetizing entries in a reference list. While Mauricio at first found his FYC instructor "cool" and funny with his awkward jokes, he was utterly bored with the course by the end of the semester because of the repetitive nature of the PowerPoint lectures and said he would have stopped coming if not for the required attendance. While he seemed more engaged at the beginning of the semester, by the end he would sit silently in the back of the class.

Mauricio's frustration with citation styles was exacerbated by his first-year seminar teacher's requirement that students use MLA style in her course, as she was an avid lover of Shakespeare and literature. Mauricio had a love/hate relationship with this course, disliking the fact that his teacher was "weird" and that the course was overly easy. However, he liked the fact that it was an easy A, the only A of his first semester. He reported only having to read a short story of several pages every other week and then posting a short paragraph response online. He did have one research paper for which he was required to turn in several drafts. He was a bit frustrated with the course as he had expected it to be more about showing him the various resources of the university, which it did not.

Like the other BU students, Mauricio did a lot of writing for his history course, although he appeared to do less than other students in the study. He reported having to write five one-page essays and a longer essay on the book *Incidents in the Life of a Slave Girl*. He disliked history with a passion, possibly stemming from his difficulties understanding history class in high school, as it was all lecturing—in English. He was excited that he received a high score on his first short history paper, but then saw his grades decline. From looking at one short paper, they appeared to be about explaining a topic from the book, as his "Short paper #2" discussed the development of British colonies in the Americas.

Of all the classes his first semester, Mauricio most disliked philosophy because of the difficulty of the readings and its focus on more abstract thinking. At the beginning of the semester, he said it was clearly the most demanding course reading-wise, as he would have to spend at least four hours a class doing the readings, and still go to class without understanding things very well. However, he noted that the other students similarly struggled and that the professor's explanations helped clarify confusion. Along with the readings, Mauricio reported having to post online for every class, but received "Neither grades, nor responses, feedback" on any of his postings. While most students stopped posting, Mauricio continued posting throughout the semester as he knew that posting was part of his grade. Mauricio's frustration peaked with the mid-term exam that required him to write a few short essays and a longer essay. Despite having done all the reading for the course up to that point, Mauricio failed the exam and disconnected with the course afterwards, only skimming the readings and calling the course and the ideas it covered "insane." Looking back at the end of the school year, he noted: "That kind of reading that I had for philosophy requires a lot of twisted thinking, you know, like, analyze things and question everything and seeing things from another perspective. So yeah, that's why it was kind of more challenging."

### Second Semester

After a disappointing first semester that ended with a 3.0 GPA, Mauricio set a goal to get a 4.0 his second semester, needing to earn at least a 3.6 in order to keep all his scholarships. In order to achieve this goal, he recognized the importance of three things: friend support, reaching out for help, and being more assertive when he received an undesirable grade.

Mauricio was thinking a lot about his major early in the semester, reconsidering his desire to go into computer science after an uninteresting experience coding and because of his desire to work more directly with people. His family had influenced his initial decision as his relatives were mostly accountants or computer scientists. By the end of the semester, he declared a major, sticking close to family tradition by planning to double major in accounting and financial statistics. He explained this decision: "I know it has to be something related with math, I like numbers, I like money. So I think that's best place for me to be at."

Unlike all of the other study students, Mauricio had two classes in Spanish: political science and history. It was not something he explicitly wanted, but he ended up in those courses because of limited class options when he registered. He was ironically pinned as a nonnative Spanish speaker after instinctively declaring "here" in English when his history teacher was taking first-day attendance in history. The teacher approached Mauricio after class and explained that he could not take the class without knowing Spanish. Although Mauricio's first instinct was to point out that he lived in Mexico, he quickly played into the nonnative Spanish speaker role. Mauricio noted that playing into this role brought him sympathy from his history instructor, who was patient when Mauricio asked dumb questions, but made other students look dumb when they did so.

On the other hand, Mauricio felt behind the other students who had been educated in Mexican schools throughout their lives. The consequence of Mauricio's years in an English-only educational environment was a struggle to understand the readings and discussions that were in an academic Spanish he had not developed in high school. He explained that the reading "sounds like I'm talking with a lawyer. You know really high terms and things I don't understand. And I have to actually go in the dictionary and look for the word." He lamented the fact that his instructors could not speak English in order to translate the more difficult words into a more familiar academic language. Despite these struggles, Mauricio felt that knowledge of academic Spanish would be beneficial.

Although he did not write at all in his Spanish history course, he wrote some in his political science class: five different three-page essays on topics such as his opinion "about whatever's happening at Colombia," "what democracy is, what it means for us," and "about my surroundings, how do I feel about it, what to expect from whatever surrounds me, and what am I doing to make a change in society." Mauricio was hesitant to share these writing samples, saying that they were really bad because he knew the instructor did not bother to read them. He found this bit of information out from the class graduate TA who said students were only given credit for turning them in. Consequently, he never received grades or feedback on these assignments.

Mauricio's second-semester FYC class was again the class that demanded the most writing. In addition to the major assignments, a genre analysis, literature review/primary research report, documentary, and op-ed, his instructor had him complete online postings of 100–200 words three times a week. He alternatively identified these as "crazy" and having nothing to do with anything to acknowledging that they focused on preparing for the major assignments.

Driven by his desire for a 4.0, Mauricio more actively came to me for feedback this semester than the previous one. He settled on a topic of college student stress and most of his projects stayed focused on this. For instance, his genre analysis focused on an article on ehow.com and a video on icyou.com, a video-sharing site. In responding to a draft of his genre analysis, I focused on getting him to analyze instead of merely summarizing the content, as he did for much of the draft: "The video 'College Stress—NJN News Healthwatch Report' shows some solution that carry to much stress because of dealing with school, their personal lives and work. It says that a possible solution for this problem is to stop spending time in unnecessary things that distract you and that take time away from your priorities the way texting for long periods of time does." He ended up with an 86/100 on this assignment, getting a B for analysis. A look at his final showed that he did not revise extensively in response to the feedback I provided. The grader of his paper noted that he could have developed the style and language section of his paper a bit more and that he had "a few minor errors regarding grammar and APA formatting." While specifics were given on some of the APA errors, nothing specific was written about the grammatical ones.

Mauricio found the literature review most important because it was worth 20 percent of his final grade. I again looked at a draft of this assignment, focusing specifically on helping Mauricio cite material and helping with the formality and clarity of his writing. A look at his draft revealed difficulty in writing about primary research, something new to him: "According to [Mauricio's last name] research about what kind of physical changes college students experience he said, 'The number of students that claim to be victims of stress is alarming. Out of two hundred and fifty volunteers that took the survey called 'My Levels of Stress,' the 90 five percentage of them feel nauseated, vomiting, and their skin breaks up before an important event at school. College students affirm midterms, final exams and test to be the creators of their stress.' (2011)"

Part of the confusion in how to reference research he conducted stemmed from a program-wide disagreement on how to reference primary research and if it needed to be cited in one's paper. Those typically teaching this IMRAD-style assignment had minimal to no experience conducting primary research and were more likely to have a background in creative writing or literary analysis. I directed him toward writing, "The author conducted a survey that was completed by 250 people from the El Paso, Juárez and Las Cruces area and found that the number of students that claim to be victims of stress is alarming . . ." but he still included some of the information above in a quote. Mauricio ended up receiving a low A, which was above the solid B he received on his genre analysis.

While the literature review may have been the most important piece of writing Mauricio did all year, he felt creating the video documentary on stress for his FYC course was the most challenging. Confident in his use of technology, he procrastinated with the rest of his group, waiting until the last few days to complete it. Unbeknownst to him, he would have to learn a new operating system (Mac) and a new piece of software (iMovie) in the process of creating a documentary. In additon, one group member was largely absent for much of the process, with his primary contribution being lending a Mac notebook to Mauricio.

Overall, Mauricio was generally unhappy with his second-semester English instructor and the grades he received via the distributed assessment system. One major complaint centered on the lack of feedback from his teacher, who he said only responded to two or so of his triweekly responses with grades or feedback and consistently directed students to the writing center if they wanted help on their writing: "If I had had a teacher that gives me just the exact feedback you [the researcher] give me, I would be happy, you know? Because she doesn't. All she says is—if I was—if I had to do her job exactly, I would just go to class, put on a PowerPoint when the deadline is, and say 'Go to the writing center' because that's what she does pretty much." Mauricio also seemed to be lacking beneficial feedback from the committee who graded his essays. He did not submit optional paper drafts for which he might have received more feedback; rather, he only submitted final papers on which the committee provided only summative comments and grades. While a look at feedback on his genre analysis and literature review found the graders pointing out general areas where his writing was lacking, the detail in the feedback was limited, especially in addressing Mauricio's concerns with his grammar as an L2 writer. Both times he was given a "B" for writing fluency but the comments said "there were a few problems with grammar" without giving any specifics.

Mauricio's complaints about his second-semester FYC instructor went beyond feedback, however. While his first-semester instructor bored him to death, he described his second-semester instructor as "nice" but really "shy" and "disorganized." He noted that she was inexperienced and did not feel comfortable teaching the class, having a background in creative writing, not research writing: "It's her first year doing English 1312. She had never done it. And she has said she prefers—I mean, she—the other day we were at the lab and she said, 'I won't ever do 1312 again.'" My observations confirmed a shy, soft-spoken teacher who was not as organized as she could have been. For instance, while she prepared a number of class activities on a Word document to use during class, she consistently made these really small so that students like Mauricio, who mentioned this as well, could not see what she was displaying. To Mauricio's frustration, she discussed cancelling at least one of the final two assignments during the last class, which upset him because they were worth 20 percent of the course grade. He said he "knew" it was because she had forgotten about them even though she blamed the English department.

In response to his disappointment with his FYC teacher and disagreement with grades, Mauricio was assertive and manipulative in this class. He appealed the grades for two out of four major assignments and reported "exploding" in class when his teacher mentioned cutting the final two assignments. He claimed only going to five or so classes all semester, which could have been very true given that he was absent from the classes I observed. However, he noted to me that he had things "taken care of," meaning that he had a friend sign in for him. He also admitted fabricating the 250-person sample for his survey mentioned earlier.

To Mauricio's credit, especially in regard to the absences, he did have a difficult and stressful semester in which both his grandfather and his

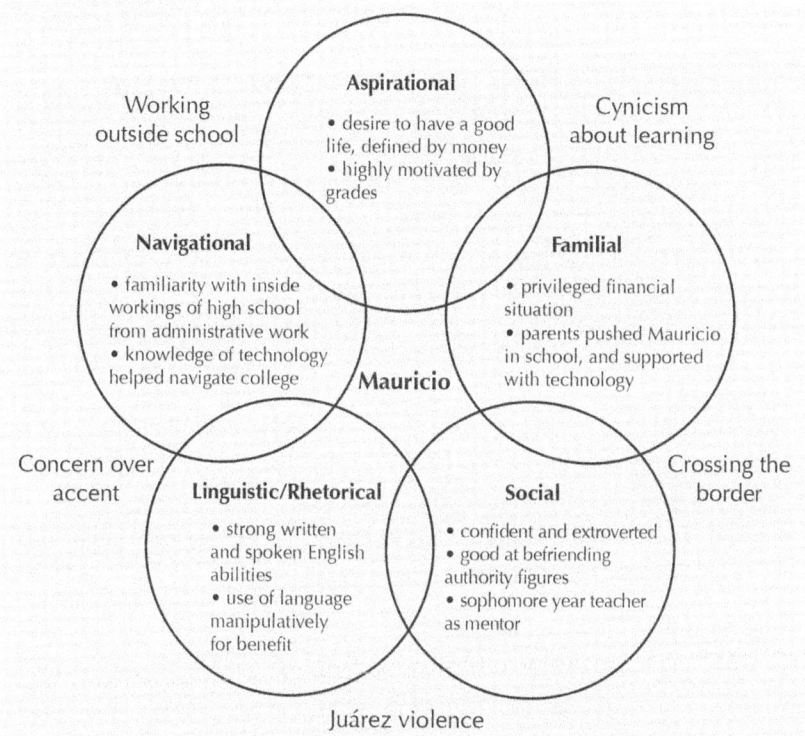

Figure 5.2. Mauricio's sources of capital and challenge.

girlfriend of several months passed away, the latter in a car accident. Nonetheless, he achieved his goal of a 4.0 GPA.

### Conclusion

Like Carolina, Mauricio had an extensive network of capital (depicted in Figure 5.2 ) supporting his success in transitioning to college despite the external challenges he faced.

Mauricio consistently commented on how easy college was even though he did not always receive an A. His comments appeared to stem in part from his desire to create a persona of a talented and smart student, which he really was. Admittance of difficulties could hurt the image he so carefully constructed. Mauricio did at times admit challenges, noting that the Spanish political science course and the documentary were both difficult experiences. His original expectations of college-level work stemmed from comments that purported the difficulty he would encounter in college, expectations he felt were unfounded given his experiences.

Coming from a privileged background and a high school experience where he showed a remarkable skill for befriending teachers and administration, Mauricio knew how to work the system and was generally much more adept in doing so than the other students. After struggling at first with the distance of his college instructors and learning that being a teacher's pet does not pay in college, he worked the system to his advantage in other ways, such as by playing the role of a nonnative Spanish speaker in his Spanish classes, appealing any grade under an "A" in his second-semester English class, and regularly having friends sign in when he missed class.

Nonetheless, Mauricio knew it would take more to succeed at college, something he had gained through learning English so quickly and succeeding so well in high school. He explained,

> "They helped me grow because I asked them to. And it's just the same way here. If I want to succeed in college, I need to ask for the help. I need to—I cannot expect them [to] come to me to help me [I] have to go to them and say, I need help here."

Whereas he had teachers like Ms. Cooper in high school, Mauricio did not seem to reach out extensively to his instructors in his first year of college, at times distancing himself by creating false personas or fabricating research results. However, he consistently sent me his papers for feedback, finding that he received more specific feedback from me than his teachers and other graders who said little more than "this paper has a few grammar errors."

In addition to reaching out to me, Mauricio discovered the importance of friend support, and worked closely with a particular friend in his English class. He described this relationship in detail: "I'm doing my paper—like all my work with a friend of mine that's in that class, too, so we all remind each other about deadlines and about stuff like that so we don't have to really worry about reading the syllabus and keeping track of it, because we know that—like I know he will tell me, and he knows I'll tell him when I know. I guess he's the only person that I text with, because we're always texting, 'Did you do homework? What was it about?' you know." Besides reminding each other of deadlines, they would read each other's postings and assignments, giving more content-based feedback since they were both L2 writers and did not feel comfortable giving each other feedback on grammar.

In discussing how SHS could make students more prepared for college, Mauricio gave a long story about when he saw SHS students visiting the BU campus. He complained that they were irresponsible and had an entitlement mentality, having come from poorer Mexico to a country with more resources. Following this example he noted that: "Students don't really need to be prepared for college. That's not something you're—you have to be prepared—like you need somebody to prepare you for. It's just your attitude, you know. The way you handle things, the way you see things, how responsible you are." Recalling that he actively sought help from others and took on responsibility for his own learning, he felt that other students needed to do the same. He noted that he "prepared myself with the help of teachers I looked to go for to tutoring. I looked for help. I looked for feedback from them." Like Carolina, Mauricio's endless motivation to excel and his willingness to reach out to others when struggling helped him immensely in making the transition to college.

### Notes

1. This being said, Carolina's first-semester teacher seemed better qualified to help Carolina on the grammatical aspects of her writing, as he was also a native Spanish speaker and lent her a book to help her improve her writing fluency.
2. United States–owned factories that sprung up on the Mexican side of the border, due to cheap labor and lax labor laws, especially in the wake of NAFTA. A worker in one of these factories can expect to earn about ten dollars a day.

# 6
## AN UNPREDICTABLE TRANSITION

While students featured in previous chapters generally stayed on consistent paths throughout their journeys from high school to college, the student featured in this chapter was never sure what she wanted. Paola initially questioned whether or not she should go to college but ultimately decided to go. She excelled the semester she was there and became very engaged in the work she was doing, but stopped out the following semester. Paola's journey helps illustrate the complexity of students' pathways to college and how they are shaped by factors beyond a teacher's immediate control.

### PAOLA: THE UNPREDICTABILITY OF STUDENTS' PATHS TO AND THROUGH COLLEGE

> *"Well I feel like obligated but I don't want to."*
> —Paola, on going to college

> *"She works hard, she tries hard, she rewrites her paper, she does her work on time. She participates in class. I think she's bright and also she's more culturally exposed to life in the United States. She writes papers about taking yoga classes and stuff."*
> —Paola's first-semester college writing teacher

### Background and Defining Characteristics and Experiences

Paola's parents came to the United States so she would have a better future, a future in which education would play an important role. She began US schooling in first grade and was placed in a bilingual program until fifth grade; however, echoing other participants, she said the subsequent transition to mainstream classes was difficult because the bilingual program was mostly Spanish. Before transitioning to SHS, she attended the same middle school that most of the other study students attended in downtown El Paso. Spanish was the dominant

DOI: 10.7330/9780874219760.c006

language in her household. While her father knew some English, her mother did not.

My first impression of Paola was one of a hard-working student who differed from most other students at her high school. Paola dressed like a hippie, carrying around a hemp bag, wearing stretched ear piercings, and avoiding make-up. She always sat with her friend, Joanne, and they worked together on various projects in their English class. Paola's senior English teacher, Mr. Robertso,n felt she always went out of her way to improve and was a "deep thinker" who was different from most of the other students.

Paola possessed an intellectual curiosity that most students I interacted with at SHS did not have. She expressed an interest in ancient civilizations and would spend a lot of her computer time reading about this topic. We talked about my experiences studying the classics, and I pointed out that she could study different styles of Greek and Roman art at college and she thought that would be "awesome." Throughout her first semester at college, Paola said reading was not a problem for her because she liked doing it, which was a different attitude from most students in this study. She read on her own outside school, and excitedly shared a story with me how she found a book she had heard about at the used bookstore at the downtown library. She wished that she had been required to read more in high school, noting, "The only thing that people tell me that's different about college and high school doesn't prepare you for is how to read."

Paola's difference was also seen in the ways she took issues with aspects of mainstream society. In one interview, she explained that she did not like money but needed it to survive. She fell in and out of cell phone ownership, partially because of the cost, but largely because she did not want to be in contact all the time. These counter-culture attitudes initially led her to question going to college. As expressed in the epigraph above, Paola did not want to go to college simply because of societal expectations. She continued to express doubts about college throughout much of senior year, saying that she might be a flight attendant instead or something similar.

However, a marked shift occurred in Paola's attitude toward college. By early March, she knew she wanted to go to college, but was still somewhat wary. A few weeks later, however, she surprised me by emailing me a scholarship essay that she wanted feedback on, the first time she had contacted me voluntarily showing a desire to work seriously toward the college application process. She explained this change to me at the end of the semester: "I wasn't sure about what I wanted in life but now I'm sure I want to get my higher education so I can succeed or have something." When asked what prompted the shift, she replied, "I think what got me encouraged was everyone going to college and getting their stuff ready. I think like the financial aid and everything. That's what probably made me think about college too." These shifts in behavior did not seem new to Paola. She had previously been a rebellious student who regularly skipped school, very different from the diligent Paola who was always present in class.

Paola was so serious about college that she and two friends, including Joanne, planned to go to a summer college prep program at the community college, for which they were to receive $200. Because of confusion with the registration process, none of them ended up going. Despite this setback, Paola's transformation continued through her first semester at college. Over the summer she found a boyfriend and she began to dress very differently, wearing more formal clothes as well as make-up. She eventually got a cell phone, letting me know I could text her. We discussed these changes at the end of her first semester at college. She described her previous self as "weird" and kind of rebellious, noting that she took out the stretched ear piercings she had at the beginning of this study. Nonetheless, her first-semester college writing professor still saw her as different from her peers, saying that she seemed more culturally exposed to life in the United States than the other students even though she still lived in an immigrant dominant neighborhood: "She writes papers about taking yoga classes and stuff. She, she doesn't live in a Spanish-speaking, um, enclave, where everything is Mexican culture. She's kind of, she's talking about . . . things that are weird."

Paola's family generally seemed to provide her with more challenges than support. Her parents seemed largely absent from her educational life, with their role limited to the following: "Just tell me that I need to go to college and to go to my classes, pay attention. That's it." While they encouraged her to do her "best," their support did not seem to go beyond verbal encouragement. They appeared to be distracted with other concerns as they struggled to find jobs to support the family. Paola had two younger brothers, and they were generally a source of concern for her rather than a source of support. One brother was married and living in Juárez, struggling to make ends meet; subsequently he became ill, straining the family's limited financial resources. The other brother, who was still in high school, disappeared and did not return to their house for a few months at one point. He would skip school regularly like Paola had done in her younger years.

## High School Literacy Experiences

Paola generally liked high school English because of her fondness for reading. She joined others in identifying the freshman English teacher, Mr. Sanchez, who had a reputation for strictness, as her favorite writing teacher. In her first semester at college, Paola actually wrote a narrative essay about her first harrowing days of school with Mr. Sanchez. After a failed attempt to get out of the class, Paola recalled an early day in class when she forgot her essay, but lied and said she left it in her locker as she furtively tried to finish it in the class. However, she got caught and recalled him yelling at her, "Do you think I'm stupid? Did you think you could fool me?" and proceeded to call her dad in front of the whole class. Paola looked back on Mr. Sanchez positively despite this early experience, saying he taught her all the things that she needed to know at that time and made students work harder than in other classes: "We did a lot of work unlike other teachers. And he like made us, made us do the work. So instead of slacking off or doing whatever, we actually learned because we were doing our work."

With the exception of Mr. Sanchez's class and her senior English class with Mr. Robertson, Paola explained that she generally wrote short and simple essays at SHS, about 300 words long. These included answers to questions that inspired personal narratives, such as "Have you ever helped someone? Why did this [event] change your life?" She explained that her senior *Beowulf* essay was the first time since perhaps freshmen year that she was required to integrate quotes into an essay, a skill she valued.

Paola's least favorite English class was a PLATO remedial class that consisted of computer-mediated instruction. She described it as "unhelpful," explaining that she would prefer an actual teacher as the program would explain the answers but could not respond to questions. Because the teacher monitoring the room was not necessarily an English teacher, they were not always very helpful. Paola's disdain for the PLATO class was possibly in part connected to her negative attitude toward technology, with an uneasy cell phone relationship throughout part of this study and an ambivalent attitude toward computers.

Paola's reputation as a deep thinker is evident in a few of her more personal senior year writings that also revealed a bit of her cynicism toward life. In her personal statement, she wrote about her parents fighting and separating, a story she later admitted embellishing as they did not actually separate. While the other students in the class would likely focus on the action and the fighting between the parents, and include extensive dialogue, something they were encouraged to do to score highly on the TAKS, Paola focused on her inner feelings throughout the page-long statement. She began, "Daily battles of rage and overflowing sadness fill my body and I feel I can't handle all the pressure, but I know deep in me, that I am strong and that I can continue, that it's necessary to have obstacles in life . . ."

For another narrative that students did for the TELPAS prompt, Paola wrote about her isolation from others and her closeness to a puppy that was killed by friends, another story that appeared fabricated. She began this essay by saying she was "Full with cynicism, a misanthrope, that's what I was. I felt insecure of everyone, especially those evil talking creatures. All my trust had been spit in my face with no mercy." When asked why she created stories, Paola explained that she was sometimes reluctant to share too many personal details about her life. She also said that she was asked to write so many personal narratives during high school that she felt she could make them more interesting by making details up.

Like the other students, Paola wrote analytical essays her senior year on *Beowulf* and *Lord of the Flies*. Her *Beowulf* essay was rather short, less than a single-spaced page, and very dry in comparison to her more personal writing. Her opening paragraph clearly came from the form that her teacher gave to the class, focusing on standard historical background of the story and failing to put forth a thesis. Nonetheless, she did manage some interesting analysis in the one paragraph where she included quotes. For instance, she introduced a quote with "He reveals his brave character when he says," indicating that she was developing knowledge about incorporating textual evidence, a skill she did not have much practice in.

Paola took her final senior essay on *Lord of the Flies* very seriously and, according to Mr. Robertson, ended up writing one of the best essays in her class. Unlike many of the students, Paola actually read the whole book, asking Mr. Robertson to let her take it home so she could finish. I noted the following observation in field notes after interacting with Paola as she prepared this essay: "She seemed like she had the ability to think more abstractly and connect the topic to the real world than other students. From what I've seen, students who have tried to connect their writing to real-world examples have done it simplistically and it has seemed forced." Unlike in the *Beowulf* essay, Paola developed a clear thesis: "[Ralph and Jack] both are born leaders, and both have initiative when controlling the British boys; however, the way they gain, use, and maintain their power differs greatly." Every paragraph was grounded in textual evidence and, with some help from me and Mr. Robertson, she learned how to introduce quotes more effectively and analyze their significance. Nonetheless, Paola's negative attitudes toward society still appeared in this essay. In the final paragraph she wrote: "*Lord of the Flies* presents us with two governments often manifested in reality, and with the clear recognition of the evil capacity humans are capable of."

While Paola wrote fairly extensively in her senior English class, she said she did not do much writing in other classes that year except Spanish.

Literacy and Learning in the First Year of College

*First Semester*

Like the other students at BCC, most of Paola's first-year writing experiences were in her FYC course, ENG 1301 (see Table 6.1 for a list of Paola's first-year writing experiences). Her professor, Dr. Thomson, spoke Spanish fluently having lived in Mexico and had a doctorate in rhetoric and composition from a major university in the Southwest. He had a high opinion of Paola, telling me in an interview that she was a "delightful young lady" and described her as a bright, hard-working student who did her work on time and rewrote her essays to make them better.

Dr. Thomson was especially fond of freewriting and seemed to have students freewrite for almost every class. In the freewriting assignments, students often responded to a story, and Paola recalled having to give her opinion or something personal that relates to the story in these assignments. Dr. Thomson regularly encouraged students to include personal elements in writing. For example, when he was teaching the descriptive essay during an observed class, he emphasized that it needed to be informative but explained that it could have some personal elements and personal viewpoints, and could also be persuasive in some way.

Paola appeared to embrace this personal element in the five essays she wrote for the course, each one about three pages long. While her first essay, the aforementioned narrative about her first-year high school English teacher, was naturally personal, she introduced personal elements in essays that could have been more formal. Her second essay was a definition essay focused on the word texting, which she described as her favorite essay of the semester, because it required giving some past and current history on the term. She skillfully worked in quotes and paraphrases of material from different websites. However, she also included some personal anecdotes such as a story about her friend who fell down stairs while texting, details about an overheard conversation of a woman talking about her sexual exploits the previous weekend, and how she chastised her friend for always texting while they were together.

Table 6.1. Paola's first-year writing experiences

| Fall Semester Classes | Writing Assignments |
| --- | --- |
| Education | 3-page article critique |
| | Two 3-page opinion essays on popular topics |
| FYC | Frequent freewriting assignments |
| | Four 3–4-page essays: Personal narrative, definition/exemplification, and comparison/contrast classification |
| | In-class mini essay on an art exhibit |
| | Final exam essay |
| Math (Developmental) | No writing |
| Psychology | Short answers on exams |

| Spring Semester Classes | Writing Assignments |
| --- | --- |
| FYC (stopped attending all classes in February, so none of the major assignments were completed) | In-class writing assignments |
| | Annotated bibliography |
| | 15-page research paper |
| | Two literary analysis essays |
| History | Copied the Declaration of Independence with a quill pen (group project) |
| Math | No writing |
| Speech | Speech outlines |

Here is a brief excerpt from the essay: "Text messaging is not limited to anyone, kids as young as eight will have a cell phone with unlimited calling *and* text messaging. Text messaging like everything else has its advantages and disadvantages." A look at passages like this reveal a strong, confident writer who is able to incorporate research and write fairly formally. She did not have the more basic struggles with spelling or subject-verb agreement that other study students did; however, sometimes she lapsed into more informal constructions such as "you" and referring to children as kids. Unlike many teachers of students in this study, Dr. Thompson gave Paola both content and localized grammar feedback throughout their essays. In the passage quoted above, he pointed out a comma splice and added in a few missing commas around the relative clause.

In another essay, Paola was required to classify different attitudes: optimist, pessimist, and realist. Making this essay very personal, she described herself as an optimist and said she could not spend much time around pessimists. In discussing pessimists, she wrote: "I knew a pessimist, this person was my mom's friend and she would always complain about men. Maybe she was only pessimistic of men, but it really made me uncomfortable when she would speak of men and generalize them, and say they are all the same, and they all want only one thing." Again, her writing was very strong in this essay, with Dr. Thompson's feedback pointing out a couple comma splices and a few issues with word choice.

Dr. Thomson was a detail-oriented professor who required students to outline and revise each essay, a time-consuming requirement but one he felt was important. On each paper, Paola received two grades, one on content and one on grammar/mechanics, which were averaged into one final grade. Dr. Thomson had been doing this for about ten years, explaining he wanted students to see that their content was strong even if their grammar and mechanics were not. In general, Paola received high Bs or As on her papers, with her content grade typically five to ten points higher than her grammar grade.

Like most FYC classes, Paola's ENG 1301 course was participatory and regularly included a mixture of group and whole-class activities. Paola had a completed peer review sheet for the first class I observed. However, she did not seem overly enthusiastic about the process, saying one peer did not even seem to read her essay. The completed sheet Paola shared with me included a checklist of key elements with room for commentary, but it seemed that the students just completed the checklists without adding commentary. An essay was due during this particular class and Dr. Thomson had three students volunteer to read their papers aloud. While Paola did not read her paper this time, she volunteered to do so in a future class, saying it felt good reading in front of others and gave her increased confidence in her writing. Other activities included peer feedback on their outlines and grammar exercises, which Dr. Thomson said were a larger part of his class than of most FYC classes at the college. Class interactions were generally dynamic and free-flowing, indicating that students were used to a participatory classroom.

The only other class where Paola did writing her first semester was her first-year seminar, where she sometimes had short answers on exams. She also had to write three essays, which initially caused her a bit of nervousness as she waited until two days before they were due to start them. One reason she waited to start these essays was because her instructor made her nervous, initially sounding very strict about the expectations. According to Paola, her instructor never explained how to write the essays, but repeatedly went through the assignment sheet she created. A look at the assignment sheet for this triple essay assignment revealed typos such as "Cover sheet will have students name," "through-out," and confusing instructions such as a required font of "14 inches Roman style." The assignments were to be graded on three categories, appearance/grade, ethics, and critical thinking. Under appearance/grade, the instructor wrote, "In addition to the instructor having full reign on grading paper subjectively, appearance is also included." One of the three papers was to be a critique of an article, while the other two were considered "personal opinion" essays. The sheet specified a number of topics, including the ones Paola wrote about: Legal Medical Marijuana, Violence in Mexico, and Immigration. Despite starting the essays just a few days in advance, Paola got 100 percent on the assignment and she felt the instructor did not really read them. The instructor commentary consisted of "Yes" on the first essay, "Fascinating!" a few check marks, and "Where did you hear this?" on the second essay, and nothing on the third essay. A sentence that read, "Now marijuana is classified as a Schedule I drug, why in the hell is that if we know it does have medicinal value!" elicited no comment.

Paola was an enthusiastic reader, regularly checking out books on her own from the library. While she said she was reading a lot for her classes, she said it was not a big deal because she liked reading. She was one of the few students who said she consistently did all the reading for her classes. Her reading experiences differed depending on the class, but included short stories in her English class and readings out of her psychology textbook. She was clearly interested in learning, expressing an interest in majoring in psychology or social work. She enjoyed learning critical thinking skills in her first-year seminar course and liked the psychology narratives her psychology instructor shared.

Overall, Paola had an excellent first semester, appeared engaged in school, and received As in three of her four classes.

### Second Semester

Paola began the second semester with speech, English, history, and math, but during our first interview seemed less engaged in school than previously, noting that she was having trouble motivating herself. She was absent from my first observation of her English class and stopped coming to school after mid-February, eventually dropping all her classes.

Paola moved in with her boyfriend in Juárez over winter break, spending the whole break with him. She returned for school as the second semester began but would head to Juárez Friday after classes and stay there until Sunday night with her boyfriend. He worked twelve hours a day, six days a week as a security guard. Balancing these two lives was difficult, as Paola had limited Internet access when across the border. This made it difficult to complete online math homework, and Paola struggled to keep awake in her history class one day because she spent all Sunday night completing math homework. Explaining why she waited so long, she said: "Cause I do it at Juárez, but it's—the Internet, it's too slow, and sometimes for the math program it needs to have program downloaded and you can't download it, so I got stuck with that, and I was really behind." Paola quickly fell behind in other homework assignments also: "I haven't even read. For the history, I need to read, and I haven't read—and I haven't even bought the book over the literature, so, no, I'm not even reading."

The Paola interviewed in early February was a very different student from the one who got mostly As the previous semester and who delayed an interview for several weeks because she was intently focused on schoolwork. Nonetheless, Paola had been doing some work in her classes. We talked about the major research paper for her English class, for which she was supposed to have fifteen sources and write fifteen pages. She wanted to write on Mayan mythology and had already done some of the research for the paper, but noted that she would have to go to other libraries because the college library only had one book on Mayan mythology and twelve on Greek mythology. She stated that the type of writing expected of her in this second-semester class would be more difficult, saying, "Oh, that was really easy, free-writings and reading and just it was—this is harder, the research."

Paola had been thinking more about her major as well, saying she was really confused. She backed off the previous desire to major in psychology, noting that "it's too many years for that." She considered being a registered nurse, but thought it would be too much work. She thought about her passion for Egypt and being an archaeologist. However, whereas she previously talked about graduate school, she now moderated her expectations, saying she wanted to complete four years of school and then continue on while working.

After the first interview, I largely lost touch with Paola. Joanne had not heard from her as well. She did not post any updates on her Facebook page for over a month. Later in the semester, we had a few sporadic points of contact via Facebook when she was in the United States. She explained that she did not want to leave her boyfriend in Juárez, who also quit his job, and was spending time with him instead of going to class. She dropped her classes and admitted to me that she made a big mistake, as she would likely lose her financial aid for the following semester and have to potentially pay back money for the classes she dropped. We talked about strategies for her to get back in school, and she definitely seemed interested in doing so, but she missed another interview scheduled with me and dropped out of contact again.

Examining the classes that Paola was enrolled in at the beginning of the semester, it appeared her only serious writing would be done in her English class. There she would have written a fifteen-page research paper that she planned to focus on Mayan mythology. She would have also been expected to write two literary analyses in the latter half of the semester, which would be around three to four pages long. The latter two observed classes had the writing center director discussing how to write a literary analysis and the course instructor analyzing sonnets with the students.

Otherwise, Paola had anticipated no major writing assignments. In her history class, they were required to copy the Declaration of Independence and a few other documents using a quill pen. They would also be reading Frederick Douglass' *Narrative in the Life of a Slave Girl* like the BU students did. However, as the syllabus noted, "the exams will be primarily multiple choice, matching, and true/false. The assignments will include short answers and perhaps one essay." While there may have been some short answer responses, it seemed unlikely that students would be writing an essay as its inclusion was qualified by a "perhaps."

## Conclusion

Paola's network depicted in Figure 6.1 is more developed than Joanne's, but less developed than those of students featured in the previous two chapters.

Paola's story indicates the unpredictable nature of students' paths to and through college. While always a diligent student in her senior English class, she was hesitant about college, feeling it was pushed on her by society. Nonetheless, she soon embraced the idea of college and grew impatient and excited to start, an energy and motivation that carried her through a highly successful fall semester. However, the turn of events in which she grew closer to her boyfriend and quickly withdrew from school was unforeseen in the scope of this study. She indicated a strong desire to go back to school in the latter part of the spring semester, but her friend Joanne questioned this. I began to wonder as well, as Paola indicated a strong interest to complete school and then subsequently withdrew from contact.

Although Paola later informed me that she did not plan to return to school right away, I imagine that she will go back to school at some point. At the beginning of the second semester of college, she felt her

An Unpredictable Transition    139

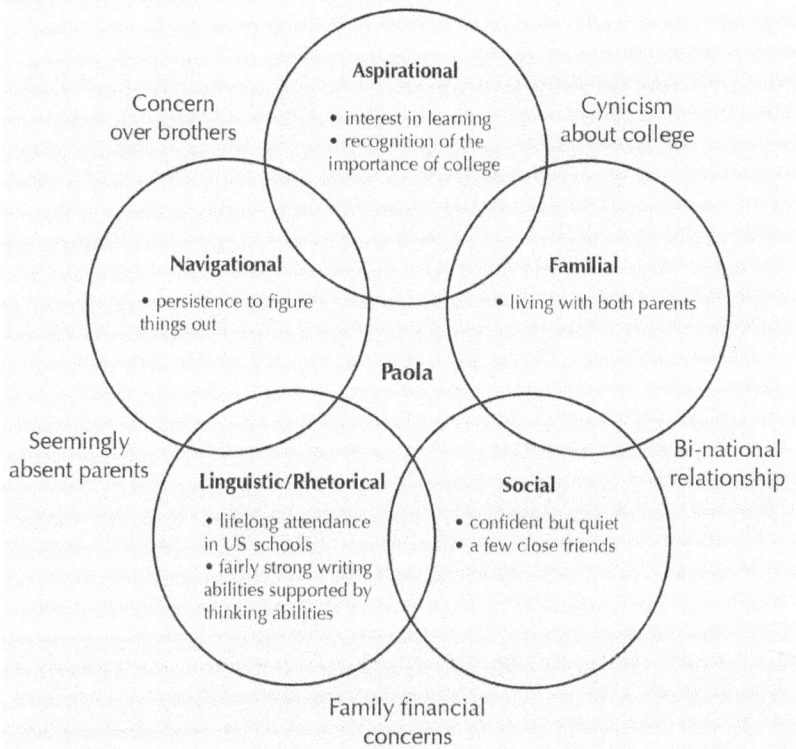

Figure 6.1. Paola's sources of capital and challenge.

decision to attend college was the right decision, citing the experience of a friend: "I did talk to [one student], and he—well, he didn't go to college. He's now working, cleaning carpets, and he said he really wants to get in school, so yeah, I think I did a good decision." She saw her boyfriend work long hours in Mexico for just over a dollar an hour, and said he wanted to attend college as well.

Paola's writing teacher explained that she seemed engaged at the beginning of the semester, and that she clearly had the ability to succeed: ". . . she is one of those tragedies because if she were having a hard time from the beginning, you know, because there's some students—like there was this one student who he was having a really hard time . . . But then you have students like [Paola] and several of the others that were doing fine, had A or B averages, and then just disappeared. And that's just tragic, I think, because like she might have—you know, they usually regret it because, you know, they lose money and they get the bad grade."

While Paola's teacher described her story as a "tragedy" because she dropped out of classes despite her academic potential, Paola's story is not over. With her first-semester successes, she proved she has the ability and motivation to be a successful college student. While it wavers and has been affected by factors such as wanting to spend more time with her boyfriend and the difficulty of crossing borders, Paola recognizes the importance of college and has demonstrated an interest in learning for learning's sake that will support her when she returns to school.

# 7
## CONTEXTUALIZING TRANSITIONS TO COLLEGE

The curricular and extracurricular experiences of Daniel, Joanne, Bianca, Yesenia, Mauricio, Carolina, and Paola show the diversity of paths Latina/o students take, even at the same institutions. Many of the stories shared were positive: high school teachers as literacy sponsors, a scholarship program for children of migrant workers supporting a student's success, and the dedication of an underprepared student helping her succeed against many odds. However, the stories are also ones of struggle. After briefly revisiting the students' writing experiences across the three institutions, this chapter explores how the students developed the habitus and networks of capital necessary to support their transitions to college.[1] It then returns to critical race theory (CRT) to challenge notions of failure while pointing to the role of systemic discrimination in hindering the success of growing Latina/o student populations.

### THE WRITING STUDENTS EXPERIENCED ACROSS INSTITUTIONS

From reading about the journeys of students like Daniel and Carolina, it is evident that writing instruction across the three institutions and even among classes within specific institutions varied greatly. Outside AP and other advanced courses, which are often limited at schools like SHS (e.g., Mayer 2012), students at SHS had minimal opportunities to write in genres beyond the personal narrative. This narrative-type writing largely faded away senior year at SHS as students had the opportunity to write some source-based analytical essays that would more accurately mirror the writing instruction they experienced their first year at college. However, students struggled in this new genre, whether in properly integrating quotations or in paraphrasing material from the book. Plagiarism was a common and unfortunate result of these struggles, with Bianca and other students lifting much of the analytical portions of their *Lord of the Flies* essays from Sparknotes. Ultimately, students entered college wishing they had done more rigorous writing throughout high school. When explaining what SHS teachers could have done to prepare her for college, Carolina suggested "give us more work, more essays, more activities that we're going to see in college. So that when we get there, we don't get scared or something."

Many FYC programs have students begin with a narrative-type essay in order to gently transition into college writing. BCC was no exception in this regard but BU had replaced this narrative essay with a more formalized presentation and discussion of one's discourse communities. Beyond these early assignments, students were primarily expected to write more formal summary, analytical, and expository papers throughout their composition classes and across the curriculum. In BU's FYC program, students who had been used to years of writing narratives came up against an expectation that they would not use personal pronouns in their writing, a practice designed to break students from the more personal writing they did in the past in preparation for more impersonal university writing experiences. As Yesenia characterized it, "You can just write whatever [in high school], and just they don't care."

It was clear that a high school writing curriculum directed toward passing a poorly designed standardized test inadequately aligned with college expectations and failed to prepare students for college writing expectations. As a result, students like Yesenia may spend endless hours writing, seeking feedback, and rewriting as they work on adapting to differing expectations in a needlessly short time period of a semester or two. Even the overachiever Mauricio had moments of panic, emailing me the following when being asked to write a memo for his workplace writing class: "I have no clue of what I am doing!!!" Yesenia and Mauricio stepped up and put in the time necessary to transition well; however, others were not as successful.

## THE ROLE OF HABITUS AND CAPITAL IN FACILITATING INSTITUTIONAL TRANSITIONS

Researchers have focused on distances between home and school discourse practices or how minority students otherwise lack the capital necessary to succeed in the educational system (e.g., Yosso 2005; Oropeza, Varghese, and Kanno 2010). In short, Boudieu's theories have been used to "assert that some communities are culturally wealthy while others are culturally poor" (Yosso 2005, 77). An examination of Bourdieu's work shows that such claims are at odds with the critical stance he took in analyzing the ways institutions perpetuated societal hierarchies. Rather, he labeled pedagogical action upholding certain power structures as "symbolic violence" (Bourdieu and Passeron 1977, 5). In *Academic Discourse,* Bourdieu, Passeron, and de Saint Martin (1996, 87) faulted academic discourse and associated practices for systematically blocking the success of students from lower income backgrounds: "Academic discourse, through its hierarchy of formal criteria, favours students from bourgeois backgrounds, who rediscover in its medium their natural linguistic milieu, and sets further obstacles in the path of working class students."

While exploring the students' stories in the previous chapters, I drew on this understanding of Bourdieu while applying his commonly used analytical framework of habitus, capital, and field. The stories of students like Daniel show that student transitions between institutional fields are not always fluid. There may be a lag that occurs when individuals move through different fields as their habitus can be slow to adapt to help them function successfully in a new environment, something Bourdieu terms hysteresis: "The hysteresis of habitus, which is inherent in the social conditions of the reproduction of the structures in habitus, is doubtless one of the foundations of the structural lag between opportunities and the dispositions to grasp them which is the cause of missed opportunities, and, in particular, of the frequently observed incapacity to think historical crises in categories of perception and thought other than those of the past" (Bourdieu 1977, 83). While students like Yesenia may work hard to overcome many of the challenges presented by these moments of hysteresis, others, like Daniel, may give up. In the words of Bianca, ". . . if they don't like adjust to the change, they'll probably quit college, BU. Because it's much difficult here than over there."

Examining the students' stories through Bourdieu's framework, it becomes apparent that the two most successful students, Mauricio and Carolina, had already been developing a habitus suitable for college in high school, working beyond school hours to ensure they were successful. This was in part prompted by the need to rapidly build their linguistic/rhetorical capital after moving to the United States in order to succeed in an English-only educational environment. It was also supported by robust networks of capital that included not only family support, but various sponsors including a community center and dedicated teachers. While Mauricio was supported additionally by economic capital, Carolina had strong familial capital with a mother who was always supportive of her educational aspirations. As the oldest sibling, Carolina was pushed to graduate from high school in three years and go to college, so that she could help the other members of the family financially and motivate her younger siblings to follow her path. These factors contributed to Carolina and Mauricio ending their first years of college with 3.5–4.0 GPAs.

While they struggled more and faced a number of challenges, Bianca and Yesenia similarly had successful transitions to college. Unlike Mauricio and Carolina, they did not have the advantage of developing a college-oriented habitus in high school, but they had influential sponsors around them during their first year in college. Supported by various forms of capital, including strong aspirations for better lives, a comprehensive scholarship program, and a supportive social network, both Bianca and Yesenia developed the habitus necessary to carry them through a successful first year and into a second with 2.5–3.0 GPAs. However, these networks may be fragile and are constantly in flux, depending on increasingly tenuous funding for programs like CAMP or the lack of a safety net when living on the edge of poverty.

Daniel and Joanne were a different story. They faced a pronounced hysteresis like Bianca and Yesenia upon entering college. In addition, they did not have a strong network of capital to support them and help them adapt. While they began college with fragile networks and potential sources of capital, many of these sources fell away as they moved through their first year. They lacked the level of familial capital that played an important role in Mauricio and Carolina's educational lives and the social capital that was important in facilitating Bianca and Yesenia's transitions. Daniel did have a few caring teachers at the college level and some supportive family members, but these caring teachers and family members appeared too few in Daniel's college life to provide the necessary impact to carry Daniel through that first year.

Paola's case was a bit different from the rest of the participants because the challenges she faced did not seem to be a question of habitus development. She did extremely well her first semester, delaying interviews so that she could focus on completing her homework. Paola's boyfriend, while supportive of her educational ambitions, was not in college. This relationship gradually drew her away, in part because he lived in Mexico, which meant time-consuming transitions across the border to balance her life with him and her college ambitions.

The experiences of students like Paola reveal that any theory of transition, such as Bourdieu's, is always limited by the complexity of human lives and the possibility of any number of factors intervening at any time. All these students passed through similar classes in the same high school; however, their paths through their first year of college varied greatly. While Paola appeared to have the habitus and capital to be successful her first semester in college, life quickly intervened as she began her second.

The results of this study might be sobering to adherents of the belief that all college students should transition smoothly to college and graduate in four years. Of the nine students who started, seven began college right after high school and four made it through their first year without stopping out. However, even students who struggled—Paola, Daniel, and Joanne—had successes that a traditional perspective of successful academic transitions would overlook. Paola excelled her first semester at college, proving she could handle the work, and made a conscious decision not to return for much of the spring semester. Joanne was considered one of the harder working students in her high school English class, taking only a month or so away from school while having a child, balancing school and home responsibilities during high school and graduating on time.

Viewing transition as a one-time move from high school to college would paint these students as failures, consequently upholding the deficit model that focuses on how certain students lack the habitus and capital to succeed in educational environments. Conceptualizing transition in this way simplifies a much more complex reality, a reality that emerges over time. Bourdieu (and Wacquant 1992, 99) himself notes this, referring to "the evolution over time of the volume and structure of this capital, that is, of his social trajectory and of the dispositions (habitus) constituted in the prolonged relation to a definite distribution of objective chances." Expecting students to immediately adapt to a radically different institutional environment shifts the blame from institutions to students by marginalizing students who do not fit within a traditional model. Working class students who leave school are seen as failures and depicted as perpetual "drop outs" even though their path through the educational system may be much different than their middle and upper class counterparts. Powell (2014) criticized traditional discourses surrounding retention and dropout as shifting the blame to the student while ignoring the fact that institutions have consistently refused to adapt to changing student populations. This is evident in the common use of the term "persistence" among scholars like Tinto (1993) that has the effect of shifting the focus from an institution's responsibility to help "retain" a student to an individual's ability to "persist" at college.

Adopting a CRT stance like Yosso (2005, 82) requires starting from the premise that "Communities of Color are places with multiple strengths." Choosing this critical orientation does not dismiss the reality that these strengths are often ignored by institutions designed around the needs of the traditional majority. As depicted throughout the students' networks of capital presented earlier, it is clear they had challenges that affected their performance across these institutions. However, they also had sources of capital, sources that were not as acknowledged and supported as much as they could have been by the various educational institutions in this study. In expecting students to adapt to different institutional demands, it is important that institutions themselves also adapt.

**REIMAGINING TRANSITIONS ACROSS INSTITUTIONAL FIELDS**

I began this study primarily interested in examining the perceived alignment or misalignment between institutional fields in terms of writing expectations and the impact it would have on student success as they transitioned and attempted to transfer knowledge between institutions. As evident from the stories recounted here, there was much more happening than I was initially aware of. In this sense, I ended much where Leki (2007, 283) did in her longitudinal work *Undergraduates in a Second Language*: "In doing this research, I came to the opinion that writing researchers, in both L1 and L2, myself included, suffered a kind of professional deformation, exaggerating the role of writing in the lives of L2 undergraduate students and in their intellectual and academic development. The academic lives I heard about in these interviews and saw in class observations could not be reduced to issues of academic literacy."

Traditional studies of literacy development in institutions have tended to focus solely on what occurs in the classroom, discussing the types of writing tasks students face, the types of reading they do, the type of teachers they have, and how their knowledge transfers from one class to another. While this model may be effective in investigating the learning of residential college students whose main responsibility is balancing academic and social commitments on campus, it does a disservice to increasingly diverse student populations who have lives outside of but interconnected with the classroom.

Goldblatt (2007), Kanno and Varghese (2010), Leki (2007), Sternglass (1997), Suárez-Orozco and Suárez-Orozco (2001), Suárez-Orozco, Suárez-Orozco, and Todorova (2008) and the findings of this study have revealed that what goes on outside the classroom greatly matters in terms of one's academic literacy development. The literacy practices of students in this study were deeply embedded in and shaped by a variety of fields: classrooms, institutions, El Paso, Juárez, Texas, the United States, and Mexico. Events happening in and across these different fields ultimately impacted the development of students' habitus and capital, consequently supporting or hindering their transitions to college. It is for this reason that Arispe y Acevedo (2008) argued that access to quality housing, food, and health care cannot be ignored in studies examining academic success. As postsecondary institutions increasingly turn to teaching digital composition, digital divides in terms of access, which is never generic (Ruecker 2012; Sheridan, Ridolfo, and Michel 2008), will become increasingly important. External factors such as the drug-related violence in Mexico, punitive immigration policies separating families, and the need to care for dependents all affect students' ability to focus on the writing they do for school. Fortunately, what happens outside the classroom is not always negative. By shifting the discourse from what certain students lack to one focused on how can we transform educational institutions into ones that support their success, we can imagine the ways high schools and universities can facilitate Latina/o student transitions into a more economically successful life.

We can recognize that the students profiled in this study, like many of their Latina/o counterparts throughout the country, are regularly making a variety of successful, complex transitions. The participants' stories revealed that they make a variety of transitions every day, transitions that a more traditional college student may not have to undergo when institutions are more closely aligned with their home discourse practices. Students in this study regularly and successfully moved between the United States and Mexico, between English and Spanish, and between home and school life. Moving between educational institutions was just one transition embedded in a larger network of successful transitions. For instance, in reading and writing, students moved from short stories to book-length historical accounts, from handwritten personal narratives to typed analyses, research papers, and even video documentaries. The habitus of students readapted as they shifted from one field to another. "Why can't I just write what I think?" was a common question students asked me when researching for papers at the college level, a question that arose because they were used to writing what they thought for so long. However, as evident from the case studies, the majority of the Latinas/os profiled in this study readily adapted to new genres of writing at college.

Latina/o connection to family is often referenced as a factor holding students back from being successful, limiting the options students consider as they plan to attend college or, in the case of first-generation parents, expecting their children to actively contribute financially to the family or provide other support, like Yesenia taking care of her younger brother (Merisotis and McCarthy 2005; Person and Rosenbaum 2006). Nonetheless, this is only part of the picture. Daniel had an uncle who stepped in to ensure he attended school while his cousin helped him navigate the college bureaucracy, both playing important roles as sponsors. Carolina's mother recognized the value of education in her daughter's life and played an important role in supporting Carolina's aspirations to earn a college degree. Instead of blaming family members for not understanding, it is important to recognize that their lack of understanding may be attributed to a history of exclusion and that institutions can be part of the solution: "Helping parents understand the level of work and expectations placed on college students as well as information on how to support their son or daughter is an important aspect in helping Latino/a students succeed" (Torres 2004, 467).

## SHIFTING THE LENS: HOW INSTITUTIONS AND POLITICS FAIL STUDENTS

Students like Daniel and their families have some responsibility to take charge of their education and become more engaged in learning. As noted in recent sociological studies of student learning and social lives at college, today's students (not just Latinas/os) are generally studying much less than previous generations and, according to some reports, learning much less as well (Arum and Roksa 2011; Clydesdale 2007). In discussing his success, Mauricio noted "I prepared myself with the help of teachers because I looked to go for to tutoring. I looked for help." Carolina referred to family support as central to her success, noting that some "parents don't care if [their children] even go to class." However, we cannot ignore the reality that many Latina/o students and their families have been beaten down with discourses labeling them as lacking capital, unprepared for college, or in other ways failing educational institutions. Echoing Bourdieu, Sacks (2007, 107) explained how they have been the victims of a class-based educational system based around an "informal system of institutional arrangements and economic imperatives that provides great rewards to the children of affluence and privilege but shutters the gates to those who have grown up without such privilege." By upholding an educational model that contributes to maintaining existing societal structures, local, state, and national institutions regularly failed the students in this study, an issue to which we now turn.

### Local Failures

Although research regularly points out that contact with professors outside the classroom facilitates student success, it appears from this study and from my own experience that the burden is often placed on a struggling student to initiate contact with a professor. Daniel's first-year seminar instructor was an exception to this in proactively asking why he was missing class; consequently, she played a role in helping him pass one of the two classes he passed his first year at college. In rethinking the expectations we have of students, it is important for professors to consider a history of silencing Latina/o students and the challenge it may be for some to approach someone in a position of authority, someone they may not identify with culturally, physically, or economically. Granted, overworked two-year college faculty or adjunct faculty at four-year institutions do not necessarily have the time to reach out to every student. Similarly, as Arum and Roksa (2011) have pointed out, there are incentives in higher education, as there are often in K–12 schools (e.g., Booher-Jennings 2005), to focus on those students who excel and are likely to succeed.

Despite admirable moves by BU to celebrate its status as a Hispanic-serving research university and developing innovative ways to support its students, students were often asked to leave their identities at the door in entering the various institutions included in this study, most notably in the area of language. Research has shown that pedagogies that actively engage linguistic minority students through using their languages as resources helps engage them more fully in the classroom and consequently correlates with success (Thomas and Collier 2003). However, the "sink or swim" attitude held by many teachers at SHS or the lack of assignments consciously building on students' multiliteracies at BCC or BU helps perpetuate a history of institutionalized exclusion that contributes to the marginalization of Latina/o student populations.

Research shows that it takes five to seven years to gain academic fluency in another language and that language fluency improves with regular feedback (Cummins 1981; Ferris 2011). Students in this study received limited feedback across institutions especially in regard to persistent linguistic challenges; however, they were consistently held accountable for this area of their writing. This situation stems from factors such as the working conditions of high school teachers or adjunct faculty and a lack of preparation in teacher education and graduate programs preparing teachers of writing—programs that have traditionally adhered to a mainstream norm, not a norm where Latinas/os are the fastest growing segment of the population. Nonetheless, it is a problem that consistently fails students like those in this study.

### State and National Failures

Individual institutions are not solely to blame for the challenges Latina/o student populations face; policies at the state and national level often hamstring educators into teaching a certain way and also lead students down a path of debt without a degree. The most obvious failure of Latina/o students in this study was the ironically named No Child Left Behind Act, which watered down instruction and expectations at SHS. Researchers (e.g., Booher-Jennings 2005; Paul 2004) have repeatedly shown that high-stakes testing policies unfairly penalize schools with a high percentage of linguistic minority students, and the findings from this study are no exception.

The incoming Common Core State Standards Initiative (2010) (CCSS) are the latest incarnation of nation-wide educational policy. Even though 35 percent of Latina/o fourth graders and 20 percent of eighth graders are labeled ELL students (Hemphill and Vanneman 2011, 4), the rapidly growing ELL student populations merit only a passing mention in the standards themselves: "It is possible to meet the standards in reading, writing, speaking, and listening without displaying native-like control of conventions and vocabulary" (6). In the words of the standards, this population is "beyond [their] scope" (6). With national standards still being designed around a native English speaking white norm in a century where minorities are expected to become the majority, can we expect the associated assessments to be any different than traditional assessments that are culturally-biased, consistently demoralizing minority students by labeling them as "failures"?

According to Ingle and Ingle (2008), well over 60 percent of Latinas/os who attend college attend public institutions, largely due to their affordability. However, funding for public postsecondary institutions has been declining at the state level for years, leading to increased tuition for those least unable to afford it. The purchasing power of Pell Grants continues to stagnate at the same time, remaining the same despite tuition increases well beyond the rate of inflation (Perez 2008). There have even been moves in Washington, DC, to dramatically cut the Pell Grant amounts. Given this anti-education political context, it is unsurprising that the President's much-lauded goals to increase degree production have been largely neutralized through a lack of funding promoting them (Marcus 2011). Researchers have consistently found a positive correlation between adequate finances to fund college and student retention (Cabrera, Nora, and Castaneda 1993; Cabrera, Stampen, and Hansen 1990; St. John et al. 2000; St. John, Paulsen, and Starkey 1996). Continued cuts to higher education funding, as well as moves by public universities to reallocate aid dollars to higher income students (Gerald and Haycock 2006), will continue to hurt students who need this support the most.

Many societal failures are not immediately connected to educational policy, but can have a huge effect on what happens in the educational system. For instance, researchers have consistently demonstrated a correlation between social class and educational attainment (e.g., Sacks 2007). While poverty played a role in shaping the opportunities of most students in this study, pregnancy was consistently one of the most disruptive life experiences faced by female participants. As I write this a few years after the last interview, all but one female in the study are either parents or expectant parents, with one facing the additional challenge of caring for three siblings. This reflects trends in broader contexts as Texas has the third-highest teen pregnancy rate in the country, with El Paso higher than the Texas average (Ballinger 2011). Latinas have the highest birth rate among all races and almost twice the national average with seventy-eight of every one thousand Latinas aged fifteen through nineteen giving birth in 2009, which is the current rate in El Paso (Ballinger 2011; Centers for Disease Control and Prevention 2011). High teen pregnancy rates in El Paso can be partly attributed to individual choices but also to the fact that Texas, like other conservative states, is known to provide little information in the way of sexual education and, when they do, it is often about advocating abstinence-only programs, which have been shown to be ineffective (Ballinger 2011; Wiley and Wilson 2009). A few years ago, all the Planned Parenthood clinics in El Paso were closed as a result of federal and state funding decisions (Maldonado 2010), making it more difficult for students to find information about their reproductive health options. A sad irony found the former Planned Parenthood clinic at the BCC campus where this study was conducted purchased by the college and turned in to a tutoring center.

### RETENTION DISCOURSES AND STUDENT SUCCESS

Given the complexity of their paths, it is almost certain that Daniel, Joanne, and Paola will not graduate in the four years that college is "supposed" to take. In fact, a minority of students nationwide actually do, with only 24 percent of students in Texas at "four-year" public institutions graduating in four years (Chronicle of Higher Education 2013). Among Texas Latinas/os, this number falls to 15 percent. Moreover, community college students take longer to finish college degrees and many struggle to make the transition into a four-year college (Cohen and Brawer 2008). Only 13.1 percent of two-year public college students in Texas complete their associate's degree in three years (Chronicle of Higher Education 2013). Unfortunately, national measures of retention and graduation, originally based off of an NCAA system designed to measure the progress of student athletes, unfairly portray institutions like BU and BCC, who serve a largely commuter population (BU's President 2007, citation omitted for anonymity). BU's President has repeatedly challenged these traditional measurements, arguing that they fail to account for 70 percent of BU's graduates because they ignore transfer students, part-time students, returning students, and students who begin in the spring semester. Similarly, a report by the Higher Education Research Institute found that public institutions actually outperformed private ones in terms of graduation rates when the type of student enrolled was factored into data analyses. Although public institutions have significantly lower overall graduation rates, they are more effective at graduating non-traditional students than private institutions (DeAngelo et al. 2011).

When I began this project, I dived into the literature on student success and retention with gusto; however, I have begun to see the darker side of this work. As Powell (2014, 23) astutely noted, retention research "motivates and justifies initiatives that perpetuate the current structure of power in higher education." While couched in the discourse of student success, it is often intimately connected with the desire for increased tuition dollars, state funding, or other financial gain for institutions. Under the guise of making sure the students who come are "successful," it can lead to misguided policies like raising the standards in scholarships targeting students of color (Lohmann 2013). Under the guise of promoting four-year graduation rates, it can lead to policies penalizing working-class students by charging less per credit hour for students taking fifteen hours instead of twelve (Galvan 2013).

While Carolina and Mauricio are currently on the four-year path, overcoming challenges and gradually building stronger networks of capital to move through and beyond college, Yesenia and Bianca are somewhere in-between, unlikely to graduate as quickly as Carolina and Mauricio. Daniel, Joanne, and Paola are on a path shared with many of their Latina/o peers, with Daniel describing a family pattern: "Yeah, well like, my uncle—well one of my uncles, he went to school right away. And oh, my dad, like, he did the same thing. Like, he stopped for a while and it took him forever but he got to where he wanted to be. And I don't know, I guess that's how it is with us." They all have ambitions to return to college at some point. These students could stop in and stop out,[2] going back to college, leaving school again, and returning again.

Understanding that Daniel, Joanne, and Paola's stories are still being created and that they are in school or have ambitions to return to school and get degrees makes it clear that labeling their cases as failed transitions is much too simplistic and premature. Looking at both the student and institution helps us see that the responsibility for successful transitions is often beyond the control of both. Institutions can develop retention initiatives to help students persist; however, not every student is going to matriculate to college and be successful. I entered this study with the naïve expectation that, as an action researcher, I would play an important role in facilitating student success. Through giving feedback on certain students' writing, I might have helped them get better grades in a few classes; however, like Blanton (2005), I felt useless in preventing the stopping out of students like Daniel, Joanne, and Paola. Many of these students participated in activities traditionally associated with student success: extracurricular activities, learning communities, religious organizations, and connecting with literacy sponsors (Antrop-González, Vélez, and Garrett 2008; Astin 1997; Barnhouse and Smith 2006; Cargill and Kalikoff; 2007; Jcynes 2002; Scenters-Zapico 2010; Tinto 1993; 1997). However, not all were immediately successful. As I discuss the role that writing administrators, teachers, and researchers can play in promoting the success of Latina/o student populations in the next chapter, it is important to recognize that there are limits to what we can accomplish. Nonetheless, we as a field and as members of a higher education system with a history of failing Latina/o student populations can do more.

### Notes

1. A successful transition is defined here by attendance into the second year of college and financial aid eligibility standards by the institutions involved in this study: at BCC, a 2.0 GPA and successful completion of two-thirds of the credit hours attempted and, at BU, a 2.0 GPA and successful completion of three-fourths of the credit hours attempted.
2. See note 9 in chapter one for an explanation of stop out versus drop out.

# 8
## THE ROLE OF COMPOSITION RESEARCHERS, TEACHERS, AND ADMINISTRATORS

The stories of Joanne, Daniel, and Paola along with the untold stories of students who began this project but never started college vividly illustrate the reality depicted by statistics shared in the introductory chapter: minority students, including Latinas/os, do not graduate at the same rate as their majority peers (Llagas and Snyder 2003; Lumina Foundation 2007). Although education is not a guaranteed pathway to economic success, educational disparities contribute to the increasing divide between the rich and the poor in the United States as unemployment rates and expected earnings between someone with a high school education and a postsecondary degree continue to widen (Bureau of Labor Statistics 2013; Carnevale, Cheah, and Strohl 2012; Julian 2012). Influential organizations such as Achieve, the Lumina Foundation, the Bill and Melinda Gates Foundation, and even the conservative American Enterprise Institute, state this argument in a way that is more likely to influence public policy: in failing to educate the fastest growing population in this country, Latinas/os, the United States will lose its dominance in an knowledge-based globalized economy where success is increasingly dependent on an educated workforce.

Discourses from prominent foundations and columnists like Friedman (2012; 2013) espousing the democratizing powers of education are by no means unproblematic, however. For instance, Lumina Foundation's (2013) work largely focuses on limited institutional change and the advocacy of more standardization and assessment, the latter of which failed the students in this study so badly. As emphasized in the previous chapter, success in college is a mutual responsibility involving a variety of agents and what occurs in the classroom is intimately connected with what happens outside the college or university. All the students who took part in this study were unprepared as they entered college, some more so than others. However, some actively worked with family, friends, community organizations, churches, institutions, and instructors to build networks of capital, facilitating transitions that helped them pass their first-year classes and move into the second year of college. Those who did not have the resources or initiative to create these networks struggled and stopped out.

It is true that institutions can and need to change. Grabill (2001, 127) has articulated this: "An institution is a well-established, rhetorically constructed design, a bureaucratic and organizational site where people live and work and where they interact with others inside and outside the institution. But just as importantly, according to this view, institutions can be changed." Scholars promoting increased diversity and success in higher education (e.g., Bamber 2008; Blunt 2008; Powell 2014; Thomas 2011) have argued that postsecondary institutions need to undergo substantial transformations to promote full minority access and success. Thomas (2011, 2–3) wrote that these transformations include "an institutional commitment in engaging a diverse student body and changing institutional structures, processes and governance; developing an inclusive culture and altering processes of knowledge creation and knowledge transfer to be more inclusive of a diverse student body." Powell (2014, 96) has forcibly argued that "we will never see the improved retention rates that administrators, scholars, and politicians claim to want, unless the institutional values become radically more inclusive."

## TRANSFORMING WRITING PROGRAMS TO SUPPORT THE RETENTION OF LINGUISTIC MINORITY STUDENTS

In writing these final chapters, I am struggling with the realization that the college writing classroom only plays a small role in students' lives. It is tempting to feel that anything we do is futile in the face of much more powerful interests actively shaping individual opportunity from birth via a system that exacerbates income and health inequalities, dictates how writing should be taught throughout our public school system, and continually diminishes support for the work we do in higher education. However, through a network of change agents spread across institutions throughout the country, we have the possibility to make some impact. Research supports this. We know that a student's first year is the most common point of student departure (Hrabowski 2005; Ishler and Upcraft 2005; Tinto 1988) and most college students pass through a first-year writing course. We have learned that curricular innovations in these courses such as the stretch program at Arizona State University, the supplemental workshop model at the State University of New York, and the Accelerated Learning Program initially implemented at the Community College of Baltimore County can lead to increased retention rates and faster time to degree (Glau 2007; Rigolino and Freel 2007; Jenkins et al. 2010).

Because our classrooms and institutions are where we as teachers, administrators, and researchers have the most immediate impact, we need to view these spaces as ones where we can begin to undertake the transformations necessary to better support the success of Latina/o students transitioning from high schools to community colleges to universities and beyond. However, recognizing that what goes on beyond our classrooms matters much more, we need to constantly seek ways to broaden our impact. To this end, I will conclude by calling those involved in writing instruction and program administration to work for much broader and ambitious transformations beyond their institutions.

**Getting to Know our Students**

The first step in transforming a writing program into one that is designed for its students is to learn about the students it serves. As Goldblatt (2007, 9) has noted: "The acquisition and exercise of language is always mediated by and reflective of conditions that can be traced to the geographical, social, and economic locations of the speaker, writer, listener or reader." Students in first-year writing programs are not "homogeneous" (Matsuda 2006) and Latina/o students "are not all the same" (Kirklighter, Cárdenas, and Murphy 2007). Students come into college writing programs from a variety of backgrounds. Some come from private preparatory high schools while others come from schools like SHS. The parents of some students pay full tuition while others are dependent on Pell Grants and other federal loans while working part or full time to support their families. Some have spent their whole lives in the United States and identify English as their first language while others may have come in third grade, eighth grade, or even in high school with little or no knowledge of English. These are only a few of the many factors that come into play as a student transitions from high school to college.

Writing teachers and administrators are often unfamiliar with university Fact Books or other resources provided by institutional data offices. These provide information on where students come from (Are they mostly local or from out of state? How many international students are there?), demographics (How many Latina/o students? African American? Native American? Males? Females?), and other valuable information such as retention rates, average time to graduation, and the most popular degrees. If the campus is primarily a commuter one, it is important to learn more about the community where the students are coming from. What are the schools like? Is the college or university's student population representative of the community population?

In addition to learning this broader information, writing program administrators (WPAs) and instructors can assess the demographics, needs, and preferences of the students in their programs, conducting surveys inquiring about previous educational experiences, educational goals, placement preferences, language backgrounds, education backgrounds, and more (see Ruecker 2011 for an example of this type of assessment). Instructors can also gain some of this information via surveys, through assigning literacy narratives, or by having students map the various discourse communities they participate in. Harder information to gain from students, but nevertheless important, is about their lives outside the classroom. Do students care for dependents, whether their own children or siblings? Do they work full or part time? Do they have Internet and computer access at home?

As I discuss in the following sections, data gathered through these inquiries should be used to shape the curriculum and delivery of writing programs in order to promote the success of students moving through them. These data can help WPAs and instructors decide the content of their classes while assessing issues such as the linguistic support they need to offer, the impact that moving to online or hybrid models will have on students, and the kind of writing experiences that students in FYC classes need in order to facilitate their transition to writing in college.

**Integrating Principles of Student Success**

Entering a college, especially a large university, can be daunting for a first-year student, especially if they do not have family members or friends who have the experience to help them navigate this new environment. The writing classroom, often part of another first-year retention initiative (learning communities), has traditionally offered a small space in which students have the opportunity to regularly interact with students and their professor. Building upon the broader steps to knowing about student populations discussed in the previous section, it is vital for instructors to focus on connecting with individual students, especially those who may struggle in their classes. For instance, when Daniel was missing school to take his grandmother to the doctor, his first-semester developmental writing instructor approached him to see what was wrong instead of waiting for him to approach her. While he failed most of his classes, he got a B in this one. While we cannot do this with all students, and as mentioned before, all students will not be successful, imagine if all of Daniel's teachers had worked with him closely that first year to motivate and engage him more fully in the classroom? Would he have stayed on for a second year? The need for these connections validates the importance of professor-student conferences commonly found in writing classrooms, one practice we can continue to integrate throughout the teaching we do.

Repeatedly, students in this study faced moments of hysteresis in adapting to the very different reading and writing demands presented to them at college. They were expected to write in new genres and consequently draw on skills they had not previously learned. Sometimes it can be easy to take these skills for granted, especially when teachers have spent years honing their own skills in integrating quotes or learning various citations styles. Some suggest that universities should not be "dealing with" students who need this kind of support (i.e., developmental), demanding that high schools do a better job or shuffling them off to community colleges. If institutions are going to be truly inclusive, it is vital that teachers work to serve all students, being conscious of the scaffolding we provide in designing and teaching various assignments, whether it be lessons on integrating quotes, formatting papers, or simply navigating the course management system.

An important part of scaffolding the development of students, especially multilingual Latina/o students, is providing feedback on their writing. Unfortunately, the findings in this study were similar to those reported by Connors and Lunsford (1993): students need more feedback, both globally and locally. Students regularly wrote for classes, but rarely received sufficient feedback for them to develop skills quickly that would place them on par with peers who had significantly more preparation. Along these lines, composition studies needs to move away from its aversion to grammar instruction, as failing to teach students the conventions of standardized written academic English perpetuates the disadvantages they already have when writing in other classes and beyond the institution.

In order to accomplish the goals described in this section, it is vital that composition teachers, administrators, and researchers continue to fight for smaller class sizes and reduced teaching loads rather than blame overworked teachers. Teaching loads among institutions and individuals in this study varied, including a high school teacher with 150 students and an adjunct at the community college teaching six classes at multiple campuses in addition to teaching for an online for-profit institution. While tenured faculty at BU taught two classes a semester, tenured faculty at the community college typically taught five classes. FYC courses at BU were capped at twenty-five while they rose up to as many as thirty students at BCC.

### Reimagining First-Year Composition Curricula

The application of habitus, capital, and field in the previous chapter revealed that Latina/o student success in transitioning to secondary school and into college is largely based on assimilating to the dominant US culture, building capital in standardized academic English while increasingly falling behind in Spanish literacy. Although the students possessed unique "traces of particular cultures, traditions, languages, systems of beliefs, texts and histories which have shaped them" (Hall 1993, 362), these were often ignored in classrooms. As Schroeder (2011, 197) argued in an institutional case study of a Hispanic-serving institution (HSI), framing linguistic and cultural difference as deficits as opposed to "intellectual resources to exploit" creates obstacles that may lead to lower retention rates among students. Out of a sense of frustration and a sense of inferiority, LM students are often pushed away from institutions that are designed for the majority when they serve the minority. Even high achieving students like Carolina and Mauricio grapple with feelings of inferiority, consequently being led into lower tracks during high school when they could take more advanced classes and questioning their ability to succeed at college when they arrive. As Hall (1998, 4) has written, "If all students are to maximize their educational potential, the institutions of higher education have to increase their awareness of, and support for, the growing diversity of students who enter higher education."

Composition studies has been slow to move away from the standardized English-only ideology that dominates writing instruction in the United States. However, the situation is improving as mainstream journals are publishing more articles focused on addressing the diversity of writing classrooms. Anthologies designed for exposing new graduate TAs to important discourses in the field are increasingly including chapters on working with linguistically diverse writers (e.g., Glenn and Goldthwaite 2013). Scholars connected with the Students Right to their Own Language (SRTOL) movement have offered ways for teachers to incorporate US varieties of English such as African American Vernacular in their classes (Gilyard 2000; Gilyard and Richardson 2001; Perryman-Clark 2012; 2013; Smitherman 2006). Well-known L2 and mainstream writing scholars such as Canagarajah (2006) and Horner and Trimbur (2002) have advocated for the inclusion of multiple languages in part through encouraging code switching in composition classrooms at the postsecondary level.[1] Matsuda and Silva (1999) described a cross-cultural composition classroom that provides a mediated integration of L1 and L2 learners.

The possibilities of assignments that build on students' multiliteracies are endless. One possibility is a relatively simple modification to a traditional FYC assignment like a rhetorical analysis. In my own classroom, I not only invite students to analyze two US standardized English-based texts in my classroom, but also give them the option to engage in cross-cultural rhetorical analysis. In this assignment, they choose articles on the same topic from two different countries and written in two different languages, conducting an analysis in which they explore how each author's situatedness changed the way they wrote about the topic. As they engage in adding options to traditional assignments and encouraging students to research in multiple languages, teachers can constantly remind their students that they are uniquely situated to conduct this type of work because of their multilingual and multicultural backgrounds. This type of encouragement can go a long way in breaking down the deficit discourses and labels (Spack 1997) that have surrounded multilingual students' past educational experiences, consequently building their confidence as students, writers, and researchers.

For WPAs and programs interested in a more radical shift, I see possibilities in a path already realized by two-way bilingual education programs most commonly seen at the K–8 level, programs that "integrate language minority and language majority students and provide instruction in, and through, two languages" (Christian 1996, 67). Traditional bilingual classrooms are like their mainstream counterparts in that they are subtractive, leading a student to advance in standardized English while stagnating in their L1. Most of the students in this study were more confident in oral Spanish than English; however, when a few of them encountered Spanish academic discourse in reading or writing tasks in college, it was some of the most difficult work for them because their development in this area had stopped years previously when they transitioned to the US educational system.

In comparison to traditional educational models and even the cross-cultural composition courses offered at several universities, two-way bilingual programs are additive, based on the belief that both language majority and minority students benefit from being multilingual in an increasingly globalized world. In a multi-decade study, Thomas and

Collier (2003, 61) found that two-way bilingual programs are more likely to close achievement gaps between language majority and language minority students while benefiting language majority students who, through the "cognitive stimulus of schooling in two languages," can advance beyond the skills of their "monolingually educated peers." BU is leading the way in this area by providing history, Spanish composition, and other classes for native Spanish speakers. The writing program at BU has already implemented bilingual professional writing courses and could bring this model to FYC classes. Nonetheless, there remains huge potential for writing programs at US universities to go down this path.

Expanding Course Delivery Options

Whether they work thirty or forty hours a week while attending school, have siblings or dependents to care for, or depend on an unreliable bus system to get to school, many Latina/o students can benefit from alternative course delivery options. Consistently making a regular two or three times a week class meeting may be difficult for students who are consequently penalized by strict attendance policies commonly found in first-year writing classrooms. We saw Daniel choosing to take his grandmother to the doctor instead of going to class. Bianca had to stay home when a sibling became sick. At BU, I regularly revised my attendance policy to accommodate students who missed class after a bus never came, waited an unusually long time at the border crossing, or had a family member in Mexico who passed away.

Innovation in terms of how non-profit colleges and universities deliver learning options is especially needed in an era where for-profit schools aggressively target non-traditional students like those in this study. A Senate report found that for-profit institutions typically spend a quarter of their budget on marketing and that "Some of the most profitable spent more per student on marketing than they did on instruction" (Stratford 2012, para. 5). I steered Paola away from one of these schools early in the study as she had received information promoting short time to degree and excellent job opportunities upon graduation. After stopping out of BCC or BU, other students in this study ended up at for-profit institutions, with a medical associates degree being the most popular (See Daniel's story in the epilogue for more on life at a for-profit college).

In response to students like Joanne, Daniel, and others that stop out of college and enter a nine-month program at a for-profit institution to speed their progress to graduation, non-profit institutions need to respond by offering options that may appeal to non-traditional students. In trying to get Joanne to consider a nurses aid program at BCC, I came across a program website that emphasized the need for a number of prerequisites as well as a low admission rate, barriers that quickly turned her off this option. For-profit institutions would likely avoid advertising barriers for admission to their programs.

Online learning, largely pioneered by these for-profit institutions, is often promoted as the magic solution to creating opportunities for non-traditional students. This discourse has been especially prominent with the recent push for Massive Open Online Courses (MOOCs), which has found a strong advocate in large foundations like the Gates Foundation and columnists like Thomas Friedman with the *New York Times*. In columns titled "Come the Revolution" and "Revolution Hits the Universities," Friedman (2012; 2013) has uncritically sung the praises of MOOCs, writing "Nothing has more potential to lift more people out of poverty—by providing them an affordable education to get a job or improve in the job they have. Nothing has more potential to unlock a billion more brains to solve the world's biggest problems" (Friedman 2013, para. 1). The Gates Foundation has seen potential as well, providing $50,000 grants to facilitate the creation of developmental and first-year composition MOOCs at several institutions (Gates Foundation 2012).

A return to decades of research on student retention calls into question the optimistic promoters of MOOCs and other online learning opportunities to democratize education and unlock economic opportunities for massive numbers of new students. We are reminded that students who connect more fully with the campus community and have interpersonal needs met are more likely to persist in and succeed in their education trajectory (Astin 1997; Tinto 1975; 1988; 1993; 1997). Early research on online learning showed that non-traditional students such as those desiring a more vocational path are "not typically-well equipped for flexible delivery" in part because they are not inclined toward self-directed learning (Smith 2000, 43; see also Boote 1998 and Evans 2000). As I mentioned earlier, Daniel chose online courses his second semester because of difficulties getting to class on time. However, he barely completed any work for these classes and felt that there was not an instructor presence he could connect with when needing extra support. As a result, he quickly dropped these courses and subsequently dropped out of college.

Online courses can be an important part of any writing program but the creation of truly flexible learning promised by online learning advocates requires attention to the learners' "needs, interests, and contexts" (Evans 2000, 221). These courses do not and cannot address the needs of every student and, as such, placing students in them should be done cautiously and include some kind of assessment for online learning readiness as explored by Smith (2005). Online instructors should be especially conscious of maintaining a presence in online courses, communicating regularly with individual students and being present in online discussion spaces (Dennen, Darabi, and Smith 2007). Alternative means, such as the hybrid format offered in second-semester FYC courses at BU, are a good way to begin integrating online learning into a writing program. MOOCs are likely never going to provide substantial benefit to students like Daniel who had trouble self-motivating for a course that came with a grade and threats of losing his financial aid dollars if he did not do well.

In addition to creating online and hybrid options that serve students with busy schedules outside school, it is important for writing programs to offer options to serve those with diverse linguistic backgrounds. As various scholars (Costino and Hyon 2007; Ortmeier-Hooper 2008; Ruecker 2011) have noted, L2 students who have spent a significant part of their life in the US educational system may not fit well into the simple mainstream/ESL dichotomy. The cross-cultural and dual-language options discussed in the previous section maybe be more fitting for such students. As with a straight ESL placement, a developmental writing placement does not always work for students like Yesenia and Daniel and can carry a similar stigma. Daniel's development in particular stagnated as he spent a full year in developmental writing classes, completing less advanced writing than he was producing by the end of high school. Yesenia fared better in a more advanced developmental writing course that was aligned with the mainstream composition program. A writing program adequately equipped to serve LM students will offer the traditional mainstream and ESL options along with online, hybrid, and stretch or studio options. This should be accompanied by some element of directed self-placement rather than the simple use of test scores, which both of the institutions in this study depended on (see Royer and Gilles 1998).

### Hiring and Training Faculty

Commitment to serving linguistically and culturally diverse students should be considered in hiring and promoting faculty. The strong English-only preferences among faculty across the institutions in this study, and the perceptions by students that their college instructors did not care about them as individuals, reveal that simply having a diverse teaching faculty is not sufficient, especially if they have been inculcated into an educational system that minimally values the diverse linguistic and cultural experiences that students bring to the classroom.

Knowledge of multiple languages, especially those common to students at the institution, should be considered in hiring and promotion decisions. The benefits of multilingual faculty teaching multilingual students are well documented (Cook 1999; Matsuda and Matsuda 2001; Thomas 1999). By going through the experience of learning another language, multilingual faculty are better able to understand the challenges their students face in mastering the conventions of academic language. In addition, learning another language helps one understand the structure of their own language better, consequently being better able to give students the linguistic help they need. Finally, and most importantly, it holds faculty to the same standards that the institution has for students and creates a culture of multilingualism and multiculturalism.

In hiring full-time writing faculty, priority should be given to people with experience and interest in working with L2 writers and other underrepresented student populations. Despite the fact that multilingual Spanish/English speaking students were the majority at SHS, BCC, and BU, monolingualism was the norm in instruction and very few instructors at both the high school and college level had formal training in working with L2 writers, assuming that experience would be enough. Throughout the different environments, students like Bianca often did not receive the feedback they needed to develop their abilities in academic English. Feedback on writing tended to be minimal, or in the case of Yesenia's draft in which every error was corrected, too much.

Similarly, institutions should hire and promote those committed to student success. One instructor reported another saying that students "have to be able to perform at a university level, and if they can't, they can't and if they flunk they have to take it over." This mentality of weeding out unsuccessful students is still prevalent across university campuses and unsustainable in an era where diversity in higher education is constantly increasing. When the President of BU began embracing the region's Mexican American population in the 1980s, faculty were concerned about the impact on the university's status as it strived toward gaining recognition for its research excellence.

Given that those coming out of graduate programs are the future of rhetoric and composition, the creation of faculty prepared to work with both linguistically and culturally diverse writers begins in graduate programs. Currently, these programs very rarely offer any required courses in working with diverse writers. Programs should offer a core course devoted to this topic as opposed to an elective that only reaches students with a strong interest in working with diverse writers. Such a course could focus on principles of giving feedback more effectively to L2 writers, working with non-traditional students who come to college underprepared, and strategies for supporting the retention of students who may have difficulties balancing home, school, and work lives. This type of knowledge can also be integrated into TA orientation courses and professional development workshops offered regularly by writing programs to ensure that it becomes part of the larger culture.

## TRANSFORMING WRITING PROGRAMS, COMMUNITIES, AND PUBLIC POLICY

This study has revealed how writing classrooms and writing programs are embedded in a much larger set of fields that includes students coming from local or national high schools or from an education system in another country. All these programs, including college and university writing programs, are thus interconnected with one another and to broader social forces at play such as the Common Core, the availability of Pell Grants, and even policies governing immigration and sexual education. While change can start locally, it is important for writing teachers, researchers, administrators, and even students to be involved in a broader project of change. In beginning this process, it is important to recall what Grabill (2001, 130) wrote: "Design is a process of creating a reality, and those interests more powerful—often because of their ability to construct more persuasive knowledge—get to create their reality." Rhetoric and composition scholars often have little influence on the way writing is taught in K–12 contexts because well-endowed and consequently more powerful organizations are the ones driving the discourses in these areas. Nonetheless, Adler-Kassner (2008, 82) has called us to be "activist intellectuals," which involves "enacting a more carefully articulated, materially based notion of progressive pragmatism" in order to "shift the frames surrounding documents like *A Test of Leadership*, *Ready or Not*, and others that assert the authority of 'experts' over educators."[2] In this final section, I articulate ways that composition scholars, administrators, and teachers can strategically formulate relations across disciplines, institutions, and beyond in order to take a more "public turn" (Mathieu 2005) and exploit "gaps or fissures where resistance and change are possible" (Grabill 2001, 128).

## Writing Programs across Institutions

Revisiting student stories in the previous chapter revealed that all participants in this study faced moments of hysteresis at different points in their education, whether transitioning from a bilingual program to a mainstream writing program, from the Mexican to the US educational system, or from high school to college. Given the very different writing experiences that students experienced at the community college in the study, it is likely that those who transfer from BCC to BU, if they make this transition, will face additional hysteresis. At the universities I have studied and taught at, those teaching in the writing program usually have little idea of the type of writing students do in high schools and community colleges.

Drawing on the "college and career readiness" mantra commonly espoused by CCSS proponents, the Lumina Foundation (2013) has proposed a solution to the challenges that students face in transitioning to college: high schools should make all students college-ready. In a form of discourse designed to appeal to a broad audience, they offer a simple understanding of what it means to be college-ready: "The definition of college-ready that states should use is simple—that students do not need remediation in college." Lumina has been a strong advocate of the CCSS and aligning college-entry assessments with these standards, stating that assessments should tell students and their teachers whether or not they are college ready. As evident from Lumina's statement and pointed out by others (Adler-Kassner 2012a; Burris 2013; Johnson 2013), assessment would be a prominent element of the implementation of the standards, with two large consortia formed to develop assessments aligned with them. The architect of the standards, David Coleman, became the head of the College Board with the goal of aligning the SAT to the CCSS (Goldstein 2012). Throughout this book, we have seen the negative effects of a system focused on high-stakes testing and associated sanctions in a school with a large number of low-income and LM Latina/o students, findings that have been validated by a number of other researchers (Assaf 2006; Gebhard, Demers, and Castillo-Rosenthal 2008; McCarthey 2008; Pennington 2007; Suskind 2007).

The implementation of the CCSS and their focus on college readiness presents both challenges and opportunities. As might be expected in standards whose creation was led by someone with limited education experience and minimal rhetoric and composition disciplinary knowledge, the CCSS draw on a very basic notion of literacy instruction. They emphasize text complexity over content and writing instruction is largely limited to two modes: expository information and fact-based argumentative writing with some narrative/descriptive writing. Johnson (2013, 520) noted the narrowness of this by explaining that the standards are based on "spiraling—returning to the same skills at increasing levels of complexity—rather than instructional coverage."

The opportunity connected with the CCSS push is that it calls for changes in how writing is taught at the secondary level. They are opening possibilities for models more aligned with college writing expectations by pushing for more nonfiction reading and writing in English and across the curriculum (National Public Radio 2013). This may provide unique opportunities for writing administrators at colleges and universities to work with high school English teachers to reimagine high school curricula in a way that incorporates narrative and literary analysis assignments alongside a more diverse spectrum of writing experiences. I agree with Adler-Kassner (2012a) in emphasizing the importance of WPAs and other rhetoric and composition professionals at the college level to form alliances with K–12 teachers actively implementing (and, where necessary, resisting) these standards. As they work on district-wide curriculum plans, specialists from rhetoric and composition can join K–12 teachers in developing ways of teaching within the confines of these standards while exploring possible ways to teach a more complex understanding of writing and learning.

Any high school/college partnerships should be approached carefully as postsecondary institutions, especially universities, often do not have the best relations with other educational institutions in their communities. Elsewhere, Goldblatt (2007; Goldblatt, Portillo, and Lyons 2008) has written about the power inequalities between universities and their communities, with some viewing them as a "force or repression or a symbol of exclusion" (Goldblatt, Portillo, and Lyons 2008, 64). A number of researchers (e.g., Jeffery and Polleck 2010; Lewison and Holliday 1997; White, Deegan, and Allexsaht-Snider 1997) have written on the benefits and challenges surrounding the formation of school and university partnerships. There is often a clear power differential between university faculty with PhDs, high school faculty, and even community college counterparts with MAs.

As a researcher, I learned always to enter various institutional contexts humbly with the belief that I had much to learn from high school teachers and community college instructors and professors. In order to lead to more productive discussions and alignment between programs, WPAs should approach educators in other local institutions in a similar way in order to begin discussions and form committees that may lead to curricular alignment that help students avoid such pronounced hysteresis when moving between institutions. By regularly reading research in journals like *English Education* and *Teaching English in the Two-Year College*, WPAs from four-year institutions can enter these partnerships more informed about the challenges faced by educators in different environments.

### Writing across Communities

In calling for institutions to play a larger role in promoting educational equity, Schroeder (2011, 212) wrote, "Such efforts can only begin if we will consider education and literacy within larger systemic contexts, particularly the intersections of individuals and institutions within multicultural communities." Like Schroeder, a number of scholars (e.g., Adler-Kassner 2012b; Goldblatt 2007; Grabill 2001; Kells 2012) have pointed out how composition has traditionally been focused on discourse practices within the institution and have failed to sufficiently engage broader communities with their work. Goldblatt (2007) has called for a broader understanding of the postsecondary literacy environment while Grabill (2001, 88) has written, "If communities and institutions are interrelated, constructed, and the source of meaning and value for community literacies, then to change the meaning and value of literacies means to change particular intersections of communities and institutions." By heeding the calls of these various scholars to more proactively and productively engage with local, state, and national communities, composition scholars can help facilitate students' transitions to college by affecting necessary change beyond the institution.

Why is this work important in the context of a discussion of students transitioning to college? Both postsecondary institutions in this study have implemented curricular changes such as the addition of learning communities to promote retention as recommended by scholars such as Astin (1997) and Tinto (1993; 1997). Nonetheless, graduation and retention rates at institutions serving large numbers of minority students continue to be low. These numbers, which were problematized in the previous chapter, result in negative publicity such as a prominent Texas newspaper decrying BU in an article headlined "BU's graduation rate among lowest in nation." The three BCC students in this study stopped out their first year and two of the BU students were at risk for doing so their second year, leaving only two of the seven students on a certain path toward graduation by the time I ended the project.

Like Powell (2014), I recognize that not every student is going to graduate from college. Nor do I hold the naïve assumption that composition scholars and teachers can have immediate and dramatic impact on sexual education and access to reproductive health care, economic and health care disparities, and restrictive educational policies that perpetuate societal hierarchies. Nonetheless, we need to continue to teach writing in a way that "supports access, voice, and impact while also acknowledging the formidable constraints that convince most people there's very little they can do . . . to affect the course of national and world events" (Welch 2008, cited in Wilkey 2012, 19). As Wilkey (2012) pointed out, in engaging students, we need to know about their lives outside of schools and the issues they care about and that impact them, rather than imposing our beliefs and our values on them. In connecting student communicators with the communities they inhabit, we can turn to innovative ideas put forth by community literacy scholars like Juergensmeyer (2011, 156) who situated student researchers in action research projects in order that they see their "academic work as a tool for addressing social problems." As Turner and Hicks (2011, 75) have illustrated, our disciplinary embrace of digital forms of writing offers new possibilities to "expose the culture of power and invite individuals and communities into broader means of expression."

### Disciplinary Knowledge Construction and Societal Change

Well-funded organizations are increasingly dominating discussions surrounding the creation and dissemination of educational policy in the United States (Adler-Kassner 2008; Hall and Thomas 2012). The Lumina Foundation president, Jaime Merisotis, has been quoted as saying, "The (Lumina) agenda is increasingly the agenda for the country" (Stuart 2010). The Lumina Foundation and Achieve espouse admirable goals aimed at promoting minority achievement: "increase the proportion of Americans with high-quality college degrees, certificates or other credentials to 60% by 2025" (Lumina Foundation 2014) and "All students should graduate from high school ready for college, careers and citizenship" (Achieve 2014). However, the policies they promote are similarly narrowly focused in that they are based on the assumptions that fixing institutions will fix educational disparities and societal inequalities. And often these "fixes" mean more standardized assessment.

In response to the systematic stripping of writing teachers' agency through NCLB, NCTE offered a statement critiquing and advocating for reimagination of this law (NCTE 2006). In 2012, NCTE responded to the CCSS with a statement that focused on urging "policymakers, school leaders, and legislators to acknowledge and respect the expertise of teachers" (NCTE 2012) as they develop policies surrounding the standards. Despite consistent policy statements from our largest organization and occasional successes such as in challenging the dominant SAT narrative (Adler-Kassner 2008), composition researchers and our organizations have not played large enough roles in shaping policy development, in part because our field does not produce sufficient wide-reaching and replicable qualitative and quantitative research that convinces leaders and policy makers. For instance, the study presented in this book provides an in-depth look into the transitions of seven students between three different institutions in one city on the US-Mexico border. However, there are millions of Latina/o students making similar but different transitions between thousands of institutions all over the United States. Many studies in rhetoric and composition only tell stories of one classroom in one institution, limiting our ability to convincingly make broader conclusions about writing instruction in the United States.

In continuing to privilege localized stories over generalizable knowledge gained from broader qualitative and quantitative studies, knowledge from our discipline will continue to be left out of national and state policy discussions. Individuals and organizations with limited experience in education will continue to label institutions as failing and impose new restrictions on the way writing is taught at all levels. Like Adler-Kassner (2012b, 172), I believe that simply dismissing narratives invoking "career preparation" is unwise. Arguments based in notions of economic growth and career preparation, while anathema to many in composition studies, can be harnessed to build our credibility and enable us to be more active in larger conversations between stakeholders within and beyond our institutions.

In order to seriously implement some of the transformations suggested here, rhetoric and composition researchers need to rethink their processes of disciplinary knowledge construction and dissemination in order to gain more credibility and a stronger voice with institutional leaders and policy makers. Although the number is increasing, many rhetoric and composition graduate programs lack required courses in methodology while their counterparts in education or psychology often have multiple core courses in quantitative and qualitative research and analysis. Haswell (2005) and Johanek (2000) have called attention to composition studies' aversion to empirical research, especially quantitative work, which Haswell (2005) has referred to as a "War on scholarship."

As Goldblatt (2007, 204) has argued in a way that reveals our continual awkward relationship with empirical work—composition studies "needs to dust off its founding commitment to empirical study not with an attitude of rigid positivism but with a sense of creativity and pragmatism." While rhetoric and composition has traditionally valued narratives, restricting ourselves to narrative alone or numbers alone fails to provide a sufficient picture of phenomena we study (Johanek 2000, 88). Our discipline is not without a history of empiricism, a history that dwindled with the rise of postmodernism and its critique of a positivist tradition with a belief in a fixed reality. Emig's (1977) and Flower and Hayes's (1981) work revealed the possibilities of aligning composition research with psychological research. Although their discomfort with a positivistic research tradition was revealed in a sarcastic comment about the "Methodology Police," Connors and Lunsford (1993) conducted a large study on teacher commentary involving 3,000 papers and a few dozen trained raters. Composition studies stands to learn from research in related fields like education, applied linguistics, and L2 writing, as researchers in these fields have consistently maintained high levels of research design, as evidenced by articles in journals like the *Journal of Second Language Writing* and the *American Educational Research Journal*. We need to increasingly read and cite the work produced in these other areas and go beyond this to develop partnerships with researchers related fields, pooling our knowledge of different research methods as well as financial resources to make a united and sustained case at the state and national levels.

The field seems to be moving in the right direction with the increased push for replicable, multi-institutional research through grants provided by organizations like CCCC and CWPA. The first such CCCC Research Initiative awarded $25,000 for an empirical study documenting the types of writing students do in high school and college, although grants offered through the program on an annual basis are funded up to $10,000 (Conference on College Composition and Communication 2013). The CWPA call for grant proposals cites Haswell (2005) in requesting research that is "replicable, aggregable, and data supported" but offers a maximum of $4,000 for an individual grant (Council of Writing Program Administrators 2013). Expanding these grant programs in terms of the size and number of awards should be a top priority for national composition organizations.[3]

In collaborating with researchers from other disciplines, those in rhetoric and composition will be better situated to seek grants from other sources. Education, a discipline which has informed much of the work in this book, has a stronger history of grant-supported research. As composition researchers increasingly turn their attention to how political policies affect adolescent literacy development in high school and consequent success in college, they can collaborate with colleagues situated in education policy research centers. At the university level, many composition scholars are already collaborating with faculty in STEM disciplines like engineering to develop writing in the discipline (WID) courses. Such researchers need to strategically position themselves to be part of grant submissions emerging from these fields. For instance, the Louis Stokes Alliances for Minority Participation (LSAMP) grant "assists universities and colleges in diversifying the STEM workforce through their efforts at significantly increasing the numbers of students successfully completing high quality degree programs in science, technology, engineering and mathematics (STEM) discipline" (National Science Foundation 2013). Scholars from our disciplines can be situated as consultants or Co-PIs on grants like LSAMP to assist in developing the writing abilities of STEM undergraduates from underrepresented backgrounds, assessing the role writing plays in supporting student success.

As our discipline increasingly directs attention to writing among graduate students, we can collaborate with graduate schools and graduate programs to apply for grants that include the development of graduate level writing instruction. One such grant program well-suited for this work is the Promoting Postbaccalaureate Opportunities for Hispanic Americans (PPOHA) program through the Department of Education (ED) and provides grants of up to $2.5 million over five years. My current institution received a PPOHA grant which has been used to develop a Graduate Resource Center that funds writing tutors, dissertation boot camps, and other activities; however, rhetoric and composition faculty were absent from the writing and implementation of this grant. In contrast, at a nearby STEM-oriented institution, a rhetoric and composition faculty member was hired through PPOHA funds in part to develop a graduate writing center. With rhetoric and composition specialists being hired with funding from multi-million dollar ED grants and $50,000 grants awarded by the Gates Foundation to composition researchers at several universities to create MOOCs, change is happening and they are increasing the possibilities to expand the impact of our research. As Kay Halasek from Ohio State University has pointed out, the creation of the writing MOOC offered by this project offers new possibilities for researching the teaching and learning of writing on a large scale (Grabill and Lindquist 2013). By developing collaborative projects and seeking funding with researchers from across disciplines and across institutions, composition researchers can make a stronger case for implementing the changes recommended in these concluding comments. We need to disseminate the results of these studies not only in our academic journals and conferences but in non-traditional ways by publishing policy reports, editorials in local or national news outlets, and by reporting to state and national legislatures.

## Notes

1. I would like to add a caveat to some of the work advocating the encouragement of code switching in our classrooms. While it is important to validate students' language varieties in various ways (and currently a very popular discussion in the field), we also are doing students a disservice if we are not talking with them about the reality they will face across campus and in the workplace, a reality that continues to privilege standardized varieties of English. It is vital that any work valuing our students' linguistic diversity does not minimize this more traditional focus in our classrooms.
2. Adler-Kassner (2008) is referring to reports produced by governmental or non-governmental organizations that claim some authority over improving the education system even though they fail to appropriately consult experts in fields like rhetoric and composition.
3. In advocating for more quantitative research, I also acknowledge the value of well-designed qualitative studies. With sufficient funding, qualitative studies can be broad reaching as well. For instance, Suárez-Orozco, Suárez-Orozco, and Todorova (2008) had research assistants in dozens of states who collected case studies of around 400 immigrant students.

# EPILOGUE AND FINAL THOUGHTS

Although I have continued to stay in touch with most of the students from this study informally via Facebook or an occasional text message, I reconnected with them more formally during their second year at college. The updates provided here about each student's ongoing college journeys emphasize the point that students' pathways to and through college are always transforming, continually impacted by forces both inside and beyond institutions.

### DANIEL

Daniel's second-year story offers a perspective of the path of what life was like after stopping out of college, a path followed by two other participants that I was unable to interview. After stopping out, he began working for a well-known fast casual dining chain as a dishwasher and later a baker. In the fall of what would have been his second year at college, he was working around fifty hours a week, at minimum wage and subject to the whims of his boss, who would not give him a raise, because, in Daniel's words, he burned six cookies. Tired of excuses for not giving him a raise, Daniel quit in March. Boredom quickly set in and he and his sister, who had stopped out of school a few years previously and also recently quit her job at the same place, decided to go back to school. However, instead of BCC, they chose Western Career College, a for-profit college.

Here, Daniel entered a nine-month program focused on becoming a medical assistant, which would prepare him to take patient vitals and enter them into a system at a doctor's office or a clinic. The school explained that it would be easy to find him a job at the end, especially given the externship experience at a clinic that would take three of the five students interning there. Making the transition to a for-profit school did not seem like a big deal for Daniel. The Financial Aid office walked him through how he would pay the $13,000 tuition: $5,000 via Pell Grants and $8,000 of federal loans, which would not be a problem because he would have a good job by the time he had to pay them

DOI: 10.7330/9780874219760.c009

back. Daniel was excited that he would graduate with a degree in nine months, much faster than his cousin who was already in his fifth year at BCC. He had plans to go back to college for a higher degree someday; however, when asked if his WCC credits would transfer, he did not know, saying "I hope so" (they do not).

Overall, Daniel seemed much more successful at WCC and liked it better than BCC: "It's like anywhere else. I mean community is cheaper but community they give you a lot of classes you don't need so . . . you stay there longer." The program was divided into six-week semesters, which Daniel appreciated because they moved fast. At the time I interviewed him, he was taking medical terminology, anatomy, art of communication, a college study class, and math. In his words, "They just give it all to us right then and there."

He would write in his art of communication and college study classes, the latter of which might be loosely equated with a first-year seminar at another school. For the communication class, Daniel wrote one-page summary papers based on the book they were reading for the communication class. These were handwritten in class and turned in. Feedback appeared nonexistent: "I don't know what happened to them . . . she told us our grade and if it was good or not and if we had to do it over." In the college studies class, he wrote two papers based on a choice of fifteen themes. One of his papers was focused on "basically introducing yourself, nothing really."

In some ways, WCC was ahead of the other schools in terms of supporting student success. Daniel noted that the first semester, his classes were all very small, about six students per class. All the classes he took throughout the program formed a learning community as he took them with the same students. These friendships were valuable to Daniel and motivated him in coming to class. He had a lot more access to technology at WCC as well. Two of his classes were in computer labs and the other instructors would always use the projectors. He would use Excel to enter patient information in simulations whereas his experiences at BCC would be limited to online tutoring or just typing papers. In making recommendations to BCC for helping students like him, he suggested that they offer mini-semesters as the norm: "I'd rather do something fast and get it over with and it's just how I learn."

### BIANCA

Bianca's second year at college was more difficult than her first. Financial issues were becoming an increasing concern. She took out a credit card the summer before her second year, ran up $500 in debt, paid it when student loan money came in, but as money ran out, ran up another $400 bill. At home, her rent was raised by $50 and the Internet was shut off because of her inability to pay. In addition, Bianca had to deal with new problems her siblings were having at school. She would miss class to attend school conferences related to her younger brother's behavior problems, eventually dropping two classes as a result.

At the beginning of the second semester, she contemplated dropping out and attending a for-profit technical school. The technical school lure was constantly present as Bianca reported being called regularly by them and hearing stories of friends who pursued this route and were earning decent paychecks. Bianca was motivated by the promise of a better future for herself and her family and resisted the temptation: "I don't know—I got so depressed at the beginning of the semester. I was planning to drop or something but no [snaps finger] something popped like no!"

Since the CAMP program is aimed at a student's first year, Bianca no longer benefited from the structure provided by the program in the form of required tutoring and participation in other campus activities. She no longer spent time with students from the program but would go to the office occasionally to use a computer or get a Scantron testing sheet for an exam. She attributed the lack of CAMP as a major source of struggle, noting that she was falling behind and was not part of anything designed to keep her going.

Turning toward the positive, one of Bianca's major sources of support continued to be church and she also identified developing friendships with other students in her classes and daily trips to the gym as important. Levels of engagement with various classes positively and negatively impacted her. Part of the reason she dropped her anatomy class was because it was so boring: "[The professor would] just talk like he was talking to himself so slow." On the other hand, her favorite class of the fall was speech and her favorite of the spring was Chicano studies. The latter course was important because she was able to learn about "her history." Also, Spanish had a stronger presence in this course than others, where it was typically non-existent.

Bianca reported doing little writing her second year. The most writing she completed were speech outlines for her fall speech class. That semester she also completed a group essay and associated presentation in her criminal justice class focused on analyzing a particular law. In the spring she wrote a two-page book review and completed exam essays for her Chicano studies class. Feedback did not seem to be a big part of these assignments. For instance, she mentioned that she got a good grade on her book review but never got it back.

## YESENIA

The summer before her second year, Yesenia took her second-semester FYC course along with a speech class and did very well in both, getting an A and a B. In addition to creating a website and other multimedia projects, Yesenia wrote a research paper on pregnancy and how to avoid it. Unfortunately, this topic would soon impact her life as she found herself pregnant by a military boyfriend at the beginning of her second year at college. She had already broken up with the boyfriend by the time we talked and her mother, upset, kicked her out of the house. Yesenia's pregnancy was by far the most impactful event her second year at college. On the positive side, it made her stop drinking and smoking; on the other hand, it negatively impacted her school and career plans.

During an interview at the end of her second year fall semester, Yesenia told me, "Being pregnant, it really changed, my mind was not on school, it was on me being pregnant and all my my goals and my dreams changed." Previously set on a business degree and an MBA, Yesenia started thinking about stopping out of BU and pursuing a nine-month medical assistant program at a for-profit college. She considered this plan after seeing a friend who was making good money in such a position and after seeing advertisements on TV for the colleges. Her revised educational plan included long-term plans for a four-year degree, however: "And I mean since I can not really get a job and I don't wanna get a job with McDonald's or Whataburger or anything. I prefer doing that short career [degree] like a month a year or something and then get that degree, get a job, get paid, survive with me and my kid and go back to school."

At the end of the fall semester, Yesenia had a 2.8 GPA and said she ended up passing all but one of her classes, albeit with grades that brought her GPA lower. As her pregnancy progressed, things got more difficult, and she found that she was often too tired to make it to class. When giving a presentation for her professional writing class, she had to cut it short because the baby was kicking too much. By the time of the last interview, her spring grades were pending because she had made arrangements to delay her final exams because she was having her child at that time.

Disappointing experiences in accounting and finance classes steered her from a business major toward nursing; however, she stuck with the idea that getting a degree from BU was more valuable than taking a short program at one of the for-profit schools, something her mother agreed with. When asked about how the university could have been more supportive in response to the challenges in her life, she replied, "I don't think the university has nothing to do with it. It's just well I mean everybody goes I mean everybody has problems I guess that doesn't involve college . . . It's just family and everything . . . So I don't think they can really do anything."

Yesenia did very little writing her second year at college and felt she developed her abilities minimally in comparison to the first year. She recalled writing a few essays in her fall economics class that focused on summarizing readings, but noted they were not really essays because they were only 250 words long. She wrote a lot of memos in her spring workplace writing course, but again did not feel like this was writing in the sense that she had done the previous year as they were very short. Ultimately, none of this really mattered much in comparison to what was going on in her life: "If I wasn't pregnant everything would be so different. It would be like probably I had better grades you know stay in my I mean my career in business but being pregnant really changed everything." Nonetheless, Yesenia considered having her baby the best thing that happened to her that year.

## CAROLINA

Carolina had a relatively uneventful second year outside of school and stayed on a strong path toward college graduation. Her family life stayed consistent and although they never had much money, she felt more or less that they were financially stable. She was even able to buy a car, which made it easier to commute to school and allowed her to stay later and study with friends. Carolina consistently felt her family played a key role in her success, largely because of the way her mother valued higher education: "I don't have that many responsibilities in my house. I have time for to focus on school . . . And sometime—like other families—their parents don't care if they even go to class." Her mother wanted Carolina to be a model for her siblings and be the first in either side of her family to graduate from college.

At school, Carolina was doing all the right things socially to continue being successful. She made friends in her classes and said they would regularly study together. She joined a few extracurricular groups including the Political Science Honors Society and Campus Christian Fellowship. All these things made her even more motivated to attend classes and continue college: "And then this semester I talk to my friends and not only going to school for the class but because I'm gonna hang out with friends."

In terms of classes, Carolina found the first semester easier than the previous year but she found the spring semester harder because she began to get into her major classes. She took fifteen hours each semester, earning mostly As and Bs but worried about getting Cs in one or two classes, particularly science ones. Professors made a big difference in her level of engagement. A history of music class titled Jazz to Rock had the potential to be very interesting but ended up being insufferably boring. As a result, she stopped reading for the course and even was a bit inconsistent on attendance, unheard of in Carolina's student life. She found the best professors would engage their students with questions, rather than lecture the whole time. Although she started college as a very quiet student due to her perception of being inadequately prepared, her growing abilities gave her new confidence and led her to participate more: "I'm like more in the level and sometimes I feel like I know a little bit more than them so I guess I feel more more comfortable giving my opinions."

As with the other students, writing played a less important role in Carolina's second year, although it was still present throughout most of her courses. In the fall semester, she had analytical and exam essays in her history class and wrote a two-page group report in her lab class. She also did some writing in her speech class: speech outlines and, for a time, mini writing assignments that focused either on finding and analyzing a speech or book work. In the spring semester, she did more writing and wrote a series of lab reports (which totaled about ten pages, including a group report), an eight-page research paper in political science, a few three- to four-page psychology essays, and several essays in her Spanish class of varying lengths, increasing from one to five pages.

Despite the fact that Carolina was writing across most of her classes, the quality of her writing instruction was inconsistent. Feedback was limited to comments on her writing in Spanish class along with a few comments on formatting her lab reports. This was most notable in her speech class, where she would work on outlines, peer review them with students, and turn in a revised version, but never receive any comments from the instructor. Even worse, the mini writing assignments in speech were required as a punishment for low attendance rates (class wide, not specific to Carolina who had excellent attendance). She never got feedback or grades on them.

As mentioned above, Carolina ended up in a junior-level Spanish writing course as she was trying to fulfill her language requirement. Here, she had the unwelcome discovery that her Spanish writing was at the same level or even worse than her English, because her instruction for the past several years had been English only. Unused to Spanish academic writing, she got her ideas confused at times, found herself thinking in English, and had difficulty finding the Spanish phrasing: "Sometimes—like some words I have—I wanna put them in like English but in Spanish it doesn't make sense how I wanna phrase it." Interestingly, her most difficult writing of the year was for Spanish because she had no experience writing a five-page academic essay in her first language.

## MAURICIO

Mauricio's second year at college started off negatively but finished positively, with plans to take three courses during the summer and a full load the following fall. As with other students, most of Mauricio's challenges stemmed from his life outside of school. During the fall semester, he sometimes worked fifty-six hours a week at two different jobs in addition to taking three classes. He was also distracted by concerns about his family business, which was not doing as well due to a drop in the price of metal and having to pay drug cartels a $500 weekly "quota" (i.e., extortion money) in order to "protect" their business, a common practice in Juárez. To make matters worse, his girlfriend at the time died in a car accident with a few of her family members and Mauricio had his own car stolen and was relegated to riding the bus on the United States side of the border to get to school and his two jobs. Partially because of all the stress in his life, he started going out on the weekends, something he had not done before, which left him too tired and hung over to pay much attention to homework. Mauricio dropped two of the three classes he was taking the fall semester as his grades started slipping.

Fortunately, the spring semester was better. Mauricio's family business started improving and he started working less at his two jobs. He also strategized in choosing his five spring classes plus an additional lab, deciding to take three classes online because of the convenience and because his online research showed that one teacher in particular gave As to over 50 percent of students. Two of these classes were at BCC instead of BU, primarily because they were easier and cheaper. Mauricio was unimpressed with his online classes in general, saying that he did not learn anything and that he would not want to take any of his major-specific courses online because of this.

Although Mauricio did not write as much his second year at college as his first, he seemed to write more than the other students. He took a professional writing class both semesters, dropping it the first time. For the first-semester class, he explained that it was primarily focused on content related to the stock market and that the writing took the form of four increasingly long memos. He found these difficult because of the unfamiliarity of the content and because the professor focused on explaining the content he wanted as opposed to basic elements such as memo formatting. He commented, "It was difficult because . . . it was something new that I didn't know and I didn't have any knowledge about you know stocks it's just really complicated and wide area at least for me so that's how I see it." His second-semester professional writing class was completely online and he was expected to complete online discussion postings three times a week in addition to other projects. These projects included a resume, web portfolio, business letter, and "something persuasive." He completed a group project focused on Best Buy but he did not remember much about it except that he wrote the first part, giving context and the history of the company, and did not bother to even read the other group member contributions because one member was in charge of bringing the individual contributions together.

He also wrote in other classes. In psychology, he had several online discussion postings over the course of the semester. As with other study participants, he wrote in history: a mid-term exam essay and an analysis essay on *Incidents in the Life of a Slave Girl*. He found writing getting easier and easier, especially shorter pieces, because he was getting "used to it" and it was becoming like a "habit." In general, he did not report receiving much feedback on his writing. He could not decipher the handwritten commentary of his first professional writing professor and said he got more feedback from peer review in his second professional writing class than he did from the professor. He did feel the feedback he received in history was better than he received in both of the professional writing classes. Nonetheless, in typical Mauricio style, he placed the blame for this more on his lack of initiative in searching out feedback: "I would like to see more of it but like in order to see more of it that you have to spend more time like looking for it, asking for it, coming to the writing center you know going to the office like with professors to ask about it so that you know that requires more time so I wish I had gotten more feedback but that's because I just didn't look for it."

## FINAL THOUGHTS

After reconnecting with various students to conduct these interviews and write their second year stories here, my emotions were mixed. It was disappointing to see that writing was a relatively small part of some students' second years. When students wrote, feedback continued to be largely absent. Daniel's description of writing instruction at WCC, which appeared to have him writing at a lower level than high school, was particularly disturbing.

Looking at the students' overall success, Mauricio and Carolina were continuing their pathways toward graduation. After stopping out of college, Daniel fell into life on the low-wage circuit, getting pulled into a for-profit school that would likely leave him burdened with debt without a good job. Bianca's and Yesenia's paths changed as well. As I worked with them the first year, they were focused, excited, and energetic; ready to overcome the many obstacles standing in their way. At the end of their second year, their worlds seemed to be caving in with financial pressures and dropped classes mounting up in Bianca's life and recent childbirth with a now absent father promising to substantially disrupt Yesenia's plans.

As I write this at the end of what would be the students' third year, only Mauricio and Carolina are still in college. Yesenia has turned to a for-profit school, pursuing a medical assistant degree like Daniel did so she can have a better job. Bianca is working for a steakhouse, hoping to go back to school. Daniel, unable to find a job with his WCC degree, is a cashier at Wal-Mart. It appears that Mauricio and Carolina will stay on the fast track and graduate within four to five years. Some of the other students will certainly find their way back to school. Nonetheless, there is work to be done by university faculty and their institutions to make these paths back to school easier and to prevent some of the leaving in the first place.

One of the final interviews in this study was conducted with two figures integral to the development of first-year student success programs at BU. Towards the end of the interview, I inquired about the responsibility that educators and institutions have in working for broader societal change to promote student success. One of them explained that the view on this came down from seeing college as a right or a privilege:

> I think no matter who you talk to, you'll get obviously one of two responses, yes or no. Because it comes back to a philosophical argument of this. Is a college a right or a privlege? And I think from talking with others, you can see we believe that it's our right and that it's our responsibility to provide young and old people, whoever comes to our doors, with, you know, a college education because it will improve the quality of their life dramatically . . . we should find every way we can to help every obstacle that students have so that they can get to school and get to class and succeed.

As writing teachers and researchers, we play a small but integral part in supporting students' transitions to college. While we can begin in our classrooms, it is vital to advocate for change in broader contexts, producing and disseminating data that convinces policy makers, voters, and others that an English-only education model, underpaid and overworked writing teachers, and poorly designed standardized tests are contributing to broader societal inequalities that will continue to threaten the United States' dominance in a globalized, knowledge-based economy. The latter part of this argument may not be popular among those in rhetoric and composition, but it is one that must be harnessed in order to play a larger role beyond the writing classroom. The need for this work is urgent and vital, not only for our country but for students like Daniel, Joanne, Bianca, Yesenia, Mauricio, Carolina, and Paola and their families dreaming of a better future.

# APPENDIX A
*Student Survey and Interview Protocols*

**BEGINNING OF STUDY SURVEY**

1. Please complete the following information so I can stay in touch with you:
   Name:
   Email address:
   Phone number:

2. How often do you speak English with the following groups of people:

   | | | | | | |
   |---|---|---|---|---|---|
   | Your grandparents | Never | Rarely | Sometimes | Usually | Always |
   | Your father | Never | Rarely | Sometimes | Usually | Always |
   | Your mother | Never | Rarely | Sometimes | Usually | Always |
   | Your brothers/sisters | Never | Rarely | Sometimes | Usually | Always |
   | Your friends | Never | Rarely | Sometimes | Usually | Always |
   | Your teachers | Never | Rarely | Sometimes | Usually | Always |

3. How good is . . .

   | | | | | |
   |---|---|---|---|---|
   | Your spoken English? | Not good | Okay | Good | Very good |
   | Your written English? | Not good | Okay | Good | Very good |
   | Your spoken Spanish? | Not good | Okay | Good | Very good |
   | Your written Spanish? | Not good | Okay | Good | Very good |

4. How often is English spoken in your home?
   Never    Sometimes    Often    Always

5. How long have you lived in the United States?
   I don't live in the United States
   All my life
   Part of my life (please specify number of years) ____

6. How long have you attended school in the United States?
   All my life
   Part of my life (specify number of years) ____

7. How many years have you attended school in English? Have you attended school in another language? If so, what language and how long?

8. Where did you go to school before high school? Please describe your English classes there. Were you in mainstream English or ESL (English as a Second Language) classes? Were you ever in a bilingual program?

9. Why do you want to go to college? What would you like to major in?

10. Where do you plan to go to college? Why?

11. Have other members of your family attended college? If so, who? Did they graduate?

12. Has your schooling been interrupted in any way because you moved, got sick, or for another reason? Please explain if you feel comfortable.

13. What do you think will be the biggest challenges for you as you make the transition to college?

## BEGINNING OF STUDY INTERVIEW
### *Previous Writing Experiences/History*

What type of writing do you do every day? How does this differ from writing you do at school?

Who has been your best writing teacher?

What do you look for in a good teacher?

What class has been the most helpful to your development as a writer?

What classes or coursework haven't you liked so much?

What has been your hardest essay to write?

What has been your favorite essay to write?

Do you feel you're a better writer in English or Spanish? What language do you write better in? What language do you write more often in?

Have you had more formal training in English writing or Spanish writing?

What kind of writing have you done for standardized tests like TAKS? Have your classes focused on the writing on these tests?

Do you feel that the writing instruction you've received here and in your previous school has prepared you for college?

### *Instructional Practices*

What kind of writing do you usually do in your English classes? What do you usually write about? If you write essays, what are their typical length? What has been the longest essay you've written during high school?

What other classes do you have writing in? How is the writing different in these classes?

Does your English teacher give you feedback? If so, is it usually given orally or in writing? What kind of feedback do you usually get? Content-based or grammar-based?

**Writing Process**

When you have a writing task for school, how do you usually complete it? Does this process change with different school tasks?

How is your process different when writing an email as opposed to something for school?

Do you make outlines?

Do you revise your papers? Have you had many chances to revise during high school?

**Outside Influences**

Does it take you long to get to school? How do you get to school? Do you ever have problems getting to school?

Do you have a job? If so, what is it and how many hours a week do you work? What do you do with the money you earn at your job?

Do you play sports or participate in any after-school activities? If so, what? How many hours a week do you spend in these activities?

Do you receive any outside help with your homework tasks? Do you attend tutoring sessions? Get help from your parents? In what subjects do you normally receive help?

How many brothers and sisters do you have? Are they older or younger than you? Do they attend school? If so, where? Who do you think is the best student in your family?

## MONTHLY INTERVIEWS DURING HIGH SCHOOL AND COLLEGE
### General

How have you been since the last interview? Have you had any really positive or negative experiences at school? In your life outside of school?

What kind of writing have you done since the last time we talked? What has been your most difficult writing task? Why was it difficult? How did you deal with this difficulty?

What is currently your favorite class? Why is it your favorite?

What is your most challenging class? Why is it challenging?

### Focused on Writing Samples

How long did you spend on this piece of writing? Do you think you had enough time to complete it? If not, how would you have improved it with more time?

Do you feel your teacher gave you enough feedback on this piece of writing?

Was the feedback helpful? If so, what feedback did you find the most helpful? What did you find the least helpful?

What did you learn from writing this piece that will help you in future writing you do?

Is this a typical assignment for your class? If not, how is it different?

### Focused on General Learning Experiences and Classroom Observation

How do you like your (class I observed or other subject) class? What influences your opinion? Your like/dislike of the subject? Of the teacher?

How would you judge your abilities in that class compared to your classmates? Better? About the same? Worse?

How do you feel the teacher treats the students in the class? Respectfully? Disrespectfully? Harshly? Fairly? Unfairly?

Does your teacher treat you like other students in the class? If not, how are you treated differently?

How do you choose where to sit in the class? Do you sit with friends? Are seats assigned?

Does the teacher ever use Spanish or is the class always conducted in English?

Which of the following does your (subject) teacher do in addressing your language needs:

    Cares more about content than grammar mistakes

    Gives thoughtful feedback on your writing

    Takes time to explain things so you understand them

    Takes time to work one-on-one with you

    Asks you to revise your papers

    Any other things?

### Semester Related

What has been your favorite part about this semester? Your time at SHS?

What has been your favorite class this semester? Least favorite? Why?

How important has writing been to you this semester?

What is the most important piece of writing you've done this semester?

Do you feel the work you've done this semester has helped prepare you for college? If so, how?

How has your knowledge of academic English improved this semester? Have you learned any new words? Phrases? Improved your writing in some specific way?

How have you felt about the interruptions to class this semester? Pep rallies? Test dates? Shortened schedules? Have you found these interruptions worth it or do you feel your schooling has been negatively affected?

How has the reading of *Lord of the Flies* compared to other books you've read at SHS? Did you read more of the book or less than typical? What could we have done to teach the book better?

How did you go about developing a topic for the essay? Did you use the materials we prepared? Did you take notes while reading?

What were you most concerned about in writing this essay? How could we have helped you with that?

Have there been any changes in your life outside of school this semester that have affected your school work?

What was the most interesting writing you did while at high school? What was the most challenging?

Did you ever have opportunities to write in Spanish at high school? Would you have liked the chance to work on your Spanish writing?

### General

Do you plan to attend college next semester? If not, why did you decide not to? If so, where do you plan to go? Why do you plan to go there?

What are you most excited about in going to college? Most nervous?

How do you think college will be different from high school? Where did you get that information?

How do you think the writing at college will be different from the writing you did for high school? How did you get that idea?

How do you think studying at high school has prepared you for college? Where do you think your preparation might be lacking?

If you had the opportunity to start again, would you choose SHS? Why or why not?

What challenges have you faced in learning English academic writing?

How has your family helped you progress as a student? Do you feel supported by them?

How have other factors outside of school helped or limited your growth as a student during your high school years? As a writer?

## BEGINNING OF COLLEGE INTERVIEW

How did your summer go? Did you attend any kind of orientation or college-related activities? How were classes?

How did the college application and registration process go? Did you get the financial aid/scholarships you expected?

How has your experience at college been different than what you expected so far? How has it been similar?

Have you had any writing assignments so far? Based on first impressions, how do you think the writing demands will be different in college? How do you think the reading demands will be different?

What has been the biggest challenge you've faced in adapting to college life?

Do you find that you have more or less free time than you did in high school? How do you feel your high school work prepared you for college?

Do you work? If so, what do you do? How many hours a week do you work?

What challenges do you have that interfere with your ability to complete your college work? How do you work with these challenges? Do you have support from anyone?

What are the advantages of attending college in town? The disadvantages?

Have all/most of your friends from high school begun college? If not, why? Have you made a lot of new friends at college?

What is currently your easiest class? Which is your hardest? What do you find most interesting? Least interesting?

How is your English class different than your high school classes? How does your teacher compare to your high school teachers? How did the class I saw today compare with your normal classes?

What is your first-year seminar like?

How is the expectation for technology usage different at college?

How would you compare your abilities with the students in your classes?

Are you happy with your college decision? Would you have preferred to go elsewhere?

## END OF COLLEGE SEMESTER INTERVIEW

How have you been since the last interview? Have you had any really positive or negative experiences at school? In your life outside of school?

What kind of writing have you done since the last time we talked? What has been your most difficult writing task? Why was it difficult? How did you deal with this difficulty?

Have you been keeping up with homework?

What has been your favorite part about this semester?

What has been your favorite class this semester? Least favorite? Why?

How important has writing been to you this semester in comparison to high school? In what class are you doing the most writing?

What is the most valuable piece of writing you've done this semester?

What is the most interesting piece of writing you've done this semester?

How would you describe the difference between high school and college to seniors at SHS?

Do you feel your high school work prepared you for what you had to do this semester? If not, where was it lacking?

How has your knowledge of academic English improved this semester? Have you learned any new words? Phrases? Improved your writing in some specific way?

Have you been offered the opportunity to utilize your Spanish knowledge in any of your classes?

Have there been any changes in your life outside of school this semester that have affected your school work?

Have you started working? If so, how much do you work?

Do you plan to continue college next semester? If so, have you registered?

Is reading important in your family? If so, what kind of reading materials do you have in the house? Are they typically in English or Spanish?

## END OF FIRST YEAR OF COLLEGE INTERVIEW

How have you been since the last interview? Have you had any really positive or negative experiences at school? In your life outside of school? Have there been any major life changes?

Have you declared your major? What made you decide that major?

Have there been any changes in your life outside of school this semester that have affected your school work?

What kind of writing have you done since the last time we talked? What has been your most difficult writing task? Why was it difficult? How did you deal with this difficulty?

Have you been keeping up with homework?

What has been your favorite part about this semester?

What has been your favorite class this semester? Least favorite? Why?

How important has writing been to you this year in comparison to high school? In what class have you done the most writing?

How important has reading been to you this year in comparison to high school? In what class have you done the most reading?

How important has technology usage been to you this year in comparison to high school? In what class has technology been the most important?

What is the most important piece of writing you've done this semester? Year?

What is the most interesting piece of writing you've done this semester? Year?

How has your knowledge of academic English improved this year? Have you learned any new words? Phrases? Improved your writing in some specific way?

Have you been offered the opportunity to utilize your Spanish knowledge in any of your classes?

Have you started working? If so, how much do you work?

What have been your biggest challenges this year? Did they interfere with school, such as gotten you a bad grade on a paper or made you miss classes?

When confronting a major challenge, have you talked with anyone at school about it such as teachers or staff? Have they been understanding or made any accommodations?

What has been your biggest success this year?

How would you describe the difference between high school and college to seniors at SHS?

What advice would you give to seniors at SHS to avoid or overcome any difficulties you have faced?

Do you feel your high school work prepared you for what you had to do this year? If not, where was it lacking?

Do you feel the high school focus on TAKS helped or hurt your college success? Explain.

Do you plan to continue college in the summer or next year? If so, have you registered? How did the registration process go?

Do you have any concerns as you continue college? Is there anything that could stand in the way of you graduating?

What have been your most important sources of support this year? What do you think will be your most important source of support as you continue?

## END OF FIRST-YEAR INTERVIEW FOR STUDENTS WHO DROPPED

- How have you been since the last interview? Have you had any really positive or negative experiences at school? In your life outside of school? Have there been any major life changes?
- What made you decide to drop your classes this semester? How did you make the decision? Who did you talk with about it?
- What was your biggest challenge in continuing college?
- What do you think the school or teachers could have done differently to help support your success?
- What could you have done differently to be successful?
- Did you let any teacher know about your difficulty or did any teacher reach out to you?
- What classes did you do the best in? Why do you think you did well in those classes and not as well in others? Was it a question of the teacher? The subject matter?
- Had you been keeping up with homework in the dropped classes?
- Do you feel your high school work prepared you for what you had to do this year? If not, where was it lacking?
- Do you feel the high school focus on TAKS helped or hurt your college success? Explain.
- How would you describe the difference between high school and college to seniors at SHS?
- What advice would you give to seniors at SHS to avoid or overcome the difficulties you have faced?
- What is the most difficult piece of writing you've done at college?
- What is the most interesting piece of writing you've done at college?
- Have you done any writing this semester? What has been your most difficult writing task? Why was it difficult? How did you deal with this difficulty?
- What has been your favorite part about college? Least favorite?
- What was your favorite class this year? Least favorite? Why?
- Have you started working? If so, how much do you work?
- What are your future educational plans?

# APPENDIX B
*Teacher and Administrator Interview Protocols*

## HIGH SCHOOL TEACHER INTERVIEWS
General

> What kind of writing assignments do you typically give your students? Why do you choose these types of assignments?
>
> What do you think are the strong points about the writing practice and instruction you provide your students?
>
> What kind of feedback do you give on students' writing? Is it usually grammar-based or content-based? Do you think students read your comments?
>
> How do you use or incorporate technology in your teaching? Do you have your students use computer technology in class? What for? What other ways is computer technology used at SHS?
>
> Do you feel that you have enough access to technology at SHS? Have you been provided with enough support and training to use this technology effectively?
>
> What limits your ability to provide students with the opportunities to practice and improve their writing?
>
> How has the focus on testing changed over the years you've been here? Has it increased? What has the increased focus on testing done for your instruction?
>
> Do you feel that students at high school are getting the writing instruction they need to be prepared for college? If not, why not?
>
> How long have you been at SHS? How has the nature of writing instruction changed over that time?
>
> How do students usually sit in your classes? Do you assign seats? If not, do students group in certain ways? Along language ability, place of birth, class or other lines?
>
> What kind of language identity labels (ESL, ELL, LEP) are in use at SHS? How do you use these labels? How does the school use them? Are you careful in how you use them?

*Student-Specific Questions*
> How does S's writing and speaking ability compare to other students in your classes? How would you describe S's language abilities?

Does S need assistance mastering spoken and written academic English? If so, do you feel qualified in providing help? How have you helped S?

How would you describe S as a student?

How do you think S will do in college? Do you think that he/she will struggle in a certain area? Where do you think he/she will do well?

## COLLEGE INSTRUCTOR INTERVIEWS
### General

Briefly describe your education background and your teaching experience.

What kind of writing assignments do you typically give your students? Why do you choose these types of assignments?

What do you think are the strong points about the writing practice and instruction you provide your students?

What kind of feedback do you give on students' writing? Is it usually grammar-based or content-based? Do you think students read your comments?

What kind of activities do you typically include in your classes?

How do you use or incorporate technology in your teaching? Do you have your students use computer technology in class? What for? What other ways is computer technology used at BCC/BU?

Do you feel that you have enough access to technology at BCC/BU? Have you been provided with enough support and training to use this technology effectively?

What limits your ability to provide students with the opportunities to practice and improve their writing?

Do you feel that students in high school are getting the writing instruction they need to be prepared for college? If not, why not?

How do students usually sit in your classes? Do you assign seats? If not, do students group in certain ways? Along language ability, place of birth, class or other lines?

Do you feel qualified to work with the ESL students in your classes? If so, why? If not, how could you feel more qualified? What kind of support do you provide for them?

Do you know Spanish? If not, how could it help you teach your students better?


### Student-Specific Questions

How does S's writing and speaking ability compare to other students in your classes? How would you describe S's language abilities?

Does S need assistance mastering spoken and written academic English? If so, do you feel qualified in providing help? How have you helped S?

Appendix B: Teacher and Administrator Interview Protocols

How would you describe S as a student?

How do you think S will do as he/she continues in college? Do you think that he/she will struggle in a certain area? Where do you think he/she will do well?

## CAMP DIRECTOR INTERVIEW

How long have you been with the CAMP program and how did you get involved?

How do students find out about the program, and what factors do you consider in their applications? What is the acceptance rate?

Why do you have the intensive summer semester? What orientation activities do you have during the summer?

How much is CAMP involved in scheduling students' classes the first year? Do you complete the registration process for them? Why?

What is your rationale for placing students in the same class? What happened with art history?

What do you do to get students involved in University community? Lip syncing, dinner theatre, etc.? Why do you find these events important?

How do peer leaders work? How are they recruited?

How does the CAMP community work? Are students supportive of each other?

What kind of problems have you had with students?

How would you compare Bianca to your other CAMP participants?

Does she have more struggles than the others? How has she been about participating in tutoring and other events?

What percentage of students go on to graduate?

What kind of tutoring requirements do students have? Do you encourage them to use other campus services as well?

What kind of support extends beyond first year for students?

I noticed that CAMP is a year by year grant. Is the application process competitive? Are you worried about the current political climate in Washington?

## HISTORY PROFESSOR INTERVIEWS

Briefly describe your education background and your teaching experience.

Why does writing play such an important role in the history curriculum at BU? Did the department develop this initiative on its own or was there collaboration with other faculty, from English for instance?

What kind of writing assignments do you typically give your students? Why do you choose these types of assignments?

What do you think are the strong points about the writing practice and instruction you provide your students?

What kind of feedback do you or TAs give on students' writing? Is it usually grammar-based or content-based? Do you think students read the comments?

Do your students write as much as you'd like them to? If not, what limits your ability to provide students with the opportunities to practice and improve their writing?

Do you feel that students in high school are getting the writing instruction they need to be prepared for college? If not, why not?

Do you feel qualified to work with the L2 students in your classes? If so, why? If not, how could you feel more qualified? What kind of support do you or TAs provide for them?

**UNIVERSITY COLLEGE ADMINISTRATORS INTERVIEW**

Please describe the role(s) you have played in supporting first-year student success at BU.

Why have you focused so much attention on the first-year experience?

How has the creation of the University College supported student success at BU, especially among low-income and first generation college students?

My students have experienced much diversity in their first-year seminars. While one reported it being one of her hardest classes, having her reading history disciplinary articles, another reported it as easy and largely a waste of time, only reading a short story every other week. How do you control the design of the courses and monitor the rigor with which they are taught? Are you generally satisfied with the courses?

How would you explain the difference between the first-year seminars offered at BU and the ones offered at BCC?

In your recent book, you describe collaboration between BU, BCC, and local ISDs. Is this collaboration still active? How has it fostered more successful transitions between the different institutions?

In that discussion, you also mentioned the Accuplacer and the different interventions that have been done to bump up student placements. How do you value the Accuplacer as a placement device? Do you think that it is by and large accurate?

In my research, I have found that various programs, ranging from the CAMP program to community organizations like La Fe, have been helpful in supporting student success. What programs has the University College started to support success among students besides the ones we've discussed?

In regard to programs like the aforementioned ones, how do you feel about the current political climate in Washington and Austin affecting these programs and what does it mean for students?

I have learned that many issues seemingly beyond the university's control (pregnancy, family responsibilities, financial difficulties, immigration status) have affected students success the first year of college. Do you think that universities, colleges, and individual instructors have any role in addressing these issues, and if so what role do they play?

# REFERENCES

Abedi, Jamal. 2004. "The No Child Left behind Act and English Language Learners: Assessment and Accountability Issues." *Educational Researcher* 33 (1): 4–14. http://dx.doi.org/10.3102/0013189X033001004.

Abedi, Jamal, Carolyn Huie Hofstetter, and Carol Lord. 2004. "Assessment Accommodations for English Language Learners: Implications for Policy-Based Empirical Research." *Review of Educational Research* 74 (1): 1–28. http://dx.doi.org/10.3102/00346543074001001.

Achieve. 2014. http://www.achieve.org.

Addison, Joanne, and Sharon James McGee. 2010. "Writing in High School/Writing in College." *College Composition and Communication* 62: 147–79.

Adelman, Clifford. 2006. *The Toolbox Revisited: Paths to Degree Completion From High School Through College*. Washington, DC: US Department of Education.

Adler-Kassner, Linda. 2008. *The Activist WPA*. Logan: Utah State University Press.

Adler-Kassner, Linda. 2012a. "The Companies We Seek *or* the Companies We Would Like to Try to Keep: Strategies and Tactics in Challenging Times." *WPA: Writing Program Administration* 36 (1): 119–40.

Adler-Kassner, Linda. 2012b. "Agency, Identities, and Actions: Stories and the Writing Classroom." In *Texts of Consequence*, ed. Christopher Wilkey and Nicholas Mauricello, 157–75. New York: Hampton Press.

Allison, Harriett. 2009. "High School Academic Literacy Instruction and the Transition to College Writing." In *Generation 1.5 in College Composition: Teaching Academic Writing to U.S. Educated Learners of ESL*, ed. Mark Roberge, Meryl Siegal, and Linda Harklau, 75–90. New York: Routledge.

Ambrosio, John. 2004. "No Child Left Behind: The Case of Roosevelt High School." *Phi Delta Kappan* 85 (9): 709–12.

Antrop-González, René, William Vélez, and Tomás Garrett. 2008. "Examining Familial-Based Academic Success Factors in Urban High School Students: The Case of Puerto Rican Female High Achievers." *Marriage & Family Review* 43 (1/2): 140–63. http://dx.doi.org/10.1080/01494920802013003.

Apodaca, Ed. 2008. "From Minority to Majority: New Education Strategies." In *Latino Change Agents in Higher Education: Shaping a System that Works for All*, ed. Leonard A. Valverde, 59–76. San Francisco: Jossey-Bass.

Arispe y Acevedo, Baltazar. 2008. "The Stakes Keep Going Up: Sustaining Latino Communities." In *Latino Change Agents in Higher Education: Shaping a System that Works for All*, ed. Leonard A. Valverde, 125–46. San Francisco: Jossey-Bass.

Arum, Richard, and Josipa Roksa. 2011. *Academically Adrift: Limited Learning on College Campuses*. Chicago: University of Chicago Press.

Assaf, Lori. 2006. "One Reading Specialist's Response to High-Stakes Testing Pressures." *Reading Teacher* 60 (2): 158–67. http://dx.doi.org/10.1598/RT.60.2.6.

Astin, Alexander W. 1997. *What Matters in College? Four Critical Years Revisited*. San Francisco: Jossey-Bass.

Baker, Tracey, and Peggy Jolly. 1999. "The 'Hard Evidence': Documenting the Effectiveness of a Basic Writing Program." *Journal of Basic Writing* 18 (1): 27–39.

DOI: 10.7330/9780874219760.c012

Ballinger, Caylor. 2011. "El Paso's Teen Pregnancy Rates Drop, but Still High." *The El Paso Times*, October 8. http://www.elpasotimes.com/ci_19067332

Bamber, John. 2008. "Maximizing Potential in Higher Education: a Curriculum Response to Diversity." In *Improving Student Retention in Higher Education: The Role of Teaching and Learning*, ed. Glenda Crosling, Liz Thomas, and Margaret Heagney, 57–66. London: Routledge.

Barnhouse, Sandie McGill, and Sherylle Petty Smith. 2006. "The Evolution of a Learning Community." *Teaching English in the Two-Year College* 34 (2): 185–193.

Beaufort, Anne. 2007. *College Writing and Beyond: A New Framework for University Writing Instruction*. Logan: Utah State University Press.

Beck, Sarah W., and Jill V. Jeffery. 2007. "Genres of High-stakes Writing Assessments and the Construct of Writing Competence." *Assessing Writing* 12 (1): 60–79. http://dx.doi.org/10.1016/j.asw.2007.05.001.

Blanton, Linda L. 2005. "Student, Interrupted: A Tale of Two Would-Be Writers." *Journal of Second Language Writing* 14 (2): 105–21. http://dx.doi.org/10.1016/j.jslw.2005.04.001.

Bleich, David. 1993. "Ethnography and the Study of Literacy: Prospects for Socially Generous Research." In *Into the Field: Sites of Composition Studies*, ed. Anne Ruggles Gere, 176–92. New York: The Modern Language Association of America.

Blunt, Richard. 2008. "Turning Apartheid Around." In *Improving Student Retention in Higher Education: The Role of Teaching and Learning*, ed. Glenda Crosling, Liz Thomas, and Margaret Heagney, 29–37. London: Routledge.

Booher-Jennings, Jennifer. 2005. "Below the Bubble: 'Educational Triage' and the Texas Accountability System." *American Educational Research Journal* 42 (2): 231–68. http://dx.doi.org/10.3102/00028312042002231.

Boote, Jeanne. 1998. "Learning to Learn in Vocational Education and Training: Are Students and Teachers Ready for It?" *Australian and New Zealand Journal of Vocational Education Research* 6 (2): 59–86.

Bourdieu, Pierre. 1977. *Outline of a Theory of Practice*. Cambridge: Cambridge University Press. http://dx.doi.org/10.1017/CBO9780511812507.

Bourdieu, Pierre, Jean Claude Passeron, and Monique de Saint Martin, eds. 1996. *Academic Discourse: Linguistic Misunderstanding and Professorial Power*. Stanford: Stanford University Press.

Bourdieu, Pierre, and Jean-Claude Passeron. 1977. *Reproduction in Education, Society and Culture*. London: Sage Publications.

Bourdieu, Pierre, and Loïc J. D. Wacquant. 1992. *An Invitation to a Reflexive Sociology*. Chicago: University of Chicago Press.

Brueggermann, Brenda J. 1996. "Still-Life: Representations and Silences in the Participant-Observer Role." In *Ethics and Representation in Qualitative Studies of Literacy*, ed. Peter Mortensen and Gesa E. Kirsch, 17–39. Urbana: NCTE.

Bureau of Labor Statistics. 2013. "Earnings and Unemployment Rates By Educational Achievement." Accessed December 3. http://www.bls.gov/emp/ep_chart_001.htm.

Burris, Carol. 2013. "Principal: 'I Was Naïve about Common Core.'" *The Washington Post*, March 4. http://www.washingtonpost.com/blogs/answer-sheet/wp/2013/03/04/principal-i-was-naive-about-common-core.

Cabrera, Alberto F., Amaury Nora, and Maria B. Castaneda. 1993. "College Persistence: Structural Equations Modeling Test of an Integrated Model of Student Retention." *Journal of Higher Education* 64 (2): 123–39. http://dx.doi.org/10.2307/2960026.

Cabrera, Alberto F., Jacob O. Stampen, and W. Lee Hansen. 1990. "Exploring the Effects of Ability to Pay on Persistence in College." *Review of Higher Education* 13 (3): 303–36.

Callahan, Rebecca M., and Dara R. Shifrer. 2012. "High School ESL Placement: Practice, Policy, and Effects on Achievement." In *Linguistic Minority Students Go to College: Preparation, Access, and Persistence*, ed. Yasko Kanno and Linda Harklau, 19–37. New York: Routledge.

Canagarajah, A. Suresh. 2006. "Toward a Writing Pedagogy of Shuttling Between Languages: Learning from Multilingual Writers." *College English* 68 (6): 589–604. http://dx.doi.org/10.2307/25472177.
Cargill, Kima, and Beth Kalikoff. 2007. "Linked Courses at the Twenty-First Century Metropolitan University." *Teaching English in the Two-Year College* 35 (2): 181–90.
Carnevale, Anthony P., Ban Cheah, and Jeff Strohl. 2012. *Hard Times, College Majors, Unemployment and Earnings: Not All College Degrees Are Created Equal.* Washington, DC: Georgetown University Center on Education and the Workforce; http://cew.georgetown.edu/unemployment.
Causey-Bush, Tonia. 2005. "Keep Your Eye on Texas and California: A Look at Testing, School Reform, No Child Left Behind, and Implications for Students of Color." *Journal of Negro Education* 74 (4): 332–43.
Centers for Disease Control and Prevention. 2011. "Teen Birth Rates Declined Again in 2009." Accessed December 3, 2013. http://www.cdc.gov/Features/dsTeenPregnancy/
Christian, Donna. 1996. "Two-way Immersion Education: Students Learning Through Two Languages." *Modern Language Journal* 80 (1): 66–76. http://dx.doi.org/10.1111/j.1540-4781.1996.tb01139.x.
Chronicle of Higher Education. 2013. "College Completion." Accessed November 15, 2013. http://collegecompletion.chronicle.com.
Clydesdale, Tim. 2007. *The First Year Out: Understanding American Teens After High School.* Chicago: University of Chicago Press.
Cohen, Arthur M., and Florence B. Brawer. 2008. *The American Community College.* San Francisco: Jossey-Bass.
Common Core State Standards Initiative. 2010. "The Standards." Accessed December 3, 2013. http://www.corestandards.org/the-standards.
Conference on College Composition and Communication. 2013. "CCCC Research Initiative." Accessed December 3. http://www.ncte.org/cccc/awards/researchinitiative.
Glenn, Cheryl, and Melissa A. Goldthwaite. 2013. *The St. Martin's Guide to Teaching Writing.* New York: St. Martin's Press.
Connors, Rogers J., and Andrea A. Lunsford. 1993. "Teachers' Rhetorical Comments on Student Papers." *College Composition and Communication* 44 (2): 200–33. http://dx.doi.org/10.2307/358839.
Cook, Devan. 1998. "Secrets and Ethics in Ethnographic Writing Research." In *Foregrounding Ethical Awareness in Composition and English Studies,* ed. Sheryl I. Fontaine and Susan M. Hunter, 105–20. Portsmouth: Boynton/Cook.
Cook, Vivian. 1999. "Going beyond the Native Speaker in Language Teaching." *TESOL Quarterly* 33 (2): 185–209. http://dx.doi.org/10.2307/3587717.
Costino, Kimberly A., and Sunny Hyon. 2007. "'A Class for Students Like Me': Reconsidering Relationships Among Identity Labels, Residency Status, and Students' Preferences for Mainstream or Multilingual Composition." *Journal of Second Language Writing* 16 (2): 63–81. http://dx.doi.org/10.1016/j.jslw.2007.04.001.
Council of Writing Program Administrators. 2008. "WPA Outcomes Statement for First-Year Composition." http://wpacouncil.org/positions/outcomes.html.
Council of Writing Program Administrators. 2013. "Research Grants Call for Proposals." http://wpacouncil.org/grants/index.html.
Cummins, Jim. 1981. "Age on Arrival and Immigrant Second Language Learning in Canada: A Reassessment." *Applied Linguistics* 2 (2): 132–49. http://dx.doi.org/10.1093/applin/2.2.132.
Cummins, Jim. 2000. *Bilingual Children in the Crossfire: Language, Power, and Pedagogy.* Bristol: Multilingual Matters.
DeAngelo, Linda, Ray Franke, Sylvia Hurtado, John H. Pryor, and Serge Tran. 2011. *Completing College: Assessing graduation Rates at Four-Year Institutions.* Los Angeles, CA: Higher

Education Research Institute, UCLA; http://heri.ucla.edu/DARCU/CompletingCollege2011.pdf.
DECA. 2012. "About Us." Accessed December 3, 2013. http://www.deca.org/about/.
Dennen, Vanessa P., A. Aubteen Darabi, and Linda J. Smith. 2007. "Instructor–Learner Interaction in Online Courses: The Relative Perceived Importance of Particular Instructor Actions on Performance and Satisfaction." *Distance Education* 28 (1): 65–79. http://dx.doi.org/10.1080/01587910701305319.
Department of Education. 2006. *A Test of Leadership: Charting the Future of U.S. Higher Education.* Washington, DC: US Department of Education.
Department of Education. 2014. "Migrant Education." College Assistance Migrant Program. http://www2.ed.gov/programs/camp/index.html.
Downs, Douglas, and Elizabeth Wardle. 2007. "Teaching about Writing, Righting Misconceptions: (Re)Envisioning 'First-Year Composition' as 'Introduction to Writing Studies.'" *College Composition and Communication* 58 (4): 552–84.
Elbow, Peter. 1968. "A Method for Teaching Writing." *College English* 30 (2): 115–25. http://dx.doi.org/10.2307/374447.
Emig, Janet. 1977. "Writing as a Mode of Learning." *College Composition and Communication* 28 (2): 122–8. http://dx.doi.org/10.2307/356095.
Enright, Kerry Anne, and Betsy Gilliland. 2011. "Multilingual Writing in an Age of Accountability: From Policy to Practice in US High School Classrooms." *Journal of Second Language Writing* 20 (3): 182–95. http://dx.doi.org/10.1016/j.jslw.2011.05.006.
Evans, Terry. 2000. "Flexible Delivery and Flexible Learning: Developing Flexible Learners?" In *Flexible Learning, Human Resource and Organisational Development*, ed. Victor Jakupec and John Garrick, 211–24. London: Routledge.
Evenbeck, Scott E., Maggy Smith, and Dorothy Ward. 2010. "The University College: A Context for Student Success and Institutional Change." In *Organizing for Student Success: the University College Model*, ed. Scott Evenbeck, Barbara Jackson, Maggy Smith, and Dorothy Ward, 157–62. Columbia: National Resource Center.
Faber, Brenton. 2002. *Community Action and Organizational Change*. Carbondale: Southern Illinois University Press.
Ferris, Dana R. 2011. *Treatment of Error in Second Language Student Writing*. Ann Arbor: University of Michigan Press.
Flower, Linda, and John R. Hayes. 1981. "A Cognitive Process Theory of Writing." *College Composition and Communication* 32 (4): 365–87. http://dx.doi.org/10.2307/356600.
Frazier, Dan. 2010. "First Steps Beyond the First Year: Coaching Transfer After FYC." *WPA: Writing Program Administration* 3 (3): 34–57.
Friedman, Thomas L. 2012. "Come the Revolution." *The New York Times*, May 15. http://www.nytimes.com/2012/05/16/opinion/friedman-come-the-revolution.html.
Friedman, Thomas L. 2013. "Revolution Hits the Universities." *The New York Times*, January 26. http://www.nytimes.com/2013/01/27/opinion/sunday/friedman-revolution-hits-the-universities.html?_r=0.
Fry, Richard. 2011. *Hispanic College Enrollment Spikes, Narrowing Gaps with Other Groups*. Washington, DC: Pew Hispanic Center; http://www.pewhispanic.org/files/2011/08/146.pdf.
Fry, Richard, and Mark Hugo Lopez. 2012. *Hispanic Student Enrollments Reach New Highs in 2011*. Washington, DC: Pew Hispanic Organization; http://www.pewhispanic.org/2012/08/20/hispanic-student-enrollments-reach-new-highs-in-2011/.
Galvan, Astrid. 2013. "UNM Tuition Hike is Anyone's Guess." *Albuquerque Journal*, April 9. http://www.abqjournal.com/186892/blogs/unm-tuition-hike-is-anyones-guess.html.
Gates Foundation. 2012. "Massive Open Online Courses (MOOCs). Accessed November 20, 2012. http://docs.gatesfoundation.org/postsecondaryeducation/Pages/massive-open-online-courses.aspx.

Gebhard, Meg, Jan Demers, and Zoe Castillo-Rosenthal. 2008. "Teachers as Critical Text Analysts: L2 Literacies and Teachers' Work in the Context of High-Stakes School Reform." *Journal of Second Language Writing* 17 (4): 274–91. http://dx.doi.org/10.1016/j.jslw.2008.05.001.

Gerald, Danette, and Kati Haycock. 2006. *Engines of Inequality: Diminishing Equity in the Nation's Premier Public Universities.* Washington, DC: Education Trust.

Gilyard, Keith. 2000. "Literacy, Identity, Imagination, Flight." *College Composition and Communication* 52 (2): 260–72. http://dx.doi.org/10.2307/358496.

Gilyard, Keith, and Elaine Richardson. 2001. "'Students' Right to Possibility: Basic Writing and African American Rhetoric." In *Insurrections: Approaches to Resistance in Composition Studies*, ed. Andrea Greenbaum, 37–51. Albany: SUNY Press.

Glau, Gregory R. 2007. "Stretch at Ten: A Progress Report on Arizona State University's Stretch Program." *Journal of Basic Writing* 26 (2): 30–48.

Goldblatt, Eli. 2007. *Because We Live Here: Sponsoring Literacy Beyond the College Curriculum.* Cresskill: Hampton Press.

Goldblatt, Eli, Manuel Portillo, and Mark Lyons. 2008. "Story to Action: A Conversation about Literacy and Organizing." *Community Literacy Journal* 2 (2): 45–66.

Goldstein, Dana. 2012. "The Schoolmaster." *The Atlantic.* http://www.theatlantic.com/magazine/archive/2012/10/the-schoolmaster/309091/.

Grabill, Jeff T., and Julie Lindquist. 2013. "Webinar Series: Teaching Writing at Scale and Online." Accessed December 3. http://wrac.msu.edu/writingmooc/.

Grabill, Jeffrey T. 2001. *Community Literacy Programs and the Politics of Change.* Albany, NY: SUNY Press.

Hall, Cassie, and Scott L. Thomas. 2012. "'Advocacy Philanthropy' and the Public Policy Agenda: The Role of Modern Foundations in American Higher Education." Paper presented at the American Educational Research Association, Vancouver, BC, April 2012.

Hall, Stuart. 1993. "Culture, Community, Nation." *Cultural Studies* 7 (3): 349–63. http://dx.doi.org/10.1080/09502389300490251.

Hall, Stuart. 1998. *It Was a Worthwhile Slog! Scottish Access Students in Higher Education.* Edinburgh: Spotlight 68, Scottish Council for Research in Education.

Hall Kells, Michelle. 1999. "Leveling the linguistic playing field in first-year composition." In *Attending to the Margins: Writing, Researching, and Teaching on the Front Lines*, ed. M. Hall Kells and V. Balester, 131–149. Portsmouth, NH: Boynton/Cook.

Harklau, Linda. 2000. "From the 'Good Kids' to the 'Worst': Representations of English Language Learners across Educational Settings." *TESOL Quarterly* 34 (1): 35–67. http://dx.doi.org/10.2307/3588096.

Harklau, Linda. 2011. "Commentary: Adolescent L2 Writing Research as an Emerging Field." *Journal of Second Language Writing* 20 (3): 227–30. http://dx.doi.org/10.1016/j.jslw.2011.05.003.

Haswell, Richard H. 2005. "NCTE/CCCC's Recent War on Scholarship." *Written Communication* 22 (2): 198–223. http://dx.doi.org/10.1177/0741088305275367.

Heath, Shirley B. 1983. *Ways with Words: Language, Life and Work in Communities and Classrooms.* Cambridge: Cambridge University Press.

Hemphill, F. Cadelle, and Alan Vanneman. 2011. "Achievement Gaps: How Hispanic and White Students in Public Schools Perform in Mathematics and Reading on the National Assessment of Educational Progress (NCES 2011-459)." Washington, DC: National Center for Education Statistics, Institute of Education Sciences, US Department of Education.

Horner, Bruce, Samantha NeCamp, and Christiane Donahue. 2011. "Toward a Multilingual Composition Scholarship: From English Only to a Translingual Norm." *College Composition and Communication* 63 (2): 269–300.

Horner, Bruce, and John Trimbur. 2002. "English Only and US College Composition." *College Composition and Communication* 53 (4): 594–630. http://dx.doi.org/10.2307/1512118.

Hossler, Don, Jack Schmit, and Nick Vesper. 1999. *Going to College. How Social, Economic, and Educational Factors Influence the Decisions Students Make.* Baltimore: Johns Hopkins University Press.

Hrabowski, Freeman. 2005. "Fostering First-Year Success of Underrepresented Minorities." In *Challenging and Supporting the First-Year Student: A Handbook for Improving the First Year of College*, ed. M. Lee Upcraft, John N. Gardner, and Betsy O. Barefoot, 125–40. San Francisco: Jossey-Bass.

Ingle, Henry T., and Yolanda R. Ingle. 2008. "Pathways to a Better Future: Reconfiguring the Educational Context for Change." In *Latino Change Agents in Higher Education*, ed. Leonard A. Valverde, 23–38. San Francisco: Jossey-Bass.

Ishler, Jennifer L. Crissman. 2005. "Today's First-Year Students." In *Challenging and Supporting the First-Year Student: A Handbook for Improving the First Year of College*, ed. M. Lee Upcraft, John N. Gardner, and Betsy O. Barefoot, 15–26. San Francisco: Jossey-Bass.

Ishler, Jennifer L., and M. Lee Upcraft. 2005. "The Keys to First-Year Student Persistence." In *Challenging and Supporting the First-Year Student: A Handbook for Improving the First Year of College*, ed. M. Lee Upcraft, John N. Gardner, and Betsy O. Barefoot, 27–46. San Francisco: Jossey-Bass.

Jeffery, Jill V., and Jody N. Polleck. 2010. "Reciprocity through Co-Instructed Site-Based Courses: Perceived Benefit and Challenge Overlap in an Urban School-University Partnership." *Teacher Education Quarterly* (Summer): 81–99.

Jenkins, Paul Davis, Cecilia Speroni, Clive Belfield, Shanna Jaggars, and Nicole Diane Edgecombe. 2010. "A Model for Accelerating Academic Success of Community College Remedial English Students: is the Accelerated Learning Program (ALP) Effective and Affordable?" *CCRC Working Paper 21.*

Jeynes, William H. 2002. "A Meta-Analysis of the Effects of Attending Religious Schools and Religiosity on Black and Hispanic Academic Achievement." *Education and Urban Society* 35 (1): 27–49. http://dx.doi.org/10.1177/001312402237213.

Jiménez, Robert T. 2003. "Literacy and Latino Students in the United States: Some Considerations, Questions, and New Directions." *Reading Research Quarterly* 38 (1): 122–8.

Johanek, Cindy. 2000. *Composing Research*. Logan: Utah State University Press.

Johnson, Kristine. 2013. "Beyond Standards: Disciplinary and National Perspectives on Habits of Mind." *College Composition and Communication* 64 (3): 517–41.

Juergensmeyer, Erik. 2011. "Sharing Control: Developing Research Literacy through Community-Based Action Research." *Community Literacy Journal* Spring 2011: 153–167.

Julian, Tiffany. 2012. "Work-Life Earnings by Field of Degree and Occupation for People With a Bachelor's Degree: 2011." *US Census Bureau.* http://www.census.gov/prod/2012pubs/acsbr11-04.pdf.

Kanno, Yasko, and Linda Harklau, eds. 2012. *Linguistic Minority Students Go to College: Preparation, Access, and Persistence.* New York: Routledge.

Kanno, Yasko, and Manka M. Varghese. 2010. "Immigrant and Refugee ESL Students' Challenges to Accessing Four-Year College Education: From Language Policy to Educational Policy." *Journal of Language, Identity, and Education* 9 (5): 310–28. http://dx.doi.org/10.1080/15348458.2010.517693.

Kells, Michelle. 2012. "Out of WAC: Democratizing Higher Education and Questions of Scarcity and Social Justice." In *Texts of Consequence*, ed. Christopher Wilkey and Nicholas Mauricello, 157–75. New York: Hampton Press.

Kirklighter, Cristina, Diana Cárdenas, and Susan Wolff Murphy, eds. 2007. *Teaching Writing with Latino/a Students: Lessons Learned at Hispanic-Serving Institutions.* Albany: SUNY Press.

Kirst, Michael, and Andrea Venezia. 2001. "Bridging the Great Divide between Secondary Schools and Postsecondary Education." *Phi Delta Kappan* 83 (1): 92–7.

Klausman, Jeffrey. 2010. "Not Just a Matter of Fairness: Adjunct Faculty and Writing Programs in Two-Year Colleges." *Teaching English in the Two-Year College* 37 (4): 363–71.

Kuh, George. 2005. "Student Engagement in the First Year of College." In *Challenging and Supporting the First-Year Student: A Handbook for Improving the First Year of College*, ed. M. Lee Upcraft, John N. Gardner, and Betsy O. Barefoot, 86–107. San Francisco: Jossey-Bass.

Kurlaender, Michal. 2006. "Choosing Community College: Factors Affecting Latino College Choice." In *Latino Educational Opportunity: New Directions for Community Colleges, no. 133*, ed. Catherine L. Horn, Stella M. Flores, and Gary Orfield, 7–16. San Francisco: Jossey-Bass. http://dx.doi.org/10.1002/cc.223.

KVIA. 2013. "El Paso Ranked No. 1 Safest City in 2013." *KVIA*, July 15. http://www.kvia.com/news/el-paso-ranked-no-1-safest-city-in-2013/-/391068/20983974/-/8gt5b9z/-/index.html.

Lee, Jaekyung, and Kenneth K. Wong. 2004. "The Impact of Accountability on Racial and Socioeconomic Equity: Considering Both School Resources and Achievement Outcomes." *American Educational Research Journal* 41 (4): 797–832. http://dx.doi.org/10.3102/00028312041004797.

Leki, Ilona. 2007. *Undergraduates in a Second Language*. New York: Lawrence Erlbaum Associates.

Lewison, Mitzi, and Sue Holliday. 1997. "Control, Trust, and Rethinking Traditional Roles: Critical Elements in Creating a Mutually Beneficial University-School Partnership." *Teacher Education Quarterly* 24 (1): 105–26.

Llagas, Charmaine, and Thomas D. Snyder. 2003. *Status and Trends in the Education of Hispanics*. Washington, DC: National Center for Education Statistics, US Department of Education. http://dx.doi.org/10.1037/e492162006-025.

Lohmann, Patrick. 2013. "UNM Modified Scholarship Plan to Begin in 2014." *Albuquerque Journal*, October 17. http://www.abqjournal.com/283812/news/unm-modified-scholarship-plan-to-begin-in-2014.html.

Lumina Foundation. 2007. *Camino a la Universidad/The Road to College*. Indianapolis: Lumina Foundation.

Lumina Foundation. 2013. "Lumina's Policy Priorities for the States." Accessed November 24. http://www.luminafoundation.org/state_work/state_policy_agenda/.

Lumina Foundation. 2014. http://www.luminafoundation.org.

Maldonado, Matthew. 2010. "El Paso's Planned Parenthoods Shuts Its Doors After 72 Years." *Borderzine*. Accessed December 19, 2011. http://borderzine.com/2010/09/el-paso's-planned-parenthoods-shuts-its-doors-after-72-years/.

Marcus, Jon. 2011. "Two Years after Obama's College Initiative, Obstacles Remain." *Miami Herald*, July 7. http://www.miamiherald.com/2011/07/07/2303983/two-years-after-obamas-college.html.

Mathieu, Paula. 2005. *Tactics of Hope: The Public Turn in English Composition*. Portsmouth: Boynton/Cook Publishers.

Matsuda, Aya, and Paul Kei Matsuda. 2001. "Autonomy and Collaboration in Teacher Education: Journal Sharing Among Native and Nonnative English-Speaking Teachers." *CATESOL Journal* 13 (1): 109–21.

Matsuda, Paul Kei. 2006. "The Myth of Linguistic Homogeneity in US College Composition." *College English* 68 (6): 637–51. http://dx.doi.org/10.2307/25472180.

Matsuda, Paul K., and Tony Silva. 1999. "Cross-Cultural Composition: Mediated Integration of US and International Students." *Composition Studies* 27 (1): 15–30.

Mayer, Anysia P. 2012. "Paving the Way to College: An Analysis of an International Baccalaureate Diploma Program Serving Immigrant Students in California." In *Linguistic Minority Students Go to College: Preparation, Access, and Persistence*, ed. Yasko Kanno and Linda Harklau, 55–73. New York: Routledge.

McCarthey, Sarah J. 2008. "The Impact of No Child Left Behind on Teachers' Writing Instruction." *Written Communication* 25 (4): 462–505. http://dx.doi.org/10.1177/0741088308322554.

McCurrie, Matthew Kilian. 2009. "Measuring Success in Summer Bridge Programs: Retention Efforts and Basic Writing." *Journal of Basic Writing* 28 (2): 28–49.

Merisotis, Jamie P., and Kirstin McCarthy. 2005. "Retention and Student Success at Minority Serving Institutions." *New Directions for Institutional Research* 125 (125): 45–58. http://dx.doi.org/10.1002/ir.138.

Mosqueda, Eduardo. 2012. "Linguistic Minority Students' Opportunities to Learn High School Mathematics." In *Linguistic Minority Students Go to College: Preparation, Access, and Persistence*, ed. Yasko Kanno and Linda Harklau, 38–54. New York: Routledge.

Moss, Beverly J. 1992. "Ethnography and Composition: Studying Language at Home." In *Methods and Methodology in Composition Research*, ed. Gesa Kirsch and Patricia A. Sullivan, 153–71. Carbondale: Southern Illinois University Press.

Murray, Donald M. 1969. "Finding your Own Voice: Teaching Composition in an Age of Dissent." *College Composition and Communication* 20 (2): 118–23. http://dx.doi.org/10.2307/354178.

National Council of Teachers of English. 2006. "NCLB Recommendations." Accessed December 12, 2013. http://www.ncte.org/positions/statements/nclbrecommendation06.

National Council of Teachers of English. 2012. "Resolution on Teacher Expertise and the Common Core State Standards." Accessed December 12, 2013. http://www.ncte.org/positions/statements/teacherexpertise.

National Public Radio. 2013. "New Reading Standards Aim to Prep Kids for College—But at What Cost?" *National Public Radio*, January 19. http://www.npr.org/2013/01/19/169798643/new-reading-standards-aim-to-prep-kids-for-college-but-at-what-cost.

National Science Foundation. 2013. "Louis Stokes Alliances for Minority Participation (LSAMP)." Accessed December 12, 2013. http://www.nsf.gov/pubs/2012/nsf12564/nsf12564.htm.

Nuñez, Ann-Marie, and Johnelle Sparks. 2012. "Who Are Linguistic Minority Students in Higher Education?: An Analysis of the Beginning Postsecondary Students Study 2004." In *Linguistic Minority Students Go to College: Preparation, Access, and Persistence*, ed. Yasko Kanno and Linda Harklau, 110–29. New York: Routledge.

Omi, Michael, and Howard Winant. 1993. *Racial Formation in the United States from the 1960s to the 1990s.* New York: Routledge.

Oropeza, Maria Veronica, Manka M. Varghese, and Yasuko Kanno. 2010. "Linguistic Minority Students in Higher Education: Using, Resisting, and Negotiating Multiple Labels." *Equity & Excellence in Education* 43 (2): 216–31. http://dx.doi.org/10.1080/10665681003666304.

Ortiz, Anna Marie, and Silvia J. Santos. 2009. *Ethnicity in College: Advancing Theory and Improving Diversity Practices on Campus.* Sterling: Stylus.

Ortmeier-Hooper, Christina. 2008. "English May be my Second Language, but I'm Not 'ESL.'" *College Composition and Communication* 59 (3): 389–419.

Pascarella, Ernest T., and Patrick T. Terenzini. 1991. *How College Affects Students: Findings and Insights from Twenty Years of Research.* San Francisco: Jossey-Bass Publishers.

Passel, Jeffrey, S. D. Cohn, and Mark Hugo Lopez. 2011. "Hispanics Account for More than Half of Nation's Growth in Past Decade." Pew Hispanic Center. Accessed December 12, 2013. http://pewhispanic.org/files/reports/140.pdf.

Paul, Dierdre Glenn. 2004. "The Train has Left: The No Child Left behind Act Leaves Black and Latino Literacy Learners Waiting at the Station." *Journal of Adolescent & Adult Literacy* 47 (8): 648–56.

Peele, Thomas. 2010. "Working Together: Student-Faculty Interaction and the Boise State Stretch Program." *Journal of Basic Writing* 29 (2): 50–73.

Pennington, Julie L. 2007. "Re-Viewing NCLB through the Figured Worlds of Policy and Teaching: Creating a Space for Teacher Agency and Improvisation." *Language Arts* 84 (5): 465–74.

Perez, Monte E. 2008. "Establishing Institutions of Higher Education that Serve Latinos." In *Latino Change Agents in Higher Education: Shaping a System that Works for All*, ed. Leonard A. Valverde, 107–22. San Francisco: Jossey-Bass.

Perryman-Clark, Staci M. 2012. "Toward a Pedagogy of Linguistic Diversity: Understanding African American Linguistic Practices and Programmatic Learning Goals." *Teaching English in the Two-Year College* 39 (3): 230–46.

Perryman-Clark, Staci M. 2013. "African American Language, Rhetoric, and Students' Writing: New Directions for SRTOL." *College Composition and Communication* 64 (3): 469–95.

Person, Ann E., and James E. Rosenbaum. 2006. "'Chain Enrollment' and College 'Enclaves': Benefits and Drawbacks for Latino College Students." In *Latino Educational Opportunity: New Directions for Community Colleges no. 133*, ed. Catherine L. Horn, Stella M. Flores, and Gary Orfield, 51–60. San Francisco: Jossey-Bass.

Powell, Pegeen Reichert. 2009. "Retention and Writing Instruction: Implications for Access and Pedagogy." *College Composition and Communication* 60 (4): 664–82.

Powell, Pegeen Reichert. 2014. *Retention and Resistance: Writing Instruction for Students Who Leave*. Logan: Utah State University Press.

Ramirez, Cindy. 2011. "El Paso's Segundo Barrio reshapes image: 'More pride.'" *El Paso Times*, May 5. http://www.elpasotimes.com/news/ci_18018779.

Redden, Molly. 2011. "Hispanic Enrollment Jumps 24%, Making Those Students the Largest Campus Minority." *Chronicle of Higher Education* 25 (August) http://chronicle.com/article/Hispanic-Enrollment-Jumps-24-/128797/.

Rendón, Laura I., Romero E. Jalomo, and Amaury Nora. 2000. "Theoretical Considerations in the Study of Minority Student Retention in Higher Education." In *Reworking the Student Departure Puzzle*, ed. John M. Braxton, 27–56. Nashville: Vanderbilt University Press.

Rigolino, Rachel, and Penny Freel. 2007. "Re-Modeling Basic Writing." *Journal of Basic Writing* 26 (2): 51–74.

Rodríguez, Cristóbal. 2012. "Top 10% Linguistically Diverse Students' Access and Success at Texas Public Universities." In *Linguistic Minority Students Go to College: Preparation, Access, and Persistence*, ed. Yasko Kanno and Linda Harklau, 93–109. New York: Routledge.

Royer, Daniel, and Roger Gilles. 1998. "Directed Self-Placement: An Attitude of Orientation." *College Composition and Communication* 50 (1): 54–70. http://dx.doi.org/10.2307/358352.

Ruecker, Todd. 2011. "Improving the Placement of L2 Writers: The Students' Perspective." *WPA: Writing Program Administration* 35 (1): 91–117.

Ruecker, Todd. 2012. "Exploring the Digital Divide on the US-Mexico Border through Literacy Narratives." *Computers and Composition* 29 (3): 239–53. http://dx.doi.org/10.1016/j.compcom.2012.06.002.

Ruecker, Todd. 2014. "Here They Do This, There They Do That: Latinas/os Writing Across Institutions." *College Composition and Communication* 66 (1): 91–118.

Sacks, Peter. 2007. *Tearing Down the Gates: Confronting the Class Divide in American Education*. Berkeley: University of California Press.

Scenters-Zapico, John. 2010. *Generaciones' Narratives: The Pursuit & Practice of Traditional & Electronic Literacies on the US-Mexico Borderlands*. Logan: Utah State University Press.

Schroeder, Christopher. 2011. *Diverse by Design: Literacy Education within Multicultural Institutions*. Logan: Utah State University Press.

Selfe, Cynthia. 1999. *Technology and Literacy in the Twenty-first century: The Importance of Paying Attention*. Carbondale: Southern Illinois University Press.

Sheridan, David Michael, Jim Ridolfo, and Anthony J. Michel. 2008. "Available Means of Persuasion: Mapping a Theory and Pedagogy of Multimodal Public Rhetoric." In

*Plugged in: Technology, Rhetoric and Culture in a Posthuman Age*, ed. Lynn Worsham and Gary A. Olson, 61–94. Cresskill: Hampton Press, Inc.

Shilling, Karen M., and Karl L. Shilling. 2005. "Expectations and Performance." In *Challenging and Supporting the First-Year Student: A Handbook for Improving the First Year of College*, ed. M. Lee Upcraft, John N. Gardner, and Betsy O. Barefoot, 108–124. San Francisco: Jossey-Bass.

Smith, Peter J. 2000. "Preparedness for Flexible Delivery among Vocational Learners." *Distance Education* 21 (1): 29–48. http://dx.doi.org/10.1080/0158791000210103.

Smith, Peter J. 2005. "Learning Preferences and Readiness for Online Learning." *Educational Psychology* 25 (1): 3–12. http://dx.doi.org/10.1080/0144341042000294868.

Smitherman, Geneva. 2006. *Word from the Mother: Language and African Americans*. New York: Routledge.

Spack, Ruth. 1997. "The Rhetorical Construction of Multilingual Students." *TESOL Quarterly* 31 (4): 765–74. http://dx.doi.org/10.2307/3587759.

St. John, Edward P., and Glenda Droogsma Musoba. 2010. *Pathways to Academic Success in Higher Education: Expanding Opportunity for Underrepresented Students*. New York: Routledge.

St. John, Edward P., Michael B. Paulsen, and Johnny B. Starkey. 1996. "The Nexus between College Choice and Persistence." *Research in Higher Education* 37 (2): 175–220. http://dx.doi.org/10.1007/BF01730115.

St. John, P. Edward, A. F. Cabrera, Amaury Nora, and E. H. Asker. 2000. "Economic Influences on Persistence Reconsidered: How Can Finance Research Inform the Reconceptualization of Persistence Models?" In *Reworking the Student Departure Puzzle*, ed. John M. Braxton, 29–47. Nashville: Vanderbilt University Press.

Stage, Frances K., and Kathleen Manning. 1992. *Enhancing the Multicultural Campus Environment: A Cultural Brokering Approach 60*. San Francisco: Jossey-Bass.

Sternglass, Marilyn. 1997. *Time to Know Them*. Mahwah: Lawrence Erlbaum Associates.

Stratford, Michael. 2012. "For-Profit Colleges' Marketers Generate Leads, and Controversy." *Chronicle of Higher Education* 22 (October). http://chronicle.com/article/For-Profit-Colleges-Marketers/135222/.

Stringfield, Samuel C., and Mary E. Yakimowski-Srebnick. 2005. "Promise, Progress, Problems, and Paradoxes of Three Phases of Accountability: A Longitudinal Case Study of the Baltimore City Public Schools." *American Educational Research Journal* 42 (1): 43–75. http://dx.doi.org/10.3102/00028312042001043.

Stuart, Reginald. 2010. "Influential Lumina Foundation Drives Higher Education Change, Innovation." *Diverse Issues in Higher Education*. http://diverseeducation.com/article/14047/.

Suárez-Orozco, Carola, and Marcelo M. Suárez-Orozco. 2001. *Children of Immigration*. Cambridge: Harvard University Press.

Suárez-Orozco, Carola, Marcelo M. Suárez-Orozco, and Irina Todorova. 2008. *Learning a New Land: Immigrant Students in American Society*. Cambridge: Harvard University Press.

Suskind, Dorothy C. 2007. "Going Public: NCLB and Literacy Practices in Teacher Education." *Language Arts* 84 (5): 450–5.

Texas Education Agency. 2006. *Secondary School Completion and Dropouts in Texas Public Schools: 2004–05*. Accessed September 9, 2011. http://www.tea.state.tx.us/acctres/DropComp_2004-05.pdf.

Texas Education Agency. 2008. "Chapter 110: Texas Essential Knowledge and Skills for English Language Arts and Reading, Subchapter C., High School." Accessed December 12, 2013. http://ritter.tea.state.tx.us/rules/tac/chapter110/ch110c.html.

Texas Education Agency. 2011a. "Enrollment in Texas Public Schools, 2010–2011." Accessed December 12, 2013. http://www.tea.state.tx.us/acctres/enroll_index.html.

Texas Education Agency. 2011b. "STAAR Resources." Accessed January 4, 2014. http://www.tea.state.tx.us/student.assessment/staar/.

Texas Education Agency. n.d. "Title I School Improvement, Stage 5." Accessed December 12, 2013. http://www.tea.state.tx.us/WorkArea/DownloadAsset.aspx?id=2147485839.

Thomas, Jacinta. 1999. "Voices from the Periphery: Nonnative Teachers and Issues of Credibility." In *Nonnative Educators in English Language Teaching*, ed. George Braine, 5–13. Mahwah: Lawrence Erlbaum Associates.

Thomas, Liz. 2011. "Institutional Transformation to Engage a Diverse Student Body." In *Institutional Transformation to Engage a Diverse Student Body*, ed. Liz Thomas and Malcolm Tight, 1–15. Bingley: Emerald Group Publishing Limited. http://dx.doi.org/10.1108/S1479-3628(2011)0000006003.

Thomas, Wayne P., and P. Virginia Collier. 2003. "The Multiple Benefits of Dual Language." *Educational Leadership* 61 (2): 61–4.

Tinto, Vincent. 1975. "Dropout from Higher Education: A Theoretical Synthesis of Recent Research." *Review of Educational Research* 45 (1): 89–125. http://dx.doi.org/10.3102/00346543045001089.

Tinto, Vincent. 1988. "Stages of Student Departure: Reflections on the Longitudinal Character of Student Leaving." *Journal of Higher Education* 59 (4): 438–55. http://dx.doi.org/10.2307/1981920.

Tinto, Vincent. 1993. *Leaving College: Rethinking the Causes and Cures of Student Attrition*. Chicago: University of Chicago Press.

Tinto, Vincent. 1997. "Classrooms as Communities: Exploring the Educational Character of Student Persistence." *Journal of Higher Education* 68 (6): 599–623. http://dx.doi.org/10.2307/2959965.

Torres, José B., and V. Scott Solberg. 2001. "Role of Self-efficacy, Stress, Social Integration, and Family Support in Latino College Student Persistence and Health." *Journal of Vocational Behavior* 59 (1): 53–63. http://dx.doi.org/10.1006/jvbe.2000.1785.

Torres, Vasti. 2004. "Familial Influences on the Identity Development of Latino First-Year Students." *Journal of College Student Development* 45 (4): 457–69. http://dx.doi.org/10.1353/csd.2004.0054.

Turner, Kristen Hawley, and Troy Hicks. 2011. "'That's Not Writing': Exploring the Intersection of Digital Writing, Community Literacy, and Social Justice." *Community Literacy Journal* Fall 2011: 55–78.

Upcraft, M. Lee, John N. Gardner, Betsy O. Barefoot, eds. 2005. *Challenging and Supporting the First-Year Student: A Handbook for Improving the First Year of College*. San Francisco: Jossey-Bass.

US Census Bureau. 2009. "Population and Housing Profile: 2005–2009 (American Community Survey)." Accessed December 1, 2014. http://factfinder.census.gov.

Valdés, Guadalupe. 2001. *Learning and Not Learning English: Latino Students in American Schools*. New York: Teachers College Press.

Villanueva, Victor. 1993. *Bootstraps: From an American Academic of Color*. Urbana: NCTE.

Wardle, Elizabeth. 2007. "Understanding 'Transfer' from FYC: Preliminary Results of a Longitudinal Study." *WPA: Writing Program Administration* 31 (1–2): 65–85.

Wardle, Elizabeth. 2009. "Writing the Genres of the University." *College Composition and Communication* 60 (4): 765–89.

Webb-Sunderhaus, Sara. 2010. "When Access Is Not Enough: Retaining Basic Writers at an Open-Admission University." *Journal of Basic Writing* 29 (2): 97–116.

Weisberger, Ronald. 2005. "Community Colleges and Class: A Short History." *Teaching English in the Two-Year College* 33 (2): 127–41.

Welch, Nancy. 2008. *Living Room: Teaching Public Writing in a Privatized World*. Portsmouth: Boynton/Cook Publishers.

White, C. Stephen, James G. Deegan, and Martha Allexsaht-Snider. 1997. "Changes in Roles and Relationships in a School-University Partnership." *Teacher Education Quarterly* 24 (1): 53–66.

Wiley, David, and Kelly Wilson. 2009. "Just Say Don't Know: Sexuality Education in Texas Public Schools." Texas Freedom Network Education Fund. Accessed December 19, 2011. http://www.tfn.org/site/DocServer/SexEdRort09_web.pdf.

Wilkey, Christopher. 2012. "Introduction: Activism in Composition Studies and the Politics of Social Change." In *Texts of Consequence*, ed. Christopher Wilkey and Nicholas Mauricello, 1–24. New York: Hampton Press.

Williams, Bronwyn T. 2010. "Seeking New Worlds: The Study of Writing beyond Our Classrooms." *College Composition and Communication* 62 (1): 127–46.

Wolfe, Paula. 1999. "Changing Metaphors for Secondary ESL and Bilingual Education." In *So Much to Say: Adolescents, Bilingualism, & ESL in the Secondary School*, ed. Christian Faltis and Paula M. Wolfe, 255–66. New York: Teachers College Press.

Yancey, Kathleen B. 2004. "Made Not Only in Words: Composition in a New Key." *College Composition and Communication* 56 (2): 297–328. http://dx.doi.org/10.2307/4140651.

Yancey, Kathleen B. 2009. *Writing in the 21st Century: A Report from the National Council of Teachers of English*. Urbana: NCTE.

Yosso, Tara J. 2005. "Whose Culture has Capital? A Critical Race Theory Discussion of Community Cultural Wealth." *Race, Ethnicity and Education* 8 (1): 69–91. http://dx.doi.org/10.1080/1361332052000341006.

# ABOUT THE AUTHOR

TODD RUECKER is an assistant professor at the University of New Mexico. His research focuses on exploring the increasing linguistic and cultural diversity of educational institutions and developing innovative ways to support student success. His work has appeared in a variety of journals including *College Composition and Communication, TESOL Quarterly, Composition Studies, Computers and Composition,* and *WPA: Writing Program Administration.*

# INDEX

*Page numbers in italics indicate illustrations.*

*Academically Adrift: Limited Learning on College Campuses* (Arum and Roksa), 8, 22n4, 148–49
academic literacy, 146
accent, 82, 113
Achieve, 154, 169
Adequate Yearly Progress (AYP), 30, 31
Adler-Kassner, Linda, 165–70, 173n2
advanced placement (AP). *See* placement, advanced
American Enterprise Institute, the, 154
AP. *See* placement, advanced
APA style, 40, 60, 73, 94, 104, 108, 119, 122
aspirations. *See* dreams
assignment descriptions, 37, 50(table), 62, 182; length, 22n4, 31, 35–36, 41, 45, 48–50(table), 59–62, 68–72(table), 73–74, 77–78, 80, 86–91, 95–96, 100, 102–4, 115, 117, 120, 122, 132–33, 137, 175–76, 179–80; prompts, 32, 34, 38, 48, 62, 74, 96, 114–15, 132. *See also* assignment feedback; assignments
assignment feedback, 13, 72, 73, 77, 86, 93, 104, 105(table), 106–10, 177, 119; limited, 34, 48–49, 61, 77, 120, 122, 123; student responses, 8, 34, 47–49, 53, 73, 86, 115, 117–18. *See also* assignment descriptions; assignments
assignments: across the curriculum, 19, 38, 41, 50(table)–53, 60(table)–62, 72(table), 77, 87–89(table), 92–96, 105(table), 106, 118(table), 120–22, 134(table); and assessment, 34; and TAKS, 34, 38, 87, 102. *See also* assignment descriptions; assignment feedback
assimilation, cultural, 159
Astin, Alexander W., *What Matters in College*, 8, 153, 162, 168
attendance, 55, 111, 119, 121, 153n1, 161; and parent involvement, 113; problems, 46–49, 61, 75, 83, 123, 124, 136, 179
AYP. *See* Adequate Yearly Progress

basics, core curriculum, 28, 29, 42, 55, 64; of APA style, 104
BCC. *See* Borderlands Community College
*Beowulf*, 33, 47–48, 58–59, 70, 75, 86, 95, 102, 115–16, 131–32
Bianca, 14, 15(table), 21, 25–29(table), 65–79, 80–81, 141, 143, 144, 152, 161, 164, 175–77
bilingual, 10; courses and programs, 14, 16, 56, 58, 128, 166; two-way programs, 160–61
Bill and Melinda Gates Foundation, the. *See* Gates Foundation
Blackboard, 75, 108
blog, 39, 71–73, 75
book work, 45, 47, 179
border: close to 1, 3, 9; crossing, 1, 112, 137–38, 140, 161, 180; other side of, 57, 63, 68; patrol, 30, 60, 64; separation/wall, 16, 144
Borderlands Community College (BCC): description and cost, 11, 28–29, 34, 42; WAC 19, 38; writing program 35–38
Borderlands University (BU), description and cost, 11, 28–29, 39; WAC, 19, 41; writing program, 38–41
Bourdieu, Pierre, 19, 21, 23n10, 142–45, 148; *Academic Discourse*, 143
bridge programs: CAMP, 27, 28, 67–81, 144, 176; Gear Up, 3; START, 96
BU. *See* Borderlands University
*BU Guide to First-Year Composition*, 39

CAMP. *See* bridge programs, CAMP
Canagarajah, A. Suresh, 4, 9, 160
capital: lacking, 19, 142, 145, 148; network mapping, 55, 63, 79, 97, 110, 125, 139; networks of, 21, 54, 141,

143, 146, 152, 155; as support, 80, 96, 125–26, 143–44, 154–55; types of, 20. *See also* field; habitus
career: plans, 25, 28, 52, 64, 68, 81, 109, 177–78; portfolio, 50–51, 59–60; preparation, 166, 170
Carolina, 14, 15(table), 21, 25–29(table), 99–104, 105(table), 106–9, *110*, 111, 127n1, 141–44, 148, 152, 159, 178–80, 182, 183
Catholic. *See* religion, Catholic
CCCC Research Initiative, 171
CCSS. *See* Common Core State Standards
challenges: crossing border, 112; dependents, 57, 63, 78–79, 151; lack of information, 24; poverty, 1, 10, 13, 66, 144, 151; studying, 53, 56, 63, 71; testing 11, 30
church. *See* religion, church
Ciudad Juárez, 1, 9–10; visiting/living in 16, 17, 57, 63, 82, 111–12, 130, 136–37, 180
College Assistance Migrant Program (CAMP). *See* bridge programs, CAMP
college degree: attainment, 5, 7, 10, 151–52, 156, 175; cost of, 29, 46, 150; earnings gap, 154, 177; interest in, 20, 25, 47, 81, 148. *See also* career
Common Core State Standards (CCSS), 150, 165–67, 169
*Community Action and Organizational Change* (Faber), 13
community center, 101, 143
community college: attendance rates, 5; deciding on, 27–29, 100–101; family member at, 46, 57; relationships with other institutions, 167; step back, 96; teaching loads, 158–59; transition (BCC), 166
community cultural wealth, 19, 21
computer lab 33, 50, 108
*Connect Writing*, online tutoring program, 88
Council of Writing Program Administrators (CWPA), 7, 171
course delivery: hybrid, 40, 76, 78, 108, 157, 163; MOOCs, 162–63, 172; online, 52–53, 55, 157, 162–63, 180–81
courses: ENG 0309, 37; ENG 0310, 38; ENG 1301, 35, 36, 133, 135; ENG 1302, 35–37; ENG 1311, 39–41, 71, 93, 94; ENG 1312, 40; film/creative, 69. *See also* course delivery; developmental courses

Critical Race Theory (CRT), 19, 141, 145
CRT. *See* Critical Race Theory
culture: school, 12, 31, 33, 68, 155, 164, 165; societal, 129, 130, 159, 169; student, 9, 14, 159
CWPA. *See* Council of Writing Program Administrators

Daniel, 14, 15(table), 21, 22n2, 25, 28, 29(table), 37, 42, 44–50(table), *51*–54, *55*, 56, 61, 63, 64, 141, 143–45, 147–49, 151–53, 154, 157, 158, 161–63, 174–75, 182, 183
DECA (extracurricular organization), 84, 92, 101
deficit, 5, 19–20, 145, 160. *See also* capital
dependents, 3, 147, 157, 161. *See also* siblings
deportation. *See* immigration policy, deportation
developmental (basic) courses, 17, 37, 40–41, 43n6, 44–45, 49, 50(table), 51–53, 89(table), 134(table), 163; and Daniel, 45, 49–51, 53; and Yesenia, 88, 93
difference, between high school and college, 37, 38, 45, 62, 65, 75, 78–80, 90, 103, 158
digital divide, 147
disciplinary practice: influences on writing programs, 30, 38, 76; knowledge construction, 169–73
disciplines. *See* writing in the disciplines
discourse communities, 38–41, 142, 157
discussion, classroom, 47, 76; in Spanish, 121
dispositions. *See* habitus
dreams, 5, 20, 25–26, 47, 68, 81, 91, 92, 109, 143, 144, 148, 177, 183. *See also* goals
drop out/stop out, 23n9, 64, 145, 153, 153n2, 161
dropping courses. *See* withdrawal

economic: disparity, 169; individual success, 147, 154; national success, 154, 170, 183
Elbow, Peter, 6
ELL. *See* labels, English language learner
El Paso, demographics, 1, 9–10
Emig, Janet, 171
English language learner (ELL). *See* labels, English language learner

exams: ACT, 69; multiple choice, 38, 51, 61, 131; TELPAS, 34, 48, 102, 132; written, 60–61, 74, 95, 106, 120, 135, 176–77, 179, 181. *See also* TAKS
exclusion, 148, 149, 167
extracurricular, 3, 19, 42, 65–66, 96, 104, 141, 153, 178
extracurricular organization. *See* DECA

faculty, diversity and hiring, 163–65
family: challenges, 15–17, 24–26, 50–51, 66–68, 72, 78, 79, 83, 112, 130, 147, 178; of study participants, 15(table), 24–48; support, 20, 25, 46, 56, 63, 83, 99–100, 111, 143, 144, 148, 178
feedback; in digital environments, 40, 75; grammar, 74–75, 122, 124, 126, 134, 135, 179, 181; limited, 41, 77, 97, 123–24, 149, 158, 179, 181; peer, 68, 73, 80, 135, 126; rubric, 41, 74–75, 77, 90; summative, 75, 91, 97, 124; on verb forms, 104, 106, 108
field, 19, 21, 23n10, 143, 146, 147, 159, 165. *See also* capital; habitus
financial aid, 24, 33, 55, 64, 130, 137, 163, 174; eligibility standards, 153n1; loans, 29, 42, 81, 92, 156, 174, 176. *See also* Pell Grants; scholarships
financial barriers, 24
first generation, 15, 42, 147
first-year composition (FYC), 2, 6, 35–37, 39–40; curricula, 19, 40, 117, 142, 159; transformation, 9, 39
first-year initiatives: engagement, 5, 7–8, 21, 176, 179; seminar, 18, 38, 41, 51, 52, 57, 59, 61, 88, 89(table), 90, 94, 104, 105(table), 106, 108, 117, 118(table), 120, 135–36, 149, 175
first-year writing experiences, 50(table), 60(table), 71, 72(table), 88, 89(table), 104, 105(table), 117, 118(table), 133, 134(table)
flagship university, 26, 114
Flower, Linda, 171
for-profit colleges, 158–59, 161–62, 174, 176–78, 182
Friedman, Thomas L., 154, 162
"From the Good Kids to the Worst" (Harklau), 1
funding: decrease in, 6, 144, 150–51; disparities, 34
FYC. *See* first-year composition

Gates Foundation, the, 154, 162, 172
Gear Up. *See* bridge programs, Gear Up
genre(s), 23n8, 32, 37, 39, 70, 73, 76–77, 117, 141, 147, 158; analysis, 40, 72(table), 76–77, 105(table), 108, 118(table), 122–24; analytical essay, 13, 70, 94, 132, 141; documentary, 40, 72(table), 76, 89(table), 105(table), 108, 118(table), 122, 123, 125; freewriting, 36, 133, 134(table); IMRAD, 40, 123; literary analysis, 35, 37, 123, 134(table), 138, 167; narrative, 31, 32, 34, 35, 38, 48, 50, 51, 70, 117, 131–33, 134(table), 141–42, 147, 157, 167, 170, 171; literature review, 40, 72(table), 76–77, 79, 105(table), 108, 118(table), 122–24; opinion essay, 39, 40, 69, 72(table), 76, 88, 89(table), 105(table), 118(table), 134(table), 136; personal statement, 47, 66, 69, 86, 87, 102, 115, 131; research essay, 36–38, 89(table), 95; rhetorical analysis, 2, 94, 119, 160
goals: graduation, 6; personal, 25, 28, 55, 56, 64, 84, 112, 113, 121, 125, 177; retention, 22n3, 150; teaching, 33, 34, 38, 39, 157–58, 166. *See also* dreams
Goldblatt, Eli, 146, 156, 167, 168, 170
Grabill, Jeffrey T., 155, 165, 168, 172
grades: expected, 67, 107, 112–13; actual, 15(table); extra credit, 62, 77, 88, 89(table), 112
graduate TAs, 74, 88, 90, 122, 165
graduation, 22n3, 49, 80, 85, 87, 100, 152, 156, 131, 168, 178, 182. *See also* rates, graduation
graduation rates. *See* rates, graduation
grammar, 37, 49–50; feedback, 74–75, 122, 124, 126, 134, 135, 179, 181; problems, 88, 91, 158
grants, 39, 73, 162, 171–73n3; Pell, 150, 156, 165, 174

habitus (dispositions), 19, 21, 23n10, 141–47, 159. *See also* capital; field
handwritten, 36, 50, 51, 61, 95, 147, 175, 181. *See also* typed
Harklau, Linda, 2, 5, 22n2; "From the Good Kids to the Worst," 1, 2
Haswell, Richard, 170–71
Hispanic-serving institution (HSI), 159. *See also* labels
homework, 33, 46, 53, 54, 57, 66–68, 71, 82, 83, 92, 101, 110, 126, 137, 144, 180
HSI. *See* Hispanic-serving institution
hysteresis, 143–44, 158, 166, 168

identity (persona), 125, 126
immigrants, 4, 11(table), 22n2, 22n7, 24, 44, 45, 93, 130, 173n3
immigration policy, 66, 76, 93, 94, 147, 165; deportation, 14, 66, 76
institutional transformation, 9, 21, 147, 155–65, 165–73
instructors: Dr. Thompson, 35–36, 134–35; Mr. Cordero, 33; Mr. Madison, 37–38; Mr. Robertson, 3, 17, 33–34, 49, 58, 67, 69–71, 86–87, 102, 113, 129, 131–32; Mr. Sanchez, 58, 68–69, 131; Ms. Carrera, 32; Ms. Cecilia, 25, 82, 85; Ms. Cooper, 111–15, 126; Ms. Flores, 36–37; Ms. Mariscal, 37, 49–52, 54, 61, 64; Ms. Morgan, 32; Ms. Ortega, 32–33; Ms. Padilla, 32–33; Ms. Perry, 71–75; Ms. Warner, 36
Internet: access, 78, 101, 137, 158, 176; for research, 60, 69, 77
interview(s): protocols, 12, 17–18, 20, 41n1, 184–92, 193–97; student participant, 17, 21, 25, 28, 34, 41n1, 48–49, 52–53, 58, 64, 73, 75, 79, 82–85, 91, 96, 100, 113, 129, 133, 136–38, 144, 151, 174–75, 177, 181; teachers/administrator, 12, 17–18, 21, 35–37, 41, 51, 54, 85
Ishler, Jennifer L., 5, 10, 155

Joanne, 15(table), 15–16, 21, 25, 29(table), 44, 56–60(table), 61–*63*, 64, 129, 130, 137–38, 141, 144–45, 151–54, 161–62, 183
job. *See* career
Johanek, Cindy, 170–71

Kanno, Yasko, 19, 22n2, 142, 146
Kuh, George, 7–8

labels, 22n2, 96, 148, 150, 153, 160; English language learner (ELL), 150; Hispanic, 11, 22n2; Latina/o, 3–5, 7, 10, 11(table), 12, 22n2, 24, 27, 42, 141, 147–53, 154, 156, 158–59, 161, 166, 170; limited English proficiency (LEP), 10, 11, 34, 45; linguistic minority (LM), 3, 5, 8–9, 19, 21, 33, 159, 163, 166
Latina/o. *See* labels, Latina/o
LEA. *See* Local Education Agency
learning community, 36, 89, 104, 175
Leki, Ilona, 2, 9, 19, 21, 146
LEP. *See* labels, limited English proficiency

limited English proficiency (LEP). *See* labels, limited English proficiency
linguistic diversity, 173n1. *See also* linguistic homogeneity
linguistic homogeneity, 4. *See also* linguistic diversity
literature, in the composition classroom, 36–37
literature review. *See* genre
LM. *See* labels, linguistic minority
loans. *See* financial aid, loans
Local Education Agency (LEA) (Samson High School), 30
*Lord of the Flies*, 13, 33, 47–48, 58–59, 70, 86, 95, 100–101, 103, 106, 115–17, 132–33, 141
Louis Stokes Alliances for Minority Participation (LSAMP), 172
LSAMP. *See* Louis Stokes Alliances for Minority Participation
Lumina Foundation, the, 5, 154, 166, 169
Lunsford, Andrea A., 158, 171

*Macbeth*, 33
mainstream: courses and programs, 16–17, 33–34, 47, 49–50, 56, 58, 73, 82, 93, 100, 115, 160, 163, 166; journals, 159; US society, 9–10, 129, 149
major, 76, 137, 179; accounting, 121; business, 92, 177; engineering, 47, 52, 102, 109; nursing, 177; psychology, 109
*maquiladora*, 112, 127n2
Massive Open Online Courses (MOOCs), 162–63, 172
Matsuda, Paul Kei, 4, 9, 156, 160, 164
Mauricio, 15(table), 16, 23n11, 25–26, 28, 29(table), 111–18(table), 119–*25*, 126–27, 141–44, 148, 152, 159, 180–81, 182, 183
median income, 10
methodology, 170–71
Mexico, Mexican, 1, 3–4, 9, 11, 22n2, 30, 68, 70, 82–83, 85, 89(table), 91, 102–3, 112, 121, 127n2, 130, 133, 136, 139, 144, 146–47, 161, 164, 166, 170
middle school, 14–16, 45, 47, 56, 100, 128
MLA style, 60, 74, 120
mode-based essay, 35, 38, 166; EDNA-style, 35
money, 92, 129, 177, 178, 180; scholarship, 26. *See also* financial aid, loans

monocultural, 9. *See also* mainstream US
MOOCs. *See* Massive Open Online Courses
Murray, Donald M., 6

*Narrative of the Life of Frederick Douglass*, 105, 106
National Council of Teachers of English (NCTE), 4, 169–70
National Survey of Student Engagement (NSSE), 7
NCLB. *See* No Child Left Behind Act
NCTE. *See* National Council of Teachers of English, 4, 169–70
networks of capital. *See* capital, networks of
No Child Left Behind Act (NCLB), 3, 30, 150, 169
NSSE. *See* National Survey of Student Engagement

Paola, 15(table), 16, 21, 25, 28–29(table), 35, 56–*63*, 64, 128–34(table), 135–*39*, 140, 141, 144–45, 151–53, 154, 161, 183
partnerships, 7, 167–68, 171
party: political, 72(table), 77, 80; social, 17, 82, 98
pedagogy, 20, 35, 143, 149: conferences, 6, 173; scaffolding, 118, 158
Pell Grants, 150, 156, 165, 174. *See also* financial aid, loans
Perez, Monte E., 24, 150
Person, Ann E., 24, 42, 147
persona. *See* identity
placement: advanced (AP), 33, 44–49, 100, 115–16, 141; developmental/basic, 17, 37, 40–41, 43n6, 44–45, 49, 50(table), 51–53, 88, 89(table), 93, 134(table), 157–58, 162–63; dual-credit, 45, 100, 102, 115; lower tracks, 159; mainstream writing, 73, 93, 166
plagiarism, 141
PLATO, 50, 131
*Pocahontas and the Powhatan Dilemma* (Townsend), 72(table), 74, 89(table), 90
political meddling, in schools, 29, 30, 34
population growth, 4
portfolios, 18, 59–60(table), 72(table), 89(table), 105(table), 118(table), 181
procrastinate, 68, 70, 82, 91, 92, 123

Powell, Pegeen Reichert, 7, 9, 145, 152, 155, 168
PPOHA. *See* Promoting Postbaccalaureate Opportunities for Hispanic Americans
Promoting Postbaccalaureate Opportunities for Hispanic Americans (PPOHA), 172

quizzes, 37, 61, 80

rates: crime, 1; graduation, 5, 10, 152, 168; teen pregnancy, 151; retention, 7, 22n3, 155–56, 159, 168; unemployment, 154
reading: amount of, 8, 22n4, 71, 104, 120, 136; overwhelmed, 33, 71, 120, 158, 160; personal, 8, 83, 97–98, 102, 104, 107, 110, 129, 136; v. skimming, 22n5, 71; strategies, 71, 158
reflection: assignments, 49, 50(table), 78; self, 78, 109
religion: Catholic, 26, 101; church, 14, 68, 78, 80, 81, 155, 176
remedial courses. *See* developmental courses
research: academic journal, 90, 104, 173; citation, 30, 40, 70, 73, 78, 94, 116, 119, 120, 152, 158; grants, 171–72; knowledge construction, 21, 169–73; library databases, 77, 104; methodology classes, 170; number of sources, 95; paraphrase, 108, 133; primary, 17, 36, 40, 72(table), 76–77, 105(table), 108, 111, 118(table), 122–23; survey, 7, 17, 25, 26, 42n1, 100, 108, 111, 123–24, 157; textual evidence, 50, 70, 75, 86, 132
responsibility, 22n3, 30, 47, 54, 66, 83–84, 114, 127, 145–46, 148, 153, 154, 182
retention, 5–8, 22n3, 145, 150, 151–53, 155–57, 159, 162, 165, 168
revision, 32, 36, 39, 49, 81, 82, 84, 85, 88, 93, 95, 114, 122, 135, 179; curriculum, 40; policy, 161
rhetorical analysis. *See* genre
Rosenbaum, James E., 24, 42, 147
Ruecker, Todd, 42, 43n4, 147, 157, 163

Samson High School (SHS), 3, 10, 11(table), 29, 30–31, 32–34, 42, 47, 50, 56, 57, 69, 85–86, 96, 98, 100, 111–13, 115–17, 126, 128–29, 131, 141–42, 149, 150, 164

scholarship(s): 24, 29, 114, 121, 152; programs, 14, 18, 27, 28, 67, 141, 144. *See also* financial aid
Schroeder, Christopher, 4, 9, 159, 168
sexual education, 151, 165, 169
SHS. *See* Samson High School
siblings, 14, 15(table), 27, 28, 65–68, 76, 78–80, 100–102, 111–12, 143–44, 151, 157, 161, 176, 178. *See also* dependents
significant other, 16, 26–27, 57, 83, 84, 92, 125, 130, 136–40, 144, 177, 180
Silva, Tony, 160
social class, 151
social media: Facebook, 13, 137, 174; MySpace, 13
source-based writing, 50, 54, 62, 70, 141
Spanglish, 1, 10
Spanish: academic writing, 94, 100, 106, 122, 125, 127n1, 160, 161, 179–80; in classroom settings, 10, 14, 16, 23, 85, 102, 111, 118(table), 121–22, 125, 133, 159, 176, 179; community, 1, 10, 44, 46; monolingualism v. multilingualism, 164; nonnative speakers, 14, 84, 121, 126; speaking, 14, 84, 160; language transition, 56, 85, 102, 111, 125, 128
*SparkNotes*, 59, 70, 141
sponsors, sponsorship, 65, 82, 141, 143–44, 148, 153
STAAR. *See* State of Texas Assessments of Academic Readiness
START program. *See* bridge programs, START
standardized academic English, 158–60, 173n1
State of Texas Assessments of Academic Readiness (STAAR), 23n8
STEM disciplines, 172
stop out/drop out, 23n9, 64, 153, 153n2, 161
studying: time, 8, 9, 44, 54, 63, 79, 148; distraction, 44, 53, 56
success: first-year, 6, 14, 16, 21, 75; literature on, 152; influencing factors, 8, 19, 21, 24, 44–48, 54, 55, 77, 80, 99–101, 109, 125, 143, 147–49, 153, 157–58, 178; promoting student, 3, 4, 7, 18, 21, 22n3, 54, 56, 65, 67, 81, 113, 125, 141, 143–44, 147–49, 151–53, 156–57, 172, 175, 182
syllabi, 18, 35–36, 88, 104, 126, 138

TAKS. *See* Texas Assessment of Knowledge and Skills
teacher: caring, 144, 169; strict, 58, 68, 102, 111, 131, 135; indifferent, 54, 85, 112, 142, 164
teaching load, 35, 158
technical school, 5, 33, 34, 57, 60, 64, 162, 176
technology: access, 35, 41, 75, 78, 101, 137, 147, 157, 175; cell phone, 112, 129–31, 134; composing, 39; computer, 13, 33, 40–41, 75, 78, 83, 88, 101, 112, 121, 123, 129, 131, 157, 175–76; drilling, 88; email, 13, 18, 112–13, 117, 129, 142; hybrid classes, 40, 76, 78, 108, 157, 163; iMovie, 108, 123; integration in instruction, 18, 38, 40, 49; Mac, 108, 123; online classes, 52–53, 55, 162–63, 180–81; text messaging, 13, 98, 122, 126, 130, 133–34, 174
TELPAS. *See* Texas English Language Proficiency Assessment System
Texas Assessment of Knowledge and Skills (TAKS) test, 11, 23n8, 31–34, 38, 45, 47, 58, 69, 80, 82, 85, 87, 102, 113–15, 132. *See also* Texas English Language Proficiency Assessment System
Texas English Language Proficiency Assessment System (TELPAS), 34, 48, 102, 132. *See also* Texas Assessment of Knowledge and Skills
thesis: development, 13, 35, 41, 48, 58–59, 86, 94–95, 116, 132; focus, 70, 74, 80, 95
timed writing, 74
Tinto, Vincent, 6–7, 22n2, 145, 153, 155, 162, 168
transition: from high school to college, 3, 29, 96, 156, 166; to mainstream classes, 58, 93, 166
tuition, 11–12, 22n6, 23n9, 29, 156, 174; increased, 150, 152
typed, 42n1, 68, 147. *See also* handwritten

*Undergraduates in a Second Language* (Leki), 146
university: classroom, classes, 9, 88, 154, 157; v. community college, 27–29(table), 100–101; faculty, 3, 35, 133, 156, 182; research, researchers, 2, 13, 149, 172; writing experiences, 4, 83, 117, 119–20, 142. *See also* Borderlands Community College;

Borderlands University; flagship university
Upcraft, M. Lee, 5–6, 155

Villanueva, Victor, *Bootstraps*, 2, 5
violence, 1, 10, 73, 93, 94, 112, 136, 147; "symbolic," 143
vocabulary, 37, 71, 98, 100, 105, 107, 111, 150
vocational. *See* technical school

WAC. *See* writing across the curriculum
WID. *See* writing in the discipline courses
Wiki, 76, 105(table), 107
Wikipedia, 62
withdrawal, 16, 53–54, 59, 61–64, 136, 176, 181
work. *See* career
WPAs. *See* writing program administrators
writing across communities, 168
writing across the curriculum, 38, 41, 179
writing demands, 3, 47, 59, 88, 90, 103, 107, 158

writing in the discipline (WID) courses: criminal justice, 77, 176; history, 51, 62, 74–75, 88–90, 103, 106–7, 120, 138; philosophy, 120; political science, 77–78, 122, 179; psychology, 62, 179, 181; science, 179; sociology, 36, 74, 96. *See also* writing across the curriculum
writing process, 39, 77; outlines, 60(table), 61, 78, 86, 106, 134(tables), 135, 176, 179. *See also* revision
writing program administrators (WPAs), 157, 160, 167–68. *See also* Council of Writing Program Administrators
writing programs, 6, 9, 21, 29–30; Borderlands Community College, 35–38; Borderlands University, 38–41; transforming, 155–73

Yesenia, 15(table), 17, 21, 25, 27, 29(table), 40, 65, 81–89(table), 90–*91*, 92–*97*, 98, 141–44, 147, 152, 163, 164, 177–78, 182, 183
Yosso, Tara J., 19–20, 21, 142, 145

www.ingramcontent.com/pod-product-compliance
Lightning Source LLC
Chambersburg PA
CBHW040324300426
44112CB00021B/2868